Samuel Royce

Deterioration and the Elevation of Man through Race Educartion

Vol. II.

Samuel Royce

Deterioration and the Elevation of Man through Race Educartion
Vol. II.

ISBN/EAN: 9783337209377

Printed in Europe, USA, Canada, Australia, Japan

Cover: Foto ©ninafisch / pixelio.de

More available books at **www.hansebooks.com**

DETERIORATION

AND

THE ELEVATION OF MAN

THROUGH

RACE EDUCATION.

BY

SAMUEL ROYCE.

THE SACREDNESS OF HUMAN LIFE INCREASES WITH CIVILIZATION.

IN TWO VOLUMES.

VOL. II.

THIRD EDITION, REVISED AND ENLARGED.

BOSTON:

LEE & SHEPARD, PUBLISHERS.

1880.

PREFACE TO THE SECOND VOLUME.

A FULL survey of the means of preventing human deterioration, as that of causing it, implies an infinite knowledge of man, nature and social conditions; we no more propose the one in this volume than we did the other in the first. If we have succeeded in opening up by our labors a comparatively new line of thought to specialists devoted to the various interests of man and society, we are rewarded.

If our first volume implied studies and sympathies of a life time, we paid more dearly than we dare tell for what we bring this time. Still, we are all debtors, and I present, not without diffidence, this, my best endeavor, to the friends of the race; may it prove its power by its work, which we trust it will by pleading for the perishing masses, upon the highways and in the byways, in the name of God and humanity, words inseparable, old and strong as the oak, and ever new as the rising sun in his morning glory.

THE AUTHOR.

CONTENTS TO VOLUME II.

PART I.

THE SOCIAL PROBLEM.

PART II.

ÆSTHETIC CULTURE.

PART III.

THE KINDERGARTEN AND THE MORALIZATION OF THE MASSES.

PART IV.

INDUSTRIAL EDUCATION AND THE SOCIAL PROBLEM.

PART V.

THE DEFECTS OF THE PRESENT EDUCATION.

PART VI.

THE NEED OF THE NATION.

PART VII.

DETERIORATION AND PROGRESS.

PART VIII.

THE REIGN OF TERROR.

EDUCATION:

A SOCIAL STUDY.

VOLUME II.

PART I.

THE SOCIAL PROBLEM.

/ 7 2 /

MACHINERY AND THE SOCIAL PROBLEM.

FOR fifty years and over manufacturers have given their foreman the order, every week's pay-day, " John, dismiss five or six hands and see if we cannot manufacture just as much as we do now with so many hands less." Science has joined capital, and has displaced, and is daily more displacing hand-labor through improved machinery to the advantage of capital. Cheapened production, no doubt, is an important factor in our civilization, and found its solution through the combined power of science and capital. But though the masses have lost day by day profitable employment, they have neither the means, the knowledge nor the position to make themselves heard, and to force upon the age what we would call the other factor of civilization, which consists in new methods for the absorption of labor that is daily being displaced by improved machinery. This is the core of the social question of the day.

That cheapened goods create a demand which calls even for additional labor, is an assumption the manufacturing statistics of Old and New England prove false, as both countries manufacture daily more goods with decreasing labor. Neither can we for a moment heed the cry against machinery; and a violent reduction of the hours of labor, in our present condition, is no wiser. For, had we adopted such a measure thirty years ago, when labor had still less adjusted itself to machinery, and consequently was more suffering than to-day, where would be the wealth or the instruments of labor the world has accumulated even by its steady industry? Four hours of factory labor, we are told, is enough to produce all we want, would give employment to all, and be best for capital as well as for labor. We say four hours; to-day at least, in the factory, means ten hours in gin or rum holes; means greater misery than that we see to-day, and soon the masses would be too demoralized to work even four hours, three, two, or even one. Crowded drinking places would breed public tumults, and demagogues would rule supreme.

CAPITAL, LABOR, AND OVER-PRODUCTION.

Capital, luxury, and over-production are complained of. But is not capital the instrument as well as the fruit of labor? Who would work, save, or gather in if it was not for the advantage he was to derive from the accumulation of his capital? Or, have we too much capital? Are not our railroads and our public debt greatly owned by foreign capitalists?

We grumble about the luxuries of the rich. But do not the poor of to-day enjoy the luxuries of the rich of a hundred years ago? And will not, in a hundred years, the poor enjoy the luxuries of the rich of to-day? And does not he who strikes at the luxuries of the rich of to-day strike at the necessaries of the poor of to-morrow? Machinery and over-production are complained of. Well, shall we burn down the factories and bring down production to what it was in the days of Henry VIII. or Queen Elizabeth, when everybody in the kingdom had a log of wood for a pillow; when lords and earls, on leaving their castles for their city residences, brought with them their windows, chairs, and tables, and ambassadors were received in royal chambers strewn with straw, after the manner of pig-sties?

No, no, this will not do. Neither can we stand still, we must press on and forward; we must manufacture more, improve in quality as well as in quantity, and bring within the reach of the poorest what was but yesterday exclusively at the command of wealth.

SOLUTION OF THE SOCIAL PROBLEM INDICATED.

When a social problem presses upon us, the solution is at hand. If one man can do to-day by the aid of machinery the work of ten, the nine thrown out of employment must be engaged in new industries which provide us with new luxuries; and consequently the problem resolves itself into increasing our wants and comforts with our increased powers; and thus, wayward children that we are, we chide the heavens that only meant to bless us, if we only would stop to think and bravely work on.

If we stupidly refuse to follow this course, the rich of to-day will become the poor of to-morrow, and perish but one day later than the poor of to-day.

If our solution is true, more labor, more skill, and more capital are needed for the production as well as consumption of a more varied and higher sort of industry.

The stomach is a brute of narrow range and limited capacity, which is soon supplied. We must seek to minister to the nobler organ of vision, which has never enough, and is a customer for the widest market.

But an industry that is to satisfy higher wants calls for a higher taste and skill, obtained only through careful training from earliest infancy.

We want more capital, more machinery, and more work, and above all a greater diversity of employment; and this last word contains the solution of the great social problem of the age, and æsthetic culture is its essential condition.

Want of a thorough and comprehensive industrial education lies at the foundation of all our present troubles.

The best ten years of our lives are wasted with a lean stock of generalities which could easily be acquired in twice as many days.

In an age of tremendous values and world-wide interests we are stuffed upon worn-out school-benches, with all sorts of trashy odds and ends, called by a misnomer Education, ending in the legitimate failure of practical imbecility or incapacity.

Capital, machinery, and even labor are cried down; and this by the very men who complain that they suffer from want of houses, food, and clothing.

Strike at the millionaire to-day and the blow falls upon the poor to-morrow. For by paying large prices the millionaire encourages the creation of articles which much-abused machinery soon brings within the reach of all. .

PUBLIC WORKS.

The modern resort has generally been the absorption of machine-displaced labor by public works. But means immediate in their results are, here as elsewhere, quackeries. Too great activity in public works increases public debts, which become, in the end, ruinous to the people through heavy taxation. Besides, they draw the masses to already crowded centers of population, and, as a rule, encourage unskilled labor.

STATE CREDIT.

Some ask capital for any and every body. Every one, however, will then be an enterpriser, and no one will do a stroke of work. How are we to single out the enterpriser with whom the money advanced will not be sunk through failure? The only conclusive criterion is, that he who has made a thousand dollars best knows how to invest them.

COMMUNISM REMOVES THE MOTIVE FOR LABOR.

Communism and even co-operation do not touch the problem arising from machine-displaced labor.

With the great stimulus of personal responsibility goading us on we can not make ends meet; and we are told to mend matters by going all to the public crib without thought or care, and we shall have plenty of everything. This certainly sounds more like a joke than an honest opinion.

The economical success of here and there a communistic society is due to their throwing upon the outside world the expense of keeping up their numbers.

THE MALTHUSIAN DOCTRINE.

Many look to Malthus' principles—upon which, in fact, all British economists more or less build— as to a remedy against the evils of the time.

But even if at the time of Malthus there had been in England a reasonable apprehension of a surplus of population, there is no ground for it there or anywhere else to-day, as the vital statistics of cities are so unfavorable to population, that only the influx from the country can keep it up; but will hardly be able to do this always under the constantly rising ratio of urban to rural population. So that, in fact, under our urban, or rather metropolitan civilization, the danger of depopulation is greater than that of over-population.

To what straits has humanity been reduced by the dismal science of the day, when the pages of sophists of high and low degree bristle with the doctrine, that the competition of labor against labor, and the pauperization of the world can only be checked by the decimation of the masses

through misery and starvation, and we are invaded
by Malthusian immorality to a degree that threatens us with the destruction sure to follow the gross
practices of Sodom and Gomorrah. What a base
and cowardly distrust in Providence, and what
want of sympathy with great humanity and the
joys of young and old to cut them off thus early,
when there is room for ten times as many homes
as there are yet in the land.

The very dog looks as big again as he swells
with the sight of the happy groupings of children,
and old and young men and women, all frolicking
merrily in the green, each and all in their own
several ways; and should not we delight in increasing the happiness of mankind and the good
feeling of all our fellow-creatures?

Or does harmonious nature, divinely impreg-
nated with self-adjusting power, rise from sphere
to sphere to break down in man, unless violating
the highest order of laws, he turns his hand against
his brother and himself in a thousand forms of
social murder in order to prevent over-population
and its wild disorders? Not to the violation, but
to the fulfillment of higher law must we look for
the correction of this or any other evil. When
every thought and fiber in us will be bent upon
high ideal creation, an exuberant, sensuous nature
will be swallowed up by divine energy, and our

progeny will be no more as numerous as to-day than that of the lion or elephant is as large as that of the cat or mouse. The Platos, the Newtons, and the Humboldts were never remarkable for the large families they have raised, even because their children were of another sort. (See page 362).

Already the intelligent avoidance of intermarriage of men and women of families of marked fertility is sufficient to reduce the fertility of the human race to any desirable minimum.

To speak of and even foster immoral and unsocial tendencies destructive of the state, in the face of the fact that neither Asia nor Europe has one-half or one-third the population they can support; that Africa has not a fifth, America not a tenth, and Australia not a twentieth of the population their territory calls for is, to say the least, unjustifiable; all our troubles spring from inefficient production and a faulty distribution.

With the approach of over-population, self-adjustments progressing unknown to us—who know so little—make the absurdly feared evil a thing of the imagination.

Over-population, over-population! this cry comes from men who badly want population, but would throw the cost of raising it upon foreign nations; it comes from families who can well afford to raise children, but lack virtue and devotion to do it.

Talk of over-population when we have not enough working force, but import it from all the world, and would even degrade our own people by the importation of pagan Chinamen in numbers that would be sure to lead, in fifty or a hundred years, to another civil war, as they would never assimilate with us.

But just as we are short of producers, even so we are wanting consumers, as our plethoric warehouses prove.

Over-population! that means, more go to the national board than can be supported; the world must, then, be rapidly getting poor; for example :

The gross assessed income of Great Britain, was in

1800	$500,000,000.
1815	650,000,000.
1843	1,255,000,000.
1855	1,540,000,000.
1855	2,080,000,000.
1875	2,855,000,000.

The assessed property, real and personal, in the United States, was, according to the Census:

1850	$7,135,780,228.
1860	16,159,616,068.
1870	30,068,518,507.

In France the real and personal property of the nation was, in

1821	$8,023,000,000.
1851	16,080,000,000.
1875	36,000,000,000.

Does, then, production not by far outstrip population, and do thy gains, oh, heartless man, not make sufficiently rapid strides that thou must begrudge the poor father the child that is to take his place, by setting aside the method of God and man and importing foreign slaves, which is sure to end in the ruin of the state with the family?

Or must we cite more figures to prove the uncalled-for alarm of over-population? Well, according to C. R. Weld, Assistant Secretary to the Royal Society of England, there have been known already, thirty years ago, 12,800,000,000 arable acres on the globe; and though in the tropical regions a very few trees are sufficient for the support of a family, give each, composed of five members, four acres—sufficient, under proper cultivation, even in our climate—and there is sustenance on the globe for 16,000,000,000 inhabitants, which is more than eleven times its present population. But have not the last thirty odd years added many hundreds of millions of newly-discovered arable acres, and will not the next thirty years add many more?

The present fertility of the race, a stumbling-block to many, is but another proof of marvelous self-adjustment; for if it were not for this great power of propagation it would have long perished under our poorly-disguised reign of violence and cunning.

The wild notions put forth as social remedies may not deserve a refutation, but they prove the madness of despair and public danger inviting our best efforts for their speedy removal. Capital as well as labor has a vicious logic. In the absence of social virtue, men think that in the general misfortune they can add to their own by taking from their neighbor; but this sort of gain is as short-lived as it is quick, and the robbery of the rich by the poor, or of the poor by the rich, is sure to end in the discomfiture of the apparently winning party, and the only method for improving the condition of the one is to improve the condition of all—a method which, of course, is as slow as it is far-reaching and effectual.

SPECIFIC SOLUTION OF THE SOCIAL PROBLEM.

The social problem, as we have put it, can only be reached by a specific principle or method which will create a demand for manual labor that is not easily superseded by machinery; a demand increased by the very supply, and that without any interference with the freedom of trade or human activity in any direction. A universal æsthetic education will do all this; as under it the demand for art and ornamental industry must ever be on the increase.

With the spread of æsthetic culture, machine-work, devoid of feeling—the requisite of beauty—will give way to manual-work. *The masses must fill the houses of men of means with art and beauty, while machinery fills their houses with cheap manufactures.*

But if the spread of taste leads to a demand for manual art-work, art-education alone can develop this national taste, above which the individual hardly ever rises.

As the manufactured products consumed by the million admit the greatest subdivision and use of machinery in their manufacture, they are daily cheapening; while manual labor, more and more approaching the character of art, is ever rising in value, the workman therefore obtains daily a higher return for his work, and pays less for the machine-work products which enter into his consumption.

An ever increasing variety of art-manual work, and most perfect machinery, the one for profitably employing the masses, and the other for cheapening manufactured articles entering into general consumption, are the two factors of universal happiness and prosperity.

The demand for articles of comfort and luxury increasing with civilization, must, under a systematic

and universal art-culture, become almost boundless.

Not an article in common use but can be improved in beauty and adaptation by manual art.

There is no end to comforts, and the liveliest
imagination can not divine those which, though un-
dreamt of to-day, will be considered common
wants at no distant day.

But we will try and give our imagination scope ;
and, by way of illustration, give but one or two
examples of new delights and pleasures, the satisfying of which might employ millions of hands.

Is it unreasonable to suppose, that with the progress of a systematic knowledge of the industries, a
dry-goods, leather, hardware, or any other large
dealer, will have each a sort of miniature museum,
illustrative of what the world has accomplished in
his line in past ages and in foreign countries?

Is it unreasonable to suppose, that as labor and
science, or work and intelligence, will more and
more intermingle, and manufacturers will take a
deep, historical, and world-wide interest in their industry, they will take pleasure in fitting up a few
rooms in their homes ; a sort of cabinet of industrial
art in their own particular line, combining elements
of instruction and curiosity?

Is it unreasonable to suppose, that as it will become more and more understood, that in old as

well as in young, the mind gets vigorous by feeding on the tangible things of art and nature, men will surround themselves and their children with a thousand instructive objects of art, industry, nature and history, and every house will become a store-house of concrete thought, putting to shame our present wordy schools and books?

There is not a science or department of human activity that may not be made quickening to us, either by being brought home to us by its very objects, or at least by its pictorial representations.

Men of means, taste, and intelligence might take pleasure in representing in different rooms the habits and fashions of different nations and epochs.

We dare predict—and most reverently we say, God is on our side—the time is coming when grog-geries will be no more, and the money saved by the mechanic will be invested in a little curiosity-shop ; the poor man's university and museum, the prac-tical man's library, where he will surround himself with the tools and processes of past ages, and foreign countries, and improve in his life-work and duty. Call this a dream who will, there is no lack of wealth, wisdom, or humanity to bring about this consummation. The capital and wages spent to-day in liquid fire, consuming the life and the brains of the people, $700,000,000 per annum, are more than enough to provide all, from the hut to the palace, with the fullest measure of comforts, museums, libraries, and everything else that instructs or delights.

Nothing at variance with the present machinery of society, unknown or doubtful, is called for.   Let the schools simply follow the pressure of social forces in full operation, and organize themselves in harmony with the industrial age we live in ; a thing they will have ere long to do if they will or not, and they will save to millions of poor men, women, and children years of bitter trials.

Capital and science ever tend to lessen labor, and the state must ever strive through industrial art education to diversify labor in the interest of the masses, and its own stability.

Machinery, with its enormously producing power, makes us look only to quantity, and we are piling up goods to the height of ancient pyramids ; but, like these, our works impose only upon children and barbarians ; held up to the quality of true art, they vanish, and their name is—shoddy.   What shame ! the masters of high art belong to the past. Familiar with nature we are strangers in our own souls.   Our only solace is, this can not last ; the interests of trade demanding that machinery displaced labor should be employed, as otherwise the fabricate turned out at one end of the machine will, for want of buyers, soon be of no more use than the smoke coming out at the other; and all men, besides, must be busied, or else, like Greece and Rome, the State will perish by the hand of the turbulent masses.

There is no other solution of the social problem than universal art culture, which will create an almost universal demand for hand and soul-made work. From the shoe we wear to the tapestry on the wall, the distance is immense between what is machine and what is hand made. There is neither fitness, nor life, nor such beauty as the soul delights in in what the machine makes. The machine gives no scope to the individuality of the operative, nor does it ply itself to the individuality of the consumer; and as wealth, culture and art spread, hand and soul made things will come more and more into requisition; and while improved machinery will ever more and more furnish the masses with cheap goods, they will, with their hand made works of art and ornamental industry, supply a market daily widening with the improving taste of the age.

SOCIAL SELF-ADJUSTMENTS.

Self-adjustment is our anchor. Infinite Wisdom has put nice balances everywhere. Division of labor, it is feared, will unite all employment under one head, and thus make kings and slaves. But, lo! as division of labor is carried to its very extreme, it pays best to separate the manufacture of one article into a dozen different branches, each carried on separately with means within the reach of almost any enterprising man.

Again, the finest machine made fabricates being brought within the reach of the poorest, manual art work alone satisfies the desire for distinction wealth seeks. The social as well as the natural adjustments are marvelous. Industry, machinery, and commerce have spread wealth among the commercial and manufacturing classes, and deprived the masses of their small trades, which however are to be replaced by manual art-work as refining in its tendencies, and as much an exercise of the higher faculties and a delight, as the former drudgery was brutalizing and a depressing burden.

One more illustration of this self, or rather Divine adjustment in the social relations of man. Manufacturers and commercial men, who made their gains by foreign trade, ever ground down their countrymen, whose cheap labor, but not patronage, they wanted. Meanwhile the wealth made by these men aroused the manufacturing spirit everywhere, and to-day we are pretty near the point when every nation supplying itself with staple goods by its own skill, foreign commerce will be forced to give way to domestic trade, which high wages alone can make profitable ; and thus the masses of our country will not always work to supply the wants of another country, but will, for the benefit of all parties, enjoy the fruit of their own labor.

Still, there is more left for us to do than the let-alone theory would fain make us believe. The spirit and facts of the age have to be rightly interpreted, the measures in harmony with them must have our support, and obstructions have to be cleared away. Judged by this rule, art industrial education deserves our co-operation, as it is in keeping with the social forces of the day, interferes with the freedom of none, arms millions with the power of creating works of art, beauty, and industry; and, while it gives comfort to many, bestows delight upon all.

ART MANUAL INDUSTRIES SOLVING MANY PROBLEMS.

The union of art manual employment with factory labor will at least partly bring back the domestic spirit that formerly attended the small trades, and moderate the haste of a hard driving age of machinery.

Trade diseases decimating the ranks of operatives—an incalculable loss to capital and the state—will disappear among intelligent work people, dividing their time between the factory and art-manual labor at their own hearth.

The apathy arising from the monotony of doing, the whole of life, one little thing, leading to popular discontent and brutal idiocy, will give way, under this new division of labor or diversity of employment, to intelligence, peace, and contentment; and God's will, written in our limbs and various faculties, having free course, will solve every problem, and work out universal happiness.

It is the unskilled and factory operatives who are the troublesome element in our present labor system. They chiefly are the victims, stand at the bottom of the social scale every way, and threaten the peace of the world; art manual labor, by diminishing this element, will lessen the danger.

Thinkers like Le Play have noticed that our greatest danger comes from the weakening of home influences and the destruction of woman's domestic nature through factory labor, and the entire absence of the man from his home. The culture of the artistic manual industries opens a wide field for home work, especially for women, and reasonably shortened factory hours will bring even man more under the influence of home, where he will engage, with his family, in art work, and joining his authority with that of the mother, rebellious children will again be brought under control, and give the state law-abiding citizens.

School opportunities for industrial art manual culture will end the corrupting influences of factories upon the young; one of the chief demoralizers of our industrial age.

If the people are not to become idle, thriftless, and partisans of the commune, we must busy them and keep their hands going; and that we can not do with the almost exclusive factory work of our day, as competition among laborers reduces wages to a point which excludes them from becoming consumers save of the barest necessaries of life, we overstock, consequently, foreign markets—which anyhow will soon provide for their own wants—bring on crises and revulsions, and hence the universal cultivation of art manual industries is the great desideratum of the state, the masses, capital, public morals, humanity, and all.

We must divide our energies between the factory and little home art shops, or between democratic machinery, working for the masses, and aristocratic art, providing luxuries for the comparatively few, and thus wipe out the double reproach of being entirely bent upon increasing poor or cheap work, or of working for art and fashion, while the masses suffer from want of necessaries.

The destruction of wealth, therefore, retarding

the demand for hand made art luxuries is as much, if not more an injury to the poor than to the rich, as it confines them to coarse and cheap labor, and deprives many of them even of that.

THE SOCIAL PROBLEM AND OUR PUBLIC LANDS.

Many think the social problem does not exist in the United States, as they believe whoever wishes can get government land at a mere nominal rate, and that we should anyhow be chiefly an agricultural nation. The fact is, of 1,902,854,400 square acres forming the area of the United States, 1,340,854,400 are cultivable, but the lavishness of the government with the patrimony of the nation may be inferred from the fact that the grants to railroads—mainly the Pacific—amount to 215,971,005, which is more than one-half of the improved and unimproved lands of the combined farms of the United States, which, according to the census of 1870, amount to 407,732,041 acres. The United States, therefore, have but little land, if any, to bestow upon settlers, who must make their bargains with companies which make prices and conditions to suit themselves.

We have passed through the agricultural state upon which younger countries have fully entered. The markets of the world are supplied with breadstuffs, and we better manufacture and get as much for a lesser surplus of produce as we would for a larger reduced in value by over-production.

It is often said that every country should restrict itself to the exploration of its own natural resources. Well, Great Britain has 9,000 square miles of coal fields, and she is a manufacturing power, and produces 500,000,000 tons of coal. The United States have already located 291,485 square miles of coal field, with probably 333,000 more in the west, together, 624,485 square miles, and produce but 50,000,000 tons of coal. Our iron fields are in proportion. There is hardly a metal or mineral, from iron to gold, or from granite and lime stone to the most precious gems, but we find it in abundance in the United States. With such manufacturing facilities, it is robbery on the soil and a crime against humanity and its future, to take from our land crop after crop, that England, France, or Germany may lay theirs in pasture and go into the more profitable form of labor —manufacturing. We are inflicting rickets upon future generations by trading away in advance their bread for our nick-nacks. The luxuries we consume should be paid for by the luxuries we produce. We smile at the savage who trades away his land for a bottle of whisky or some trinkets, and trade away the vegetable soil of our broad acres for champagne or other foreign trifles.

Let nations manage their sewage and return it to the soil instead of poisoning the streams with it, and the equilibrium between taking from the soil and returning to it being restored, mother earth will never tire giving.

We can not become again a purely agricultural people, no more than we can go back to the hunter state. From common manufacturers we must advance to art industries and high art. With agricultural prosperity towns sprung up with factories formerly located in distant large cities, which can to-day only maintain themselves by excelling in ornamental industries and high art, hitherto the boast of foreign countries.

In proportion as the new education spreads the spirit of industry over the country, the raw material will be manufactured into articles of use nearer the place where it is raised; there will be, consequently, less trading, less rapacity, and less over-reaching.

With the spread of industry, producers and consumers are brought together, their interests are blended, and their mutual rights respected. The absorption of capital, the uncertainty of commerce, and outside profits are diminished in proportion as unnecessary middle-men disappear from the scene. An over growing commerce, aiming at extended markets, and meeting foreign competition, must necessarily sell low and in great quantities, which requires cheap production, or slop work, which more than any other cause deteriorates the laborer and the public taste, and injures thereby most materially the interests of the work-people.

CAPITAL INTERESTED IN THE EFFICIENCY OF LABOR.

Unless labor is made more efficient by scientific and art industrial education, capital can get no return for its daily increasing investments, and high professional skill will look in vain for its proper remuneration. Hittel, in his " History of Culture," shows that the poor of the world pay annually in interest or profit, to the rich, about $11,000,000,000 including $4,000,000,000 on large estátes in land; $2,000,000,000 in the excess of the salaries of high officials above the average income of the people; $1,200,000,000 on large manufacturing establishments; $800,000,000 on public debts; $500,000,000 on private debts and railroads; and $1,000,000,000 on large capital invested in the commercial and financial business not included in the foregoing items. This taxes every producing laborer—whose number we may put at 200,000,000—with fifty-five dollars per annum; which certainly he can not produce over and above his living, unless his efficiency is increased by an improved industrial education.

2*

The same author estimates that one in two thousand adult males is a high professional man, with an average income of thirty dollars per day; the second class of professional men, perhaps one in two hundred, have an income of ten dollars per day; third-rate professional men, perhaps one in forty, get four dollars per day; all of which must ultimately come out of labor, which it only can if the education of the masses is completely changed and brought into harmony with the new era in agriculture, trades, means of communication, and commerce, all of which have undergone a complete revolution.

.THE RATES OF WAGES.

A high rate of modern wages, which may any how be reduced in favor of capital, is an assump. tion contradicted by unquestionable facts of history. To be sure, common wages were but four-pence per day in England during the fourteenth and fifteenth centuries, but then an ox sold for twelve to sixteen shillings, or a farthing and a half per pound; a sheep for fourteen to sixteen pence; butter for three farthings per pound; cheese for a half-penny; eggs, twenty-five for a penny; and a quarter of wheat for five shillings; so that an English day laborer could procure about half a quarter of beef or four bushels of wheat with his weekly wages, which is, after all, a great deal more than he can get to-day.

According to Hallam's statement, laborers were better provided with means of subsistence in the reign of Edward III. or Henry VI. than at present. And in place of many similar authoritative statements, we will quote but that made in Parliament by Lord John Russell, an English premier: " If we compare the condition of this country with what it was a century ago, it is impossible not to see, that while the higher classes have advanced in luxury beyond measure .... while the middle classes have made a very great advance .... if we look to the quantity of necessaries which the wages of the laboring classes would buy in the middle of the last century, and that which they can buy now, I think we must be convinced that they have not participated in an equal degree in the advantages which civilization and increased knowledge have conferred upon us."

Another English premier, Gladstone, expressed himself equally emphatic against the inordinate gains capital had made in our day. " The growth of wealth," he says, " has been such that in the moral sphere it would not be too much to call it a revolutionary change. .... Progress of all kind is good ; but our instinct tells us that there are certain rates of progress which it is necessary to observe."

We admit manufactures have been brought within the reach of many; but of what avail is the cheapness of comforts to laborers short of means for procuring necessaries? And hence, with the daily growing scarcity of necessaries, and the increase of investments looking for a favorable return, there remains but one thing for capital as well as for labor, which is the increase of the productiveness of the latter through industrial education.

CLASS AND NATIONAL ANIMOSITIES.

Class prejudices intensified by national animosities towards our mostly foreign working population blinding us, we consider their great misery—if we notice it at all—as self-inflicted by shiftlessness or other willful causes, forgetting that the average income of their families is but between $300 and $400 per annum ; that much mismanagement is the result of poverty, and that the squandering of wages is but an exception. We must discard an indiscriminate condemnation of the poor as well as of the rich ; the miseries of the one are, as a rule, not their own fault, nor are the riches of the other always robbery. Let us be just to the poor, that they may be just toward us.

THE NATURAL EQUIVALENT FOR LABOR.

We have assumed nothing in setting out in our inquiry into the condition of the masses, but having found their death rates, and every sort of defectiveness, excessive, and having upon a minute study of their mode of living, ascertained an almost universal want of proper food, air, and other hygienic conditions, we form, by connecting the one with the other, a body of truth, unimpeachable, whether we study our subject in its causes or in its effect.

Social science as well as mechanical philosophy has to learn, from the doctrine of the correlation of forces, that man, as well as machinery, can *distribute*, but not *originate* power; and what has not been absorbed by the one as fuel or by the other as food, can not in either case appear as force, be the mechanical ingenuity ever so great or the taskmasters ever so severe.

The work a mill driven by water-power performs is neither more nor less—making allowance for friction—than the weight of the water impinging on the wheel multiplied by the velocity or fall of the stream. The same is true of windmills. In the steam engine the unit of heat that will raise the temperature of 1 lb. of water 1° Fahrenheit, will lift by the steam it generates 1 lb., 772 feet, or 772 lbs. 1 foot, and this mechanical equivalent of heat is ever the same, and not a pound can be lifted, be it but a fraction of a foot, but the fuel furnishing this much heat has been consumed.

It is plain, the same is true in reference to man. Whatever physical labor he engages in, either he has to overcome the power of gravitation or cohesion, as in lifting the hammer or digging, filing, sawing or planing, and this force is but another correlation of power engendered in the human body by a combustion, to which food furnishes the requisite fuel; and yet, in all ages and countries, have men tried, and are trying to-day, to get out of their fellows as much work as possible, without troubling themselves in the remotest if the equivalent of the work exacted is afforded to the work people in the shape of food or not. And herein man is at a disadvantage compared with a machine. If labor is exacted of him and its equivalent in food is not furnished, it is taken out of the constituent parts of his body, which is thus deteriorated.

Dr. Engel conclusively shows that if laborers do not receive in the shape of wages what has been expended in their rearing, insurance of this very capital with the interest on it, insurance, likewise, against loss of employment, sickness, old age and death, the nation itself is doomed to perish; for all this belongs to the cost of labor, and as a business man is bound to be ruined if he derives from the sales of his wares less than cost, so a nation must be ruined if a smaller return is made for its labor than its natural cost.

But do laborers get· even the small modicum requisite for keeping up the human economy, and the equivalent of the expenditure of force attending their daily labor? They certainly do not ; as the fewest of the laborers of the world get sufficient wages to indulge in the consumption of a sufficient quantity of wholesome meat, which, however, is indispensable to the steady workman, as the best of them, when deprived of it, sink in effectiveness down to the lowest ; while the poorest, when furnished with it, rise in effectiveness up to the standard of the best.

We do not cull our information from the sullen pages of social malcontents, but from the official correspondence of high diplomatists.

In Belgium very many of the work-people have for their entire subsistence potatoes with a little grease, brown or black bread, often bad, and for their drink the tincture of chicory ; sugar is seldom seen ; so is milk, except with the better class of workmen. When the wife has to work she has not time to attend to the cooking of the food, such as it is, nor can she mind the children, who, therefore, grow up in a state of misery, both physical and moral. The hucksters constantly adulterate everything they sell, and undermine the health as well as the pocket of the unfortunate workman. The children are employed from six to seven years. Many of the huts are unfloored.

In Holland meat is rarely tasted by the working-classes, and the average wages are far below the average bare necessaries of an ordinary workman with an average family, leaving a deficit to be made up by over-work or the help of wife and children. They live chiefly on potatoes, cheap vegetables, such as carrots, turnips, onions, etc. Labor is cheap, but performed without energy, and of comparatively poor quality.

In Saxony laborers take pork or other meat once or twice a week. What the man does not earn with his low wages must be made up by his wife, and if she is disabled the household gets into debt. The women nourish themselves with weak coffee often made from roasted barley, or grounds bought in hotels or taverns.

The food of the work people in Norway is of an inferior description, consisting in coarse rye or barley bread, porridge of barley or oats, potatoes or salt fish. Fresh meat is but seldom seen.

In Wurtemburg, many workmen can procure a warm meal but on Sunday, living all the week on brown, black, or rye bread, cheese and cold sausage.

Though labor is nominally cheap it comes in the end higher than in England.

In Prussia, fresh meat is with the work-people an exceptional luxury; their household economy is of the humblest kind.

In Denmark, the food of the common laborer chiefly consists of black bread. Of ten old work-men nine have to go to the parish for relief.

In Italy, at Genoa, the diet of the workman consists in soup twice a day, and a piece of bread with a piece of cheese, or lard, or fruit, or a pint of their wine. The Neapolitan lives on bread and vegetables, and is not fit for heavy work. The Sicilian artisan indulges in meat but once a week.

In Spain the laboring classes live on scanty food —bread and a cold soup of slices of cucumber, and bread steeped in vinegar and water.

The Wallachian lives on porridge made of maize, and seldom eats bread or meat.

In Russia the living of the operatives is very wretched, the food consisting hardly of anything else beside black bread and water, and occasionally only, a little tea; they work on an average thirteen hours per day, but accomplish little, and the children work as many hours as the men.

In Switzerland the working classes live principally on bread, cheese, potatoes, vegetables and fruit. They seldom eat meat above once a week, and even then in very small quantities.

In France the workmen live mostly on vegetables, but they never can perform two-thirds of the day's labor of an Englishman.

British workmen receive better wages than the workmen of any other European country; they are greater meat consumers, and their work is decidedly more efficient; and even they are outstript in effectiveness by American workmen, who consume still higher meat rations.

In turning our attention to the condition of the laboring masses in the United States, the only reliable statistics of labor we have present the following results:

The majority of the workmen of the State of Massachusets do not support their families by their individual earnings alone, but have to depend upon their children for from one-quarter to one-third of the entire family earnings, without which they would be in poverty and debt. Men and women are paid no more for their labor than the bare cost of subsistence, and are left to shift for themselves when they are sick, infirm, or without employment. And the last statistics of labor, as stated elsewhere —not to speak of the late hard times—showed the average income of average families below the average expenses for bare necessaries.

What a commentary this description of labor forms to its fearful death rates, its universal discontent, and universal communistic madness!

Execration of the inhumanity, and contempt for the folly returning from abroad with the eureka, *" Our masses must be fed on black broth like European laborers,"* that a few thousand princely merchants may engage in a profitable foreign trade to the ruin of the home market with its millions of small traders, is not all that is to be gathered from this sad picture of the masses, put by misery outside the pale of civilization, in the full blaze of the Christianity of the nineteenth century. There is a more fruitful lesson to be gathered from this almost universal poverty, and that is the comparatively unproductiveness of labor, which suffers from want of universal art and industrial education, in the absence of which there is a perfect insecurity of bread and comfort among the masses, into which, under the ever-shifting prosperity of trade and commerce, *all* sink sooner or later, so that in fact we are *all* but paupers, if not of to-day, of to-morrow or the day and generation after; against which doom universal art and industrial education alone can secure us and our children after us.

"A sin," says Hood, "committed against a member of the social state is a sin against the whole state. There cannot be a large share of happiness where there is not an equal share of happiness. A man's property in his muscles should certainly be as sacred as that he holds in real estate, and yet he may work and work and not get for it the jail comforts of a criminal. The poor always pay more for what they get than the rich, and everybody knows tenement-house property pays the highest profits. The phrase is old : there is one law for the rich and another for the poor. It must be admitted that the laborer is in the main shamefully paid ; his risk of life and expenditure of strength are not at all considered. There is but little of comfort among the hard laborers of the land, and if they complain it is but a happy sign, that they have not fallen to the state of the savage who has no idea of higher wants."

INDIRECT TAXATION.

The very idea of graded taxation, or taxation in direct proportion to wealth, is scouted as robbery ; but, reader, has it ever occurred to thy mind, that all indirect taxation of commodities is graded taxation, or taxation in direct proportion to a man's poverty? Thus the government statistics of England, where indirect taxation is carried out, show, that men whose annual incomes amount to

$1,000,000		are taxed of the same 5 per cent.
50,000—$100,000	" " " 10 "
5,000—$25,000 .	" " " 15 "
1,000—$1,500	" " " 20 "
125—$250	" " " 30 "

What a commentary on human legislation! taxing a man who has a million of dollars to spend per annum 5 per cent of his spending money, and the poor man, who by toiling earns for his family $125—$250 per annum, 30 per cent of his hard earned wages. And this is the philosophy of indirect taxation.

HOME THE FOUNDATION OF THE FAMILY AND THE STATE.

We must kindle a passion for home and land. A plot of but one half or quarter of an acre is the most profitable and desirable investment, especially as a homestead, near a great city, where a man is confined to the factory during working hours. Such retired and thrifty country homes are a school of virtue and moderation to the family and the state, while the vicious company of crowded tenements is a school of vice which cultivates in the children of the honest poor criminal tendencies beyond their power to arrest.

The law of separating health from the contagion of disease and corruption holds as good in the moral as in the physical world; and our tenement houses, into which the workmen are crowded, are an infraction upon this inexorable law, sandwiching parents, who yearn to see their children grow up into noble men and women, between moral lepers, who render all their better efforts nugatory. The love of virtue and of their own offspring being daily and hourly offended by the inevitable moral deterioration eating into the flesh and bone of their family, they are filled with unutterable anguish and a gloom bordering on insanity.

Oh, let us arouse ourselves on behalf of men and women who love virtue and their children as well as we do ours, lest the contagion spread, and, drawn into the vortex of universal corruption, we too perish. If we do not recognize the law of the solidarity of mankind by saving one another, we shall have to bear witness to it by perishing together.

Wherever thou gambolest, God and scene enchanted, with thine own, in flowery lawn or on hillside, think on the poor woman, bent and broken with too much duty, in the sickening atmosphere of her darksome abode; think on the husband with the manly heart bursting within, at the thought and the sight of his worthy wife and innocent children pining away in a world full of light, joy and happiness for everybody but him and his own.

The delights of nature, the pleasures of art, and its own domestic bliss, to the sensitive mind, are but sermons of the bereavements of the poor, whose specter will ever haunt it until misery is haunted out of the world through universal moral and art industrial education, and rural homes for the producers of the land, who are, after all, men, aye, the children of God, like the best of us.

The double vice of commerce of over riding the interests of agriculture and humanity, is corrected by suburban or country homes for our factory population, a measure facilitated by our means for quick transit, and demanded by the interests of labor as well as capital.

We must encourage homesteads, or it will soon be in America as in the British Islands, where four-fifths of the soil is held by some 5,000 owners, or nearly one-half by less than 1,000; or as it is in Scotland, where more than one-fourth of the whole country is in the hands of 21 individuals; nearly one-half is the property of 49 individuals; more than three-fourths is owned by 583 persons; and one proprietor holds as much land as three millions of population.

With a population thus deprived of comfortable homes, rendered neat by the love with which we cherish the family hearth we call our own, the pitiful sight, common there, of children in numbers, dirty in rags, painfully amusing each other in the gutter, is not uncommon ; and gutter children has become a national phrase there, significant of the condition of the land, which is filled with misery, squalor, drunkenness, and anything but thrift.

There is not a land where the people are so torn from the soil as in England, and the result is, that in spite of its wealth and its industry, *according to the official statement of the medical officer of the Board of Health, one-fifth of the population have not the minimum of food requisite for the preservation of life and health.* This ought to be a warning to us, and stimulate the masses to acquire homes with small plots, the only security against bitter poverty and the relentless grasp of capital and its growing power of reducing wages to the point of starvation through the competition of labor against labor, in order to keep together body and soul.

Possessed of art industrial skill and property, workers would meet their employers as free and independent men, and no more odium would attach to their labor or wages than to the services or fees of lawyers or physicians.

It is time that we should awake to the common danger. Scores and scores of farms, covering from fifty to over a hundred thousand acres, each, foreshadow the day, not far off, when the land famine that has enthralled the masses of the British Isles, will turn even here the joy of life to sadness; when this fair land, broad enough for all the world, the sky that over-arches it, the forest and the gladsome prairie, the song of birds, and the enrapturing murmur of the stream winding its way through the peaceful meadow, will all taunt us with the reproach, that such wealth, such beauty, such a life estate has been taken from us, and that in our poverty the mercies of God do not avail us ; but slaves, we only half live by the sufferance of men. The warning has gone forth—let men who have children, who are fathers, and upon whom God has laid the responsibility of future ages, get a home and a green spot where generations of free men may bless their sires.

Individual estates are growing to proportions that ought to arouse men to thoughtfulness. According to the *Worker* founded by the liberality of Mrs. Elizabeth Thompson, in the interests of co-operative farming—an enterprise, by the way, in which she has been anticipated by twenty-two members of the English Parliament, who clubbed together for the same purpose just forty-five years ago—there are in Texas whole counties belonging to a few great cattle raisers. There is one estate in California half the size of the State of Rhode Island, and a single farm in Kansas which is re-

3

ported to have a river frontage of over thirty miles.
Of course, small farms can no more compete with
such estates than small capital can with large, and
hence co-operative farming alone can save us from
a country proletariate swelling that of our large
cities.

Quick transit is fast becoming a universal feature
of all large cities; let men secure country homes;
there is not an economical, sanitary, or moral consideration but urges this course.

Our crowded city homes outrank by their deadly
effect upon the pulmonary condition of sedentary
women the combined attack of a hundred fatal
trades, and loudly call for a removal to the more
healthful environments of suburban locations.

The great mortality from consumption among
domestics shows the tendency of sedentary life in
our present homes. The mothers among our
middle classes, the most noble type of humanity,
are to-day decimated by this plague, and transmit
their feebleness to their offspring. Can our cry to
heaven and humanity remain unheard in behalf of
these incarcerated mothers and martyrs? Let their
prison life and service be at least in country homes ;
that, cheered and invigorated by God's light and
air, their work and their duty in the family may
not prove death and destruction to them.

There is not a measure that regulates population

as well as the habit of providing a neat homestead for the family.

Professor Cairnes shows that Ireland doubles its population in twenty years, England in sixty-three, and France in two hundred and sixty-five. And why? Because the prevalence of small properties and the general good taste of the French people, have accustomed them to consider a comfortable home the indispensable prerequisite of a family.

COMMUNISM DESTROYS LIBERTY.

Communism curiously advises us to expunge individual responsibility; we insist upon extending it by extending facilities for proprietorship. The history of the world is but the history of liberty, and civilization has ever kept pace with the march of liberty. Individuality, energy, invention, commerce, wealth, art and science, with the rest of the social forces, and the whole of civilization, are but the evolution of liberty. The power of the rich and the few is, therefore, not to be broken through the destruction of wealth and liberty communism aims at; but civilization must march on and extend liberty to all classes and increase thereby their energy, their wealth and their power.

Tyranny is odious under any name, call it communism, monopoly or what you may. What we want is honest competition between free and inde-

pendent men.   Let work people have country
homes, raise their vegetables, milk, butter, meat,
etc., etc., and they will, as men of education and
property, deal with employers as equals, and get
just terms.   As men of education and property the
masses will not only be a numerical power used for
party purposes, but will contribute to the formation of a public opinion which will protect them in
their rights and interests.   *Even herein is our present public danger, for when large masses are precluded, as they are to-day, from making themselves
heard through public opinion by reason of their abject
condition or poverty and ignorance, revolution becomes
inevitable ; and hence the necessity that all the citizens
should share in the wealth and intelligence of the
community, that they may all share in the formation
of public opinion, and in the protection which this
great power affords in the modern state.*

When artisans, trained by men of science and
practical wisdom, will, as men of property and responsibility, affect public opinion, as they ought to
in matters that affect them vitally, our currency,
commercial, and railroad legislation will prevent
periodic financial crashes, which fully as much deteriorate and destroy the masses in our day as famine
did in the past.

The present murderous competition will be sufficiently checked without arbitrary interference with

individual liberty, by laborers owning and living in their own homes. Laborers living upon their own property improve the home market in a double way, by expending more of their wages in the purchase of their own fabricates, and by forcing better wages through greater independence.

The consideration property and education bestow, the assimilation with the best elements of the nation, and the consequent favorable public opinion, will call forth a wise factory legislation, extending its protective care to the sons and daughters of toil; character and dignity attaching to permanent homes will stop the deterioration that springs from loose morals, and the higher moral tone among the masses will lift higher the leaders and rulers of society, who never are but one or two grades above the common level; and the universal sentiment of temperance accompanying such a state, will turn yearly a half a billion dollars, and even more—our present annual liquor bill—into useful channels of trade, education, property, and its management will develop the character and the means of the work-people, and fit them for the formation of co-operative societies.

PRISON LABOR AND ART INDUSTRIES.

Things apparently of little moment in themselves are often of importance as disturbing ele-

ments, such is the prison-labor contract system,
and should be indirectly eliminated from our labor
market by art industrial education. In Pittsfield,
Massachusetts, the county received in 1878 $12
each quarter for the labor of each man sent to the
shop ; the labor thus costing the contractor one-
thirteenth of the usual price. At Ipswich, in the
same state, a contract was made for the labor of
twenty one men at fifteen cents per day each, and
at ten cents for the balance of the prisoners ; at
Springfield a contract for three cents per day was
made with the privilege of two years extension at
five cents per day. At Northampton the prisoners
have been hired at six cents per day, with the
privilege of five years extension. What a story of
despairing men, hollow-eyed women and children
in the gutters out of prison ; and what a tale does
this tell of pauperism, crime and barbarism among
men who have to compete with these sham wages,
which but poorly cover official bribes only the ill-
gotten gains of prison contractors can afford to pay ;
or, to put on a more charitable construction, it tells
a tale of heartless unconcern for the poor, and a
culpable indifference for pauperism with all its
criminal and race deteriorating tendencies. If the
state can not get just wages for prisoners' work
nor can employ them itself in trades, nor will make
them raise agricultural produce, let it educate the

masses for the higher industrial arts in which they will not be crushed by the sham wages of criminals who are supported by taxes wrung out of the sweat and poverty of honest laboring men.

TRADE UNIONS.

In the strife and pressure of the hour, workmen look for relief exclusively to their trade unions, which during 1824–1876 have grown in England from a few thousands to 1,250,000 in 3,000 independent societies, having a yearly income of $10,000,000, with their total reserve funds hardly less than that sum, and hardly this expresses their entire strength, which embraces the best part of the entire artisan population. Since the right of public assembly has been almost universally granted, trade unions are growing fast in number and influence everywhere. We admit, these powerful societies give to a poor isolated workman—who else would have no show of justice, nor could contract like a free man with capital—the dignity and independence of a man. We grant these powerful societies have forced important factory legislation protecting women and children, and called forth wholesome sanitary regulations and kindred measures. Still, though workmen might be worse off without such backing, they best know, their situation is far from being rendered satisfactory by it.

CO-OPERATION.

The ablest thinkers of the day look to co-operation as the settlement of our labor troubles. Co-operation, it is maintained, is not a thing of yesterday. Birmingham had a co-operative tailor shop as far back as 1777 ; Hull had a co-operative mill in 1795 ; Woolwich had a co-operative store in 1806, and Davenport in 1815. About 1830-35 there existed in and about London forty six co-operative societies. Manchester and Salford had then ten, and the whole of England about four hundred. According to a parliamentary return of 1874, there are in England and Wales, 790 co-operative societies, with 340,930 members, having a share capital of $16,670,520, and a profit of $4,793,605 for 1873. But this account does not include many societies which have not registered, nor those of Scotland which has 255 registered societies.

The town of Oldham has eighty joint stock co-operative mills. In the county of Lancashire there are one hundred and fifty. The most important of these associations is the Industrial Co-operative Society of Oldham, founded in the year 1850-51 ; which, beginning small, paid to its members in 1872 a dividend of $200,000, and does a yearly business of $1,250,000. The Sun Mill Company, another co-operative association of Oldham has a capital of $500,000. The Oldham Industrial Society had in 1874, 5,344 members with a capital of $430,000. (Holiyoke's History of Co-operation).

The celebrated Rochdale Pioneer Society was formed in 1844 by seventeen poor weavers, with a total capital of $140, and their business amounted in 1876 to $1,525,950.

The profits in 1876 were, in the

Rochdale Store	-	-	- $253,346
Halifax ,,		-	- 99,100
Leeds ,,		-	- 172,550

According to the Registrar's return, the purchases of the co-operative stores in 1877 amounted to $53,047,575. The Co-operative Wholesale Society of Manchester sold in the same year to 588 co-operative societies goods amounting to $13,957,385. This co-operative wholesale society has a boot, biscuit, and soap factory, as also engine works; besides which it holds shares in seventeen manufacturing, printing, coal and insurance companies. There is hardly a respectable town in the United Kingdom but has a co-operative store, and large towns such as London, Manchester, Liverpool, and Glasgow have large co-operative wholesale societies owning dairies, flour mills, and similar branches.

In Germany, Schultze—Delitzsch started in 1859 co-operative credit societies for furnishing honest

3*

workmen capital upon liberal terms. There were
of these societies in

	Duly Reported.	Members.		Loans.
1861	340	133	50,000	$12,500,000
1865	890	455	135,013	36,110,619
1871	2,059		1,200,000	300,000,000
1875	2,763	815	418,251	498,549,479

Already in 1872 there were reported aside of
these credit associations 440 productive associations, 902 co-operative consumptive stores and 37
building societies.

Paris had, according to Levasseur, in 1866–1867-
120 credit associations, seven consumptive and
fifty one productive societies. Lyons had at the
same time twenty two consumptive stores, besides
many productive associations. There were then
large productive as well as consumptive associations at Pau, at Poully on the Loire, at Moulereau,
at Saint Etienne, at Elfent, at Alger, at Guebwiller,
at Dienz, at Havre, Marseilles, Mulhouse, Passy,
Vienne on the Isère and at Toulouse.

There are to day at least forty productive associations in Paris, of which several do a very large
business ; every province in France has them.
Lyons has 1,800 co-operative members, and Saint
Etienne 1,200 ; a sufficient evidence of the capacity
of workmen to be their own masters.

There certainly is a remarkable success of co-
operative societies of consumption in England, of
co-operative societies of production in France, and

of co-operative societies of credit in Germany, though the latter have spread beyond France and England to Denmark, Russia and Italy, and even to Spain, in which industrial societies were introduced in 1862, and have increased in 1870 to 196 with 25,000 members, and an aggregate yearly business of $22,500,000.

Co-operation has never been lost sight of by the sons and daughters of toil in New England since 1845, when the New England Protective Union was started.

In 1849, 73 divisions did a co-operative business of $638,636.53; in 1852, 403 divisions did a co-operative business of $1,696,825.46.

The sales of the American Protective Union, a branch of the New England Protective Union, amounted in 1853 to $1,100,000; in 1854 to $1,536,000; in 1855 to $1,400,000; and in 1856 to $1,492,000. This union counted in 1859 about 600 co-operative stores.

After the war the co-operative spirit revived again, and twenty workingmen's co-operative associations, among which a number were manufacturing companies, were organized during 1866–1871 in various New England towns, and in 1874 the Sovereigns of Industry organized, who counted in 1875, 153 councils and 12,077 members. The average monthly business of twenty nine of the co-operative stores of that order amounts to $49,806.

Beside these co-operative provision stores the Sovereigns of Industry managed about fifty to sixty co-operative enterprises, as cigar, chair, foundry and the like undertakings.

The seventy-two communistic societies, representing a capital of $12,000,000, which Nordhoff met with in the United States, can find no place in a survey of co-operation, as communism crushes the individual which co-operation seeks to strengthen. While co-operation, by securing to everybody property, favors responsibility, moral power, character and individuality, communism destroys every one of these chief elements of human nature and civilization.

The very nature of co-operation and its spread, make it the hope of many, who consider it the solution of the social question and the future of labor, a view advocated by men like Lord Brougham, John Stuart Mill, Gladstone, Bright and Cobden.

Industrial partnership, or a fixed share in the profits of an enterprise constituted the reward of labor at different times and places, and has lately been added to the common wage system, to improve and modify it, by interesting the laborer in his work, and giving him a chance to accumulate capital. We cannot enter at length upon the various forms of industrial partnerships, premiums or bonuses paid in addition to wages, and in proportion to profits and labor, in the shape of a contribution to the workman's sick and the like funds, or as a starting capital ; but as they are a step in the direction of co-operation, a resumé of their success in various countries and industries as presented in Böhmer's excellent work on the subject cannot fail to interest, and is given in the following table :

Distribution of 120 industrial partnerships in different pursuits and countries.

Groups	INDUSTRIES	Germany	Switzerland	France	England	Belgium	Austria	Denmark	Norwegia	Sweden	Russia	Italy	America	Total
I.	Agricultural and management of forests	8	1	3	1									13
II.	Fisheries and Navigation	1	1	1										3
III.	Mining, Foundries, Quarries, Potteries and Porcelain factories	8	1		4	1								14
IV.	Metal industries, Machinery, Tools and Apparatus	4	4	1	1	1		1					1	13
V.	Chemical Industries, Heating & Illuminating Material	4	1									1		6
VI.	Textile, Paper and Leather Industries	16	14		2		1	1	1		1		1	37
VII.	Woodwork Industries	1								1				2
VIII.	Building Trades	2	1	2										5
IX.	Industries of Food & Consumption, Tobacco, &c.	5			1		1							7
X.	Clothing Industries, Shoes, &c.												1	1
XI.	Book-printing, & Engraving			5										5
XII.	Commercial, Railroads, &c.	5	2	5	1	1								14
		54	25	17	10	3	2	2	1	1	1	1	3	120

Admitting that co-operation, uniting the laborer and capitalist in the same person, removes industrial strife and class feeling, that all profit being pocketed by the laborer he will be all honor and industry; that, studying the enterprise he is interested in, he will become an intelligent agent ; that, being his own master, he will avoid processes, methods and conditions destructive of his health or nobler characteristics of manhood; that he will improve in dignity with his more independent position—admitting that co-operation means universal justice, industry and improvement, we must first of all moralize the masses by an education which is to prepare them for co-operating with one another, or we bring co-operation into discredit by the inevitable failure which must follow the unfitness of its members. Co-operation requires the greatest confidence of the co-operators in one another, the greatest harmony among them, strict discipline and voluntary subordination, qualities not apt to prevail among a population growing up fighting and quarreling in the gutters. We want an infant education specifically aiming at a state of mind and morals, which are the soil in which co-operation finds its natural growth.

Again, the co-operative performance of unskilled individuals amounts to but little ; and if the laborer is not merely to live by his work, but to accumu-

late capital and reserve funds he must possess the
highest industrial efficiency; and hence co-operation,
next to a social and moral education, demands a
thorough art industrial training.

If our work is to be co-operative, not only must
the school start us rightly, but the education of the
world must fit and prepare us for it ; and that it
does through associations in which the individual
finds a safeguard against dangers, of which to bear
the risk he is too weak. Our civilization has certainly been tending that way for the last fifty years ;
and the increase of insurances—life, fire, marine,
against rail-road, and other accidents, of crops
against storms, of live stock, etc., etc.—all this is
preparing us for co-operation in the main work and
business of life, and hence the importance of work-
ing-men's associations and benefit societies, which
must insure him against all possible risks, the premiums upon which we have elsewhere shown to
form an integral part of normal wages. The table
following shows the ratio of the insured to the
population in various countries.

Italy	.	.	.	1 in	195
Belgium	.	.	.	1 "	104
France	.	.	.	1 "	2S
Switzerland	.	.	.	1 "	25.7
England	.	.	.	1 "	3

THE REAL PROBLEM AND ITS SOLUTION.

Communists and all make a mistake in thinking
the social question to be merely one of distribution,
namely—how shall the people be supplied with the
necessary articles of consumption, and the first
mean to cut the Gordian knot by making the state
the proprietor of all capital in the name and for the
benefit of all. In truth, however, the difficulty
arising from machinery displacing labor is not how
shall the people be fed, clothed and housed, but
how shall men be kept busy? Think of thirty
thousand idle hands and brains in a city, or of a
couple of millions in the land; who is wise enough
to foresee all the forms of mischief, folly, madness,
strife, war and revolt, such enforced idleness must
involve a nation in such an unnatural condition,
and which certainly would soon terminate in general imbecility and national decay through weakness
and corruption? Struggle means strength and
energy, inactivity means weakness, defeat and
death. The want of industrial occupation, which
invention and machinery are daily narrowing, is,
therefore, the main problem, which has to be met,
and that can only be done through the creation
of a general demand for hand and soul made work;
this being accomplished, and all being kept busy on
higher forms of art manufacture, the question of

subsistence finds its solution without dangerous interference with the present system of exchange, which, to say the least, is intimately interwoven with every fibre of our individual and collective nature, and cannot be disturbed without a revolution, the end of which is beyond our conception.

The question is not what shall the people eat, and wherewith shall they be clothed, but what shall they do, and wherewith shall they be employed? To employ our entire urban population on machine made goods, implies an activity in machinery and inventions which would continually throw them out of work by new methods of manufacturing constantly superseding each other. Beside, the endless multiplication of little comforts and conveniences brings with it a sort of Asiatic barbarity, overlaying life with too much that is artificial, unnatural and cumbersome. As to turning all agriculturalists, and producing bread stuffs in much larger quantities than we can consume for foreign markets, we have shown to be as great a crime against the future as it is a folly and unprofitable. Every extreme has its dangers, and our only safety is in the harmonious employment of our forces in the pursuit of agriculture, art and manufacture; and that of art we may increase to any degree necessary to employ the forces not absorbed in the other pursuits, if we only cultivate a severe taste and a pure feeling for the beautiful.

We must make the school as industrial as the age in which we live, and double the two great factors of demand and supply by an universal art industrial education, which does equalize the distribution of wealth as well as increase it, and by giving each a home with pure air to breath in, wholesome food and a clean shirt, give him a clean heart. Every effort we make to elevate man blesses us, but only he who follows in the lines in which Providence moves serves humanity efficiently.

The millions which are spent to-day in doling out a pittance to comparatively a few favored poor, and in the maintenance of the organizations of endless charities, their secretaries and numberless persons, would do infinitely more good if spent in the cultivation of industries which would put the masses above the necessity of seeking relief, and increase the wealth and prosperity of the land.

Our present method makes a hundred paupers for every one it but half relieves.

In adding annually to the wealth of the nation two or three thousand millions by a method which equalizes distribution as well as enhances production, we increase the moral quality of the nation as well as its riches, and only universal art industrial education can achieve this double result.

Co-operative farming may improve the condition of farmers, the twenty millions of people which our cities will ere long contain, the most suffering, most dangerous, and most influential part of the nation as far as the nature and progress of our civilization are concerned, universal art industrial culture alone can elevate above the present degradation of the masses.

The more we study the tendencies of art manual industry, the more we shall find it the only corrective of a centralizing industrialism which to day crowds, pauperizes and destroys the masses.

At present fraud and scheming are drawing elements to our large cities which demoralize the whole country; let us make them centers of art manual industries, and skill and honesty will soon become characteristic of the age.

Machinery aims at gain with as little labour as possible, the age of machinery is, therefore, very apt to be one of fraud and scheming, in which labor ceases to be considered a moral element; while art manual industry aiming at quality, recognizes in labor a moral element of human nature, and cultivates a love of skilled labor and honesty.

Work, the requisite of the health of the body and of the mind, as well as of society, failing to conform to our present high state of civilization, is ostracised, and hence the many ills that afflict us, and which can only be corrected by art manual culture, that alone can make men find in labor the satisfaction they seek to day in gain and pleasure, which lead to fraud and corruption.

Factory labor, by its endless division of labor, atomizes the masses ; under the regime of art manual industries, men working up to the same ideal will organize into guilds and societies, which foster a specifically communal life, bind men together for higher human purposes, prevent decay, and develop the seed of a new and healthful social growth.

PART II.

ÆSTHETIC CULTURE.

HEREDITY AND THE ÆSTHETIC ELEMENT.

Race Education looking to hereditary race improvement cannot neglect the culture of æsthetic impressions which, according to Herbert Spencer, are largely a "growth rising with the advance of intellectual culture from the crude enjoyments of sensation to the more refined and subtle delights of the cultivated mind."

Carpenter, the physiologist, remarks upon the universality and the hereditary tendencies of the æsthetic feelings: "They exist in very different intensity in different individuals . . . . they constitute a fundamental part of our nature . . . . and are peculiarly susceptible of development, however, by appropriate culture; under the influence of which, they not merely grow up in the individual, but manifest themselves with increased vigor and more extended range in successive generations of mankind."

In a list of forty two great painters twenty one had relatives illustrious in that art, and there are plenty of families of painters, as the Landseers in England, the Bonheurs in France, the Bellinis in Italy. Van der Weldes in Holland, etc.

That the imagination, projecting all that is grand in art, as well as in science and government, is automatic or chiefly organic, and hence largely hereditary and falling within the domain of a permanent and progressive Race Education, is plain from Carpenter's researches on Mental Physiology. The very exuberance of the productive power of the imagination betrays its automatic nature, which is best illustrated by the effusions of a Walter Scott, a Hook, a Coleridge, a Mozart, or a Wordsworth, whose imagination has become automatic by severe training, and who says, "All good poetry is the spontaneous overflow of powerful feeling, and the best is produced by obeying blindly and mechanically the impulses of cultivated habits."

A truly great work of art, says Carpenter, tends to develop in successive generations an ever increasing capacity for refined enjoyment which will thus add largely to the happiness of the race, and there can be no doubt that the present taste for the picturesque is a growth of landscape painting scarcely three hundred years old.

The same writer dwells upon the important fact

that all great practical inventions or discoveries in science are the work of a sublime imagination. To cultivate the imagination is, therefore, to increase the power of invention and scientific discovery, and, in fact, to furnish leaders and master minds in every great work, be it government, religion, art or science, especially if this culture be coupled with steady application and serious training. Upon the wings of this divine faculty do we rise to man's ideal state, or the Kingdom of heaven, the highest, brightest and holiest conception, without which life is not worth living.

Galton concludes his great labors on hereditary genius with the practical remark, if we could but raise the character of the masses one grade, our eminent men would be ten times as numerous, and we would get, besides, some illustrious beyond the present measure, who would give the age an altogether higher direction. Another of his inductions is, that steady, energetic and industrious application characterizes the higher civilization. Early industrial Education advocated in these pages supplies the training that will lift the masses beyond the present grade of mentality. We must join in the Education of the masses the inspiration of art with the steadiness of persevering industry, and thought with sentiment or quickening emotion.

ART, HER NATURE, CLAIMS AND EMPIRE.

An industry inefficient for the employment as
well as for the support of the masses has led us to
æsthetic culture as an economical necessity. Still,
we confess art has broad claims aside from all utili-
tarian considerations.   Art, science and religion,
says Hegel, embrace each the whole of life and
the Absolute.   Art duplicates man's inner life and
places it before his reflection as the embodiment
of his thoughts, feelings and experience.

The past of art, which is so much extolled to
us, will pale before its great future.   The abnormal
and the spasmodic draw more attention than the
normal and the steady, still the latter have more
breadth and importance.   Once we read the fate
of men and empires in the stars, it was a magnificent science, now lost—well, astronomy has taken
the place of astrology ; it is the same with alchemy,
or the art pretending to make gold, which has
given way to chemistry that makes precious
stones ; the once pompous rites of religion have
given way to a spiritual power, the very culmina-
tion of religion, which controls to day our very
thoughts and conduct of life, and so art, .which
once meant statues, pictures, songs and music, is
but patch work when held up to what we call to
day, or soon shall call, art—*the perfect work as full*

of beauty as of use in every line of human life or activity.

The childhood of the race is often spoken of as the period peculiarly proper for art. All the relations of life, the social, religious and political, were then, we are told, poetical, while with us all is sober science. We forget that past views appear only to us poetical, because we do not consider them as matters of fact, for which, however, they were taken in their own day. Neither is art a matter of fastidious taste and fickle fancy, but has its science and stern facts. An age of science far from being adverse is absolutely favorable to art, and it was so in ancient Greece. A correct knowledge of art, as well as of the mental states attending the creation, or the enjoyment of a work of art requires deep reflection. It calls for a clear head, a feeling heart and a ripe life full of experience, in short, it calls for a full and perfect life and not for flippant amateurship. True art is even impossible without mature reflection. The latest works of Göethe and Schiller were their most perfect, and in his old age blind Homer gave us his Iliad, as Hegel observes. Facts are grander and more poetical than illusions, and nature is full of beauty and poetry though she is all fact and science.

In our view of art, as the perfect work, as full of beauty as of use, in every line of human activity,

4

her empire must widen with the ages until all men are brought under her sway. As science and religion have enlarged their spheres of usefulness until nothing escapes them, so will art extend her empire until she embraces the whole of life.

THE INFLUENCE OF ÆSTHETIC CULTURE.

There is not an aspect of life æsthetic culture does not improve, be it the individual, the family, or the state. Art enhances life from infancy to old age. It softens the asperity of man, and prevents the natural softness of woman from degenerating into effeminacy. Morals, religion, commerce, manufacturing, literature, the theatre and every other department of human life and activity improve under its influence.

Æsthetic culture ennobles our wants, it translates us through art into the ideal world of beauty, which if it is not the same as that of the good is at least its symbol.

Surrounded by nature, her harmony, universality and immutability steal in upon the æsthetically cultured soul and stamp it with her own divine attributes. Deprived of such culture, insensible in the great school of nature and unaffected by her lessons, we grow narrow, partial and out of accord with eternal love, truth and beauty.

Well may, therefore, all lovers of their kin advocate the equal importance of æsthetic education as an efficient means for the elevation of mankind. The signs of the times are, æsthetic culture will be made universal, a new road will be opened to American genius, and the coming ages will witness the rise of an art before which that of ancient Greece and Italy will wane as the morning dawn does before the full splendor of midday.

Æsthetic pleasures, though mild and gentle, form in the aggregate a not inconsiderable part of the sum of human happiness. The lower passions may stir us deeper, but are also oftener turned into agents of human misery.

Æsthetic culture fills us with delight at the sight of art touches, of which each calls to mind pleasures reaped from past studies of one or another of the masters, and every present enjoyment of the beautiful in nature is intensified by association with similar past emotions.

Art making us happier makes us better. That is not all, but art taking its motives from home— religious — or public life, the ethical and the æsthetical blend into one, whereby morality loses its sternness and becomes fairer, and art loses its seductiveness and becomes more noble and dignified.

ÆSTHETIC CULTURE THE MEASURE OF OUR CIVILIZATION.

The æsthetic culture of a nation is the measure of its civilization. The architecture of a people gives the foreign traveler his first impressions of a country, and its remains impress the archæologist with the character of the extinct race. Neither is this a superficial judgment. As we are, so we build. Houses, temples, churches and other public buildings, landscape gardening, etc., are the projections of our thoughts and feelings and as true to us as our shadow is to our body.

Architecture, home and costume are all the outgrowth of the æsthetic culture of a nation. In antiquity the forum and the temple had architectural beauty, the home was hardly known, public life swallowed up the individual. Woman was a slave and hardly the companion of man. There is no home without woman, and only since she has attained her position man has got a home, which adorned by the art tastes of a people of universal æsthetic culture, will assign to us our place among the civilizations of the world. We do not mean to slight the mind, spirit and culture reflected from the ancient temple, but what are they compared with the mind, spirit and culture reflected from private houses, each representing a temple with many compartments, of which each is a shrine of Godlike men, women and children.

Tenement houses, filthy streets, rum holes, gambling houses, unclean hearts and lips, polluted hands, neglected bodies and souls, what a multiplicity of work æsthetic culture will find among us to do! Our police stations, jails and Blackwell's Island, barefooted and ragged children, mothers disfigured by hard work and poverty, garrets with poor men, women and children starving or violently throwing open the gates of death with a suicidal hand; who will dare say all this and more, which we pass by for decency's sake, could exist but a day in a community of universal æsthetic culture? This Augean stable is too much for a few hands, but were our entire respectability truly refined, such a world would be too soul harrowing for its comfort, and things would soon be changed.

Men unfitted by natural defectiveness for continued hard work have to day no other alternative than pauperism and crime. Æsthetic culture while it adds the new higher motive for work—the love of the beautiful—introduces also work of a more facile and less exhaustive nature, and thus doubly lessens the present fatality of pauperism and crime.

Æsthetic training stimulates the demand for works of pure art, for ornamental goods made and finished by hand, as also for a finer grade and a greater variety of machine made fancy goods.

GREEK ART AND NOT GRAMMAR WANTED.

While we would take the Greek grammar out of the hands of nine young men in ten who are to day crammed with it, we insist on spreading art opportunities until not a poor man in the land shall lift his eyes to the ceiling of his modest room but he shall meet there the elevating influence of the severe intellectual-beauty of the works of art of Greece. We discard the soul killing grammar, but plead for Phidias, Praxiteles, Apelles, etc.

ÆSTHETIC EDUCATION AND MORAL ELEVATION.

The æsthetic education of young pupils, says Eugene Véron, requires that we expand their moral qualities, the very source of art; refine their sensibilities, elevate their conceptions and warm their imagination by liberal ideas, familiarity with masterpieces of art, a comprehension of what constitutes the basis of human society and the grandeur of man's nature, and by whatever is calculated to awaken and develop enthusiasm and poetic sentiment, for as the imprint of the individuality of the artist upon his work constitutes his style, the elevation of art must depend upon the generosity and loftiness of the individuality of the artist.

In the æsthetically cultured State the inbred regard for what is honorable and beautiful makes men fly from whatever is mean and unsightly in character or action. Greece, therefore, had as many heroes and patriots as sculptors and poets. A nation whose ideal in art is next to perfect has necessarily a high ideal of private and public life, and hence the importance of æsthetic culture to the State. Art when guarded by science against the excesses of an unruly imagination is the most effective school of morals for the people, and the French—like the old Greeks—are often safely directed in their moral conduct by their delicate feeling for the beautiful.

Æsthetic growth implies, according to Schiller, moral freedom and sociability as its conditions.

Æsthetic culture trains us for perceiving the beautiful in this best of possible worlds, as Leibnitz calls it, a faculty most essential for our peace in a critical age naturally leaning to pessimism.

ÆSTHETIC EDUCATION IS LIVING CULTURE.

The æsthetic education we are entering upon must avoid the old vice of cramming with words or even with examples; we want spontaneous activity and real art work. Words have only a meaning if they follow work and things, but not if they precede it.

Bright objects, beautiful colors, forms and sounds,

cleanliness, order and a certain symmetry of conduct, regard for what is beautiful in manners, the recitation of stories and songs, are all conducive to the development of the feeling of the beautiful; but all these, and the like means of æsthetic culture will suggest themselves, and form, in conjunction with design, and other parts of a complete industrial art-culture, a system of æsthetic education which will give us the æsthetic State, in which there will be no place for corrupt officials or the low greed of mammon worshiping citizens. A mere babbler may be a master in scholastic teaching; industrial, æsthetic and ethical training require a thorough man and character. The world has hardly yet conceived a complete education of the hearts and hands of all the people, one not only for general purposes, but for definite usefulness in life; and may we not hope democratic America, in its power and wisdom, will realize it? In Europe, we fear, the court, the army, the church and the aristocracy eat up the State, and leave but very inadequate means for the education of the masses.

ÆSTHETIC EDUCATION UNREASONABLY NEGLECTED.

Religion, art, literature, private and public amusements, public buildings, customs, manners, dress, conduct, our very frame of body and mind, and entire character—in short, what we are and do, greatly depend upon the degree of our æsthetic culture.

There is beauty in form, magnitude, number, relation, color, light, shade, organization and function, in short, it is the perfection of being, and the very soul of whatever is pleasing in thought or sensation.

It is in sky, earth and ocean, in sun, moon and stars, in whatever lives or is; it endears to us men, nature and all things. And this faculty of the beautiful, so potent for what we are, create, or enjoy, and which more than any other determines our civilization, wealth and happiness, we neglect. Of course, this, like every other faculty, grows by spontaneous exercise, but its full strength is only attained by persistent, methodical culture. Our education may be ideal and subjective, looking to man; or practical and objective, looking to his work; in either case it ought to be æsthetic, training him to harmony of feeling and action, without which neither he nor his work can be perfect.

How much happiness do we lose, and how much less do we bestow through our lack of knowledge and training in the elements of beauty which are scattered all around us and within us. A general æsthetic culture would far more sustain a correct moral deportment than the present culture of the intellect. A man clean and neat in his tastes and habits, is, in nine cases out of ten, a good man; which is more than can be said of men noted for their intellectual attainments.

Beauty thrills body and mind, its impressions are deep and lasting, and improve our character, while intellectual conceptions pass over the mind as a shadow does over a sheet of water.

It was the conjunction of art culture with environments that developed the superiority of the Greek character.

The National Government stirs up the nation to intellectual activity through its great departments of State, the treasury and the interior, each of which sends out daily a thousand messages of vast importance. To show up properly the work of any one of these great departments, and their influence upon the nation, would require volumes, and they are the great college of the people in matters of greatest import, our civil, economical and political existence, and keep the intellect of the nation active.

Legislative assemblies and courts of justice may be said to stimulate the moral life of the nation, and are a practical school of morals, as the church develops the religious feelings; we, therefore, plead for the systematic culture of our neglected æsthetic faculty, which is allied to all that is elevating and inspiring, and making life charming and beautiful.

ÆSTHETIC CULTURE AND NATIONAL TYPE.

With the spread of æsthetic culture, and a higher ideal life and its work, the very type of the nation improves in beauty of form as well as in physical strength. Assyrians, Persians, Grecians, Etruscans, all who left monuments of an art life, were races of beauty and strength; and governments should cultivate the sense of the beautiful in the interest of a nation's strength and preservation.

ART THE MONUMENTAL RECORD OF THE RACE.

Who but takes literature for the embodiment of human sentiment in all its depth and variety, as the flower of civilization; well, art represents the feelings, struggles, and higher life of men and races, in the past and present, a sort of monumental record that needs but to be glanced at to be taken in as a whole, and to inspire us with the power of creating works of an equally high art. Science, religion and art form the complete trio of civilization. Our schools sacrifice all to a few shreds of science. Art is in fact the realization of every element of civilization. It speaks through the eye to the heart and mind, and busies the hands of millions with work, the making as well as the possessing of which is a pleasure.

THE ELEVATION OF WORK INTO THE SPHERE
OF ART.

The stern realism of the age calls for art, which mediates the ineffable, and is as serene and cheerful as the light of day. Not the mere knowledge of the laws of nature, but the creation of works of art, the beauty of which uplifts and inspires the beholder, is the acme of human power and ability. The school must make us productive, or the world will discard its wisdom altogether. Our ten fingers are so many of God's commandments admonishing us to work, and the education of the masses can aim at nothing higher than at rendering them useful and happy by lightening their burden and their drudgery through the elevation of work into the sphere of art. We repeat it—the elevation of work into the sphere of art must be the aim of education, and no other aim is worthy of it—next to that of the preservation of the race—in this cosmopolitan age, which must extend the blessings of the few to the many left to perish in other ages.

Our cities are reflecting a higher civilization, and with the eye the heart is uplifted by spire and palace ; but O, for the dilapidation of that temple of God—man, crowned by his Maker with beauty and elegance of form above any other creature. Good men do unprofitably wear themselves out in hunting down this, that or some other evil, but here is the hydra we must unite our attacks upon— pauperism, nursed by what are very properly called "*grammar*" schools.

Days, nights and years consumed in deep thought and meditation, dear lives given up, and happiness, and all else, are well spent in the struggle with the monster our schools foster, if we only thereby carry some of the light and joy of God's beautiful creation into the homes of the poor.

SOURCE AND POWER OF THE NATIONAL STANDARD OF BEAUTY.

Genius, wealth and happiness cannot but spring up from the Divine Power cropping out in the infinitude of forces, forms and developments, spiritual and physical, progressing through the ages, which by a sort of divine alchemy, combining and uniting again in the conception, sentiment or aspect of a nation concerning the moral and material universe, form the standard of perfection and beauty from which rise a truly national art and literature, inexhaustible fountains of life and inspiration to many generations.

The marriage of body, soul and nature and what is divine in them, the union of infinite elements and the full activity of our powers to the highest degree of health and vigor constitute the nature of art or beauty and its heavenly thrill.

What a silent admonition has for our restless and artificial world the beautiful, which according to Winkelman, consists in noble simplicity and quiet grandeur.

The contemplation of art is the best training for solving difficult intellectual problems, as the beautiful is undistinguishable from the true, says Plato.

Language, expression, gait, thought, action and everything else is but art and perfected by æsthetic culture. Pythagoras with true philosophical vision discovered the cause of all in numbers, as rhythm is the very soul of things, the motion of the stars is the music of the spheres, and the world is a veritable cosmos or universal order and beauty.

INSPIRATION MUST TAKE THE FORM OF WORK.

Inspiration with the masses must take the form of work; all may become artists, but not metaphysicians. Philosophy may suggest to the few the absolute; the many, beauty alone can lead to the perfect. And even a mind like Aristotle declares poetry more philosophical and serious a matter than metaphysics, and Schelling's estimate of art is the same.

FURTHER EXPLANATIONS ABOUT THE BEAUTIFUL.

Art, says Taine, is philosophy made sensible. Art is the poetry of work as well as of religion. It is the worship of strength and beauty.

Make the masses through judicious early training art workers, and the diffusion of energy and beauty will give rise to the creation of a new heaven and a new earth.

A universal reign of art would elevate the standard of character lowered to day by the vulgar estimate put upon wealth.

To the good and the useful predominating in our ideal of to day we must add the beautiful, which is but another rendering for the spiritual, as "it is mind alone that is beautiful, and in perceiving beauty we only contemplate the shadow of our own affection."

ART IS THE CORRECTIVE OF MATERIALISM.

Art is the idealization of the senses and their corresponding feelings and impressions, which, as Taine says, form our character, and hence it is the corrective of the materialistic tendency of the age. As the beautiful requires an ideal motive as well as a perfect form, the just balance between mind and matter is the constant lesson of art. As every art seeks the perfect and the pure, but the work cannot rise above the master, the artist must himself be perfect and pure, neither can the contemplation of art give pleasure to the unwise and impure. And as a work of art must be the honest expression of the soul and feeling of the artist, as Véron says, the cultivation of art is a school of integrity. The admiration of the beautiful, Kant justly remarks, is the most unselfish of feelings, and even herein is the elevation of art, that in the contemplation of its works we get rid of ourselves.

PHILOSOPHY IS FOR THE FEW, ART FOR THE MANY.

Mankind are not to be plodding forever like the ox, nor can they become all pure thinkers, of whom the philosopher of Königsberg said that there are but a very few in any generation, while habit, education, strong feeling and temperament, which interfere with pure thinking, form the marked artist. Philosophy is for the few, art for the many; and fine feeling, the twin of art, becomes much more a part of ourselves, and is so much more a safe guide for truth as well as conduct than abstract reason, that it is by far the more preferable to aim for, at least in the education of the masses.

And there is certainly food enough in art which already years ago filled with its productions and philosophy 14,791 works, catalogued by the Kensington Museum in two volumes of 2,129 pages, of which works there are written in

English..............................2,545
French..............................7,935
German..............................1,346
Italian..............................1,786

It certainly is not unworthy of notice that the French nation, which according to this showing excels in works on art leads the world in the ornamental industries.

ART CORRECTS THE TEMPER OF DEMOCRACIES.

Homage, reverence, devotion, faith, trust, confidence, allegiance, calmness, repose, self possession and moderation are all cultivated by the contemplation of works of art and are a counterpoise to the irreverent haste, vulgar restlessness and exaggeration so apt to invade the temper of men in all levelling democracies.

ART AND RELIGION IDEAL AND INSEPARABLE.

Law and proportion in all parts or union in variety in art or nature, coupled with emotion, constitute beauty and lead on to the sublime conception of God, who is the Law and Union and Eternal Father of all. Art and religion are both ideal and inseparable, and Hellwald, an unquestionable authority in this matter, well says, it is doubtful if there ever lived an atheistical artist.

Our age is too practical to be affected by abstract formula, art mediating between the ideal and the real, corrects both extremes, that of an one sided phantastic spiritualism as well as that of a dead and cold hearted materialism.

Law, order, freedom and purity are the very soul of beauty, principles at the very foundation of character and leading to happiness in the family and to greatness and peace in the state. Of course to whom consciousness is but matter the æsthetic thrill is but a certain geometrical curve and Plato a fool. But the mention of this sort of unmeaning gibber is all the refutation it calls for or deserves.

Love of art is love of man. Or does he care for a statue who does not care for man ?

The indirect moral effect of art was greatly weakened by the impure paganism of antiquity, its general want of education and universal slavery.

Art education can be but salutary in our day. Were we more bigoted it might lead to idolatry; were we less religious, it might corrupt our senses. Art, in these days of machinery, does not interfere with the useful industries, but is rather an economical necessity, and rigid science is panting for the warm breath of art.

Art separate from religion and chiefly used in this industrial age as ornament or to decorate the houses of the rich, is bound to degenerate as it once did in ancient Rome, into barbaric pomp unless universal æsthetic culture does unlock the inner world, and genius be impelled to give form to its ideals, as it once did to the religious myths of the past.

ART INDUSTRIAL EDUCATION, NOT CONQUEST, OUR GREATNESS.

Art, as Leckey expresses, once a fetich, next religious symbolism, then æsthetic worship of the beautiful and at last the servant of the lower senses, must be purified and elevated by science and the memory of its own great past ; it must instruct, reform and inspire us by its historical, moral and literary illustrations. As ornament it must occupy the millions as much as the common industries do. Not conquest nor the leading foreign populations captive, nor ten thousand millionaires building up a foreign commerce at the expense of their own country which they use as a slave colony, but the complete education of the masses, which can only be of an art industrial nature, is to day the greatness and glory of a nation.

ART THE PURIFIER OF MORALS.

Only when science and art or wisdom and beauty will be wedded to each other in the popular mind through universal industrial art Education, will the theater become a safe institution and a school of morals as well as a place for recreation as it was among the ancient Greeks.

Rum, tobacco and every other excess are but sins of grossness, and best corrected by art, the twin of refinement and the most effectual element in the Education of the individual and the race.

Art is not only the child, but also the parent of peace. Essentially creative, it shrinks from the vandalism of destructive war. Art delights, instructs, reforms, purifies and refines us; it cultivates the soul and calms the passions.

Art without machinery leaves the people in want of necessaries, machinery without art leaves the people soon without work. Art without science and religion demoralizes through excess of sensibility and wild passion, exclusive industrialism ends in greed and cruel heartedness; only art, science, religion and industry combined develop a harmonious civilization.

ART AND ORNAMENTAL INDUSTRIES.

It is by her study of art that France leads the world in the ornamental industries, and has the preference in all markets, to which she greatly owes her prosperity.

The effect of art upon ornament is manifest from ancient Greece, " where the commonest furniture, lamps, pots and pans, chairs, stools, were all designed with singular grace and elegance ; . . . . boorishness was considered a crime, and want of sensibility a disease."

High art must not stand aloof in haughty isolation. By its intimate association with the ornamental industries in schools of design, in art museums and exhibitions, in France as well as in England, these countries have succeeded in obtaining a favorable judgment of their styles, and in gaining a wide market for their goods.

The ornamental industries exhibited in the great international fairs of the world show that the nations of Europe have become convinced that a flashing and arbitrary or roccoco fashion cannot hold the markets of the world. The realistic school may be too imitative, the historical too slavish, the critical and æsthetical too fanciful ; still, we must know and examine whatever preceded us, and form our style upon sound principles, based upon methodical art studies of the past as well as of the present ; and hence the universal demand for schools, museums of art, and ornamental industries.

The art-remains of the age of stone, and even of. the reindeer epoch, as well as the popularity of the ornamental domestic industries among the hardly half civilized nations of the past or present, show the universality of the art taste, and the extent to which it may be cultivated. In many cases again, rude ornamental industries are traceable to specimens of high art of bygone ages, or to other nations, as to the mother of the more common ornamental industries.

We can produce nothing worthy of the age without nobler conceptions of life, a high national feeling, and the study of art in the past, its progress, decay and revival, as well as the causes that led to the one and to the other in various ages and countries. In France, Germany and England, as well as everywhere else, the success in the ornamental industries dates from the promotion of high art, great schools of design, and the founding of museums rich with works of art, and kindling a taste for what is pure, beautiful and chaste in style.

THE ECONOMY OF ART.

The economy of art is an important element of national wealth ; like wine, it gets more precious with time, and its growing skill and genius are a most valuable capital. As a family relic or work of art attaches us to the homestead, renders us more domestic and careful in the management of our affairs, public works of art foster the same spirit in reference to the State, to which they attach us and render us more patriotic. Art ties us by a golden chain to the past, and fosters a conservatism steadying us in the onward rush that tears us from ourselves.

Art gives us the admiration of the world, which is an element of national strength. Through her art Greece, though conquered, has made her own terms with Rome, and Rome has, in her turn, endeared herself to the world through her art.

Art refines. Its objects are enjoyed at a respectful distance, and are not destroyed in the enjoyment which is shared with others. We invest in art without looking for a return of so many dollars and cents, a lesson not unimportant in a commercial age.

ART CULTURE HARMONIZES ALL INTERESTS.

The idealism of art culture strips industrial education of its low materializing tendencies, while it, at the same time, enhances the economical value of labor, and thus harmonizes all interests.

The fetichism of Greek and Latin Grammar must give way to an art culture which will enter into the spirit of antiquity, its literature and works, beyond anything even a Lessing or Winkelman ever anticipated.

THE CULTURE OF MUSIC.

In regard to music we will quote from a competent authority, who well says, " strange that what was deemed a grace, a gift, and a necessity, in ages we call barbarous, should be neglected in times which boast of their enlightenment. Begin and end the labors of the school with music, the softening and purifying power of which will do what neither dogma nor discipline can accomplish."

THE LOVE OF ART RETURNING.

Ecstatic love of the beautiful made Greece excel in art, and gave her that grand civilization in which she was pre-eminent ; all is conspiring to bring back the race to this her first love, the necessities of the body, industry and commerce, as well as our cultivated imaginations, teeming with high conceptions clamoring for suitable vestments and haunting us like ghosts ; the grace and beauty that are sleeping in the unchisled marble and unformed clay, they beckon us with irresistible power to end that spell and burst the prison that keeps them captive. Every creature wants to preach the gospel of joy and of purifying love. Let then mind and matter come together again and commingle in works of high art, and when the sons of God come to the daughters of man we shall have again a progeny of giants ; every hamlet will have its poet, prophet and artist ; and when there will be plenty of the bread of life, daily bread will not be wanting. The widow's haggard countenance will no more be turned heavenward, with her tears falling down as a reproach upon earth to mingle with the tears of her hungry little ones, but there shall be plenty for all and to spare.

THE POET-PAINTER'S STAND-POINT.

The picture of man and nature seen by the artist from the stand-point of the soul of things, is a volume of divine philosophy, inexhaustible in delight and instruction.

The manners, the habits, the passions, the vices, the virtues, the weakness, the strength, and reach, and quality, and entire individuality of men in all ages, stations, and countries the pencil of the artist gives them at a glance in all their totality, as only life can, unapproachable by tedious descriptions, doling out fragments but few know how to reconstruct into a whole.

The eternal verities of the mind of God, hid in star and flower, in bog or mineral, in the heat of day, in noon splendor or setting sun, in hazy spring, gorgeous summer, rich autumn or snowy winter, in the open valley, steep mountain or ravine, in burning desert, in lake, river or ocean, in lofty tree or humble moss, in gigantic animal creations, or in the mote dancing in the solar beam ; in short, the divine idea in the depth of every form and energy of nature, the poet-painter artist brings it out of

5

the heart of things, and pours it over them where it may be seen by all.

PAINTING THE MEMORY OF ALL TIMES AND PLACES.

Take a pensive walk through an art gallery, and then say if painting is not the living memory of all times and places. It brings before us in all vividness forest, plain and mountain, lake, river and sea ; it takes us into the battle field, makes us partakers of public hilarity, give us access at court, the secret council chamber, and the private family circle. A glance at the people in the public square, or into the workshop, or political meeting at some city remote in time or space, teaches us more than all histories can. It gives—to tell all in a few words— the world of man and nature, past and present, with all its variety, depth and reality, to the eye and to the heart.

Do we want all men to become painters? Not by any means. But they shall all learn to draw, which is the foundation of ornamental industry as well as of painting. We want the appreciation of painting and the other fine arts to be as common among Americans at it was once in Greece, Italy, or the Netherlands, and much more so, because we are a better educated people, and given to manufactures, and have to cope with the commerce of the advanced nations of Europe.

With Ruskin, we maintain that illustrated school rooms will put life and reality in what are to-day barren words not deserving the name knowledge. Why should we not educate the people to read pictures as well as books; the process is quicker, more attractive and less fatiguing, prints and lithographs are within their reach, galleries are becoming numerous, and every innocent pleasure is a battle won against vice.

Does the print or engraving on the wall not cheer the poor man's room, and shed over it an air of elegance? Does it not by divine homilies read at his hearth elevate, strengthen and comfort him?

Ministers, teachers, lawyers, physicians, judges, politicians, employers and employees, in short all ages, ranks and sexes call for another Hogarth, to shame them out of their sins and follies by the good natured wit of his inimitable pencil; verily Punch and Nast perform an important moral part in society, and there is hardly a judge on the bench whose verdict is more feared by evil doers, or who does more towards purging the community of its vicious elements.

THE HIGH MISSION OF ART.

When religion appeared upon earth as witchcraft the worldly wise discarded it as an idiosyncrasy of the savage mind, until it at last burst the shell and broke forth as the life power of the world. Art too appeared first as a mere toy and play of fancy. But even as the great men of the race and bearers of heaven's messages, so do the Leonardo Da Vincis, the Michael Angelos and the Raphaels by their lofty natures show the reach of their mission, which will be better understood when the Scriptures of art will find a shrine in every home and all men will be workers, artists, prophets and apostles. That day is coming as true as God is our father and as the old seers have not been mocked in their visions of the glories of the later days.

HISTORIC ART STUDIES.

Not to speak of the deadening materialism of our days, except the few bright spots, like the age of Pericles, Augustus, Elizabeth or Louis XIV., which were the summing up of the labors of the past, the life of every generation is but fragmentary, and only the study of the grand development of the history, art and philosophy of the ages can give us a complete and living knowledge of men and things. And even so, art in its idea and execution, like every other department, can only be comprehended if studied in its development through the ages.

The art idea of the Egyptians was religious and symbolical, the Greeks saw divine perfection in beauty of form, the Romans aimed in art at sublimity and grandeur, in the Middle Ages art aimed at religious emotion and culminated in Leonardo Da Vinci, Michael Angelo and Raphael in the expression of intellectual grandeur as well as emotion and beauty and perfection of form, and to day the art idea is striving to become as broad as nature, as deep as the soul, as high as heaven, as comprehensive as human history and reaching from the epic to the genre, and from sky and ocean down to the daisy.

The close imitation of nature makes mechanical slaves, and even more so does closely following in the traces of men. Still, the defects and excellencies of art in all ages have their lessons, and we may study design in the Roman school of painting, color in the Lombard, motion and shade in .that of Venice, learn what power is in Michael Angelo, purity in Corregio, truth in Titian, decorum and solidity in Tebaldi, learned invention in Primaticcio. And this lesson of the eclectic school of Carraci might be indefinitely extended to schools out of Italy.

In the spasm of action of the age we live in, the character and union of all parts expressed in antique art are of moral service. But even the perfect beauty of form in the plastic arts of Greece leads through its sensuous nature to weakness and debasement.   Roman art impressing us with grandeur and dignity, corrects this defect, but leads to barbaric splendor and pride.   Gothic art turns our vision within and to holier things and ends by excess in this direction with caricaturing the soul.

When the sanctuary was all ideal art, and life bare misery, the contradiction begot a high passion in the soul which ended in the terrible folly of religious conflict with man for the love of heaven. It is time art, like religion, ceased to gild the pinnacle and deepen the gloom of the valley, but like the sun in mid sky, bathe all in genial light.

Under the inspiration of Leonardo Da Vinci, Michael Angelo, Raphael and Titian, art has burst through the thick walled cloisters and churches and waits to day for universal art industrial education to prepare all for its reception and application in every sphere of life.

We confess the history of words tells the history of the race.   Well, so does the history of theology, laws, customs and political institutions, but all this is not to be thrust upon the children of the masses. To bring them into living contact with the humanity of the past that they may better understand themselves and their own work, we must acquaint them with the industries, inventions and

arts of the past, which indicate the historical relations of individuals and nations, the unity, progress, labors, sacrifices and achievements of the
race, and are the prophecy and the assurance of a
future transcending the loftiest imagination of the
most ardent lover of man. By studying the arts
and industries of the past we trace the march of
civilization among the nations, and their degree of
indebtedness to each other ; their history and even
our own becomes clearer to us, and literature
acquires a fullness of meaning and puts on flesh,
where without this knowledge it was but words.

With crayon and pencil in hand the scholar must
retrace the art industrial history of the past that
he may resurrect the part that fits into the present, or significantly suggests what may properly
take its place. Clear and pure art conceptions once
formed in the mind will chase away whatever is
confused or impure in the imagination, everything
will stand out clear and sharp, every blade of grass,
tree or flower, the animal world and the starry
heavens above will become a new revelation of
beauty, purity and truth to the art instructed eye
and imagination, and guided by such faculties the
hand will execute designs which will make our arts
and our industries the delight of nations.

In Greece and in the Middle Ages high art in
which the human figure is the theme of statuary

and painting preponderated and led to the ex-
travagancies of passion and imagination arising
from a constant morbid feeding upon ourselves.
As the going out of ourselves into the objective
world is the condition of self consciousness, so
does it lead to healthfulness of soul and a deeper
self knowledge. Ornament entirely objective holds
the balance to the excessive personal in high art,
which is so apt to degenerate into morbid fancy
and the caricature of passion.

A writer speaking of ornamental art has said not
infelicitously it is an incarnation, and is a sort of
petrified poetry, or concrete rhetoric. It is the
blossom of the art tree, whose root is Thought,
and whose trunk is imagination. It is inventive, imitational and composite. Gothic is imitational, Greek inventional, and Byzantine composite.
Egyptian ornament is thoughtful, and always alle-
gorical. The Assyrian is still quainter, simpler
and more primitive. The Greek revels in noble
sweeping curves and in fretted foliage, highly con-
ventionalized. The Oriental types in their art lost
their symbolic character, and became enriched and
idealized by fancy ; harmony and a sweet grace are
in every line. The Etruscan is rude and Asiatic,
with Greek luxuriance. The Roman is strong and
vigorous, leafy, luxurious and voluptuous. The Byzantine is barbarian, rich, knotted, linked and

studded like embroidery. The Moorish is the poetry of geometry and the mathematics of color, varied and changed as nature. The Gothic is nature subdued and limited by rules and space. The Indian is varied, strange in its blendings and studded intermixtures, arranged by the instinct of men of a hot climate; but the Persian is the most graceful and poetical of all Oriental work; gorgeous and yet delicate in color, it is full of the broadest effects of contrasting hues and wreathed and blossomed with threads of flowers, bright as those of a missal. In the harmony of dyes there are invention and imagination. Let our student follow nature boldly and lovingly, but not servilely, —learning to compose as she does—not following her laws without laying down his own. Above all, let him remember that ornamentation is to art what words are to thought, and that if design and architecture are dead, no ornamentation, however beautiful, can give them life. It will be at best but a wreath of flowers around the pale brow of a corpse.

The grace of form and high intellectual cast of antique beauty are cold and heartless without the expression of the spiritual nature of man ripened in Judea, and add even to this the romantic element of chivalrous manhood developed in the Middle Ages and art is still incomplete, as

5*

inexpressive of the scenic beauty of nature, the theater of man. But even this is not all, for we cannot separate from the æsthetic contemplation of man the world he creates for himself in objects of use delighting by their symmetry or geometric beauty. But art in our day must rise higher or leave the mind unsatisfied and thus mar our impressions. History has unfolded the high capabilities of man, and unless art expresses his universal energies and aspirations, which with one mighty sweep take in all nature and human possibilities, reaching up even to the throne of God and touching as it were the hem of his garment, unless it expresses all this it falls short of its high end, but this is above the power of the isolated individual, who can create but a mongrel art by mixing up all schools, epochs, and tendencies. It requires the hearts, brains, and hands of a whole people to assimilate into its own great life through a process covering ages, the countless glories radiating into every direction from God, man and nature, and this alone can give us a national school of art, outside of which all individual effort is of necessity abortive, and hence the necessity of universal art culture, that all the nation may help weaving the garment of beauty that is to deck the future of humanity, and help square the block and build the structure of the new national art which is beyond the power of any individual to rear by himself.

But even as there is no true art without national life, neither is a true national life possible without art in which it finds its most permanent and highest expression, neither is the highest individual development possible outside of the true national life.

ART IN EDUCATION.

Art, the civilizer of the world and the poetry and inspiration of the masses, must have its proper share in their education. Art is not an incident. We are beholden to it in our first Education which in the infancy of individuals as of nations, is all pictorial.

Once science was thought to belong to the privileged few, to day the same mistake is made with reference to art. We cannot make all men great designers, no more than great scientists, but their art industrial Education will anyhow enhance the quality and commercial value of their work.

Art is said to be the gift of genius and to need no schooling. This is a mistake. Genius is perfected by study and labor. We are not to study the past for the sake of imitating it; the very reverse; we study it that we may not waste ourselves in doing over what was done before us, and that we may be sure to begin where our predecessors have left off. Of course, imitating is easier than the striking out a new path, and the copying of great masters is apt to lead us into a slavery we ought to guard against, by developing our own individuality before we make an all absorbing study of one or another of the great masters.

We materially differ from Herbert Spencer, who puts upon the fine arts but a low estimate, and will allow them but the leisure part in education, as they occupy but the leisure part of life. Æsthetic culture and love of art make, as we have shown, a demand for the art manual industries, and keep busy millions of hands. It gives daily bread to the masses engaged in the production of articles of ornament, and feeds their minds while thus engaged, as well as their bodies. If, therefore, the value of a thing in life is to be the measure of its importance in the school, the arts of design and æsthetic culture in general must occupy an important place in the Education of the masses.

Let us not transfer old blunders to the new field, by spoiling artisans in the vain endeavor of bringing up everybody for high art. We frequently reverse the order of Providence, and end as often in failure; the great Architect of the universe began His work with the more material portions of it, progressed through the higher organic forms, and

finished with man. We begin where he left off—
with man—instead of beginning with geometrical
drawing, and schooling our pupils well in that, as
the foundation of ornament—as far as ninety-nine
in a hundred anyhow will ever go.

Every mechanic should be proficient in geometrical drawing, which is the language and grammar
of science and the shop, and the soul of industrial
ornaments ; though he need not wander through all
the mazes of high art, from the antique through
the catacombs to Raphael.

A spiritual art Education alone can save us from
the barbarism in which the heartless instruction of
our public schools must end.

The cultivation of science to the exclusion of art
in the general Education of the people has led to
the displacement of labor by improved machinery.
Our axiom is, science and art must be cultivated
together, that improved machinery may work
cheaply for the masses, who must profitably employ
themselves in the art manual industries.

It is not the belly of the masses we worship, no
more than our own, but we would fain share with
the million the glories and triumphs of the race
achieved in the long cycle of past ages by lofty
genius.

Prostrate in darkness and misery great humanity
is beckoned upward by divine apparitions of beauty,

grandeur and truth, to which it can only rise through art, the earliest teacher of nations, best adapted to children and the masses, whose brains are best reached through their hands, which for reasons of state, as well as their own interest, are best busily employed.

President Theodore D. Woolsey, in his work on Political Science, admits the right of the government to establish polytechnic institutes, and especially schools for the fine arts, which are altogether beyond the reach of private means, just as libraries and museums are.

The popular interest in art was always its measure of success ; witness Greece, Italy, France, England, Germany and the United States, and every fact of history bearing upon this subject is an argument in favor of universal art Education.

The broad intention of the Greek artists to please all and not a small clique of partial admirers, is the main cause of the universal effect of their work even to-day, and hence the necessity of a universally cultivated taste, which must give art its laws.

MANUAL LABOR AND MACHINE MADE WORK.

Richard Redgrave, the late inspector general for art, science, and the art department at Kensington, emphatically declares himself against the low art character of machine made ornaments, in which

there is a " tiresome sameness, a sickening monotony, and a degraded style and execution." The
best workmanship and the best taste is in hand
made ornaments. One of the best tendencies, says
the same competent judge, of the present age, and
also the one holding out the best promises for the
future, is a desire in some manufacturers to return
to the typical forms of hand worked ornament, and
to bring into its due prominence the superior value
of honestly hand wrought decoration.

Gladstone, the far seeing statesman, dwells upon
the necessity of cultivating handicraft which has
been too long neglected in this our age of machinery, and that ever will be the foundation of civilization.

The poet and artist, William Morris, traces many
of the present troubles to the lack of the art element in our labor. The work is ugly and without
taste, and hence the men have no liking for it,
and hence it is a rarity to get anything well done.
Ruskin is of the same opinion ; if men are to take
more interest in their work more of the art element
must enter it.

Elizur Wright, that bold thinker and lifelong
lover and defender of his race, openly gave, at the
social science meeting of 1878, the Chinese the preference, who encourage hand labor that supports
the masses, rather than machine work which starves

them.   We have sufficiently shown how much of truth there is in this assertion, and how by striking the golden mean the evil may be corrected.

The study of the ornamental industries, exhibited at the great international fairs, shows that manufacturers have hardly studied art, that nothing has been added to the styles of the ancient world, or those of Egypt, Greece and Rome; to those of the middle ages, or the Byzantine, the Saracen and the Gothic, and to the modern styles, or the Renaissance, the Cincento and the Louis Quatorze, and at last this study reveals to us that we have but three decided expressions of taste, the Greek, the Italian and the French, or the Classical, the Renaissance and the Louis Quinze.

ARTISANS MUST BECOME ARTISTS.

Economical reasons and the effect of machinery have convinced us of the necessity of combining art with the common trades, or of transforming the artisan into an artist; and it is no little satisfaction to us to see the possibility of this transformation supported by no less a scholar and critic than Cardinal Wiseman in his discourse on the connection or relation between the arts of production and the arts of design; or the identification of the artisan and the artist. Dr. Wiseman establishes by numerous examples, that wherever in antiquity,

Italy, or the East, there has been real beauty and perfection of work, it has been in consequence of the practical arts, and of the fine arts, which ought to work together, being most closely combined, and as nearly as it can be done in the same individual, and that the separation of the artisans or workmen and artists in our day is the cause of our inferiority; and that, therefore, the Education which we are to prepare for those who are to carry productive art to its perfection must be one which will combine, closer than is now done, these two departments which are one and the same thing. The jewelers and silversmiths of the fourteenth, and even to the seventeenth century, were educated as artists of the highest class, and often turned out most eminent sculptors, as Benvenuto, Cellini and others. Pompei and Herculaneum have been found full of innumerable objects of beauty for common use, showing that the braziers, brass founders, potters and the like artisans were able to do what now defies almost our most superior workmen.

It is equally important that the artisan be artist and the artist artisan. The greatest artists formerly stamped the highest impress of art on the smallest work they made great and noble, and Rafael did the work of a common house decorator. He did not disdain to draw patterns for carpet weavers; and it is the same tendency which gives the French their superiority in the more delicate operations of art applied to manufacturing.

Dr. Waagen, the director of the Royal Gallery at Berlin, before a committee of the House of Commons made the same statement as Dr. Wiseman: "In former times artists were more workmen and the workmen were more artists, and it is very desirable to restore this happy connection between these two, the productive and the beautiful arts."

The blending of the character of the artizan and of the artist, therefore, far from being a problematic novelty is the normal and historic condition of the two, to which we must return as to the only refuge from general want of employment, in this age of machinery, if we are to escape universal pauperism.

DRAWING AN INDISPENSABLE ACCOMPLISHMENT.

A child, says Prof. Walter Smith, who cannot draw the forms of objects which his eye sees, as readily as he can write or repeat the words his ear hears, is only half educated. Every child can be taught drawing, which should precede writing than which it is more natural, and, therefore, more easily acquired, and for which it is the very best preparation.

A man who cannot work from drawings loses time, wastes material, and produces a poor article. Prof. Thompson, of the Worcester Technical School, says, " It is calculated that the productive efficiency of every machine shop would be increased thirty-three per cent if every journeyman could read any common working drawings and work by it."

Prof. Bail, of Yale College, speaks of grey haired men who, knowing the value of drawing, learn out of books for children of eight years.

"A teacher," says Prof. Walter Smith, " who can illustrate a lesson in physical geography by sketches of the natural products of the country and character of the people, and their habits, or who accompanies his historical exercises by drawings of the costume, architecture ; portraits of eminent men, weapons and implements used in war and agriculture ; or maps of contested ground, or charts of geographical distinctions, is twice as powerful a teacher as he who appeals only through the ears to the understanding without illustration of forms or display of visible peculiarities."

" People whose eyes," says the same author, " are constantly, or even occasionally, seeing beautiful forms, are receiving an education, whether they know it or not, and the withdrawal of such influences is destructive of art power."

RUSKIN ON UNIVERSAL ART.

We call for universal art, not for that of the Middle Ages, the pride of the so-called superior

class, as Ruskin eloquently says, " a pride which supported itself by violence and robbery, and led in
the end to the destruction both of the arts themselves and the States in which they flourished. . . .
for us there can be no more the throne of marble,
for us no more the vault of gold ; but for us there
is the loftier and lovelier privilege of bringing the
power and charm of art within the reach of the
humble and the poor ; and as the magnificence of
past ages failed by its narrowness and its pride, ours
may prevail and continue by its universality and
lowliness. . . . . We want no more feasts of the
gods, nor martyrdoms of saints ; we have no need
of sensuality, no place for superstition or for costly
insolence. Let us have learned and faithful historical paintings ; touching and thoughtful representations of human nature in dramatic painting ;
poetical, and familiar renderings of natural objects,
and of landscape ; and rational, deeply-felt realiza-
tions of the events which are the subjects of our
religious faith. And let these things we want, as
far as possible, be scattered abroad, and made
accessible to all men.

So also in manufacture ; we require work sub-
stantial rather than rich in make : and refined
rather than splendid in design. . . . . If in jealous
rivalry with neighboring States or other producers
you try to attract attention by singularities, novel-

ties and gaudiness, to make every design an adver-
tisement, you may snatch the market, or by energy
command it. But whatever happens to you, this at
least is certain, that the whole of life will have been
spent in corrupting public taste and encouraging
public extravagance. . . . . Let the duty and ambition of forming the market and restraining its follies
as well as to supply it, be once accepted in all its
fulness and the best glory of European art, and of
European manufacture, may yet be to come. . . . .
The steel of Toledo and the silk of Sinna did but
give strength to oppression, and luster to pride ;
let it be for the furnace and for the loom of to-day,
as they have already richly earned, still more abun-
dantly to bestow comfort on the indigent, civilization on the rude, and to dispense through the peaceful homes of nations the grace and the preciousness
of simple adornment and useful possession."

ART EDUCATION ABROAD AND AT HOME.

No government has ever so quickly and energetically increased the facilities for the art instruction
of its people as England has done, as may be seen
from our statement pp. 162—165, and the following
table :

	Schools in which art is taught.	Art students.	Works of art produced by the schools.
1871	2,100	203,638	102,467
1874	2,811	281,400	157,636

This art training told as quickly on the exportation of art industrial productions in England, which increased 1856–1868 to 855 million of francs, 505 million francs more than in France, and an increase of 442 million francs above its own art industrial exports of the preceding decade; while those of France decreased during the same time 68 millions. What a commentary upon the influence of art industrial education of a nation upon its commerce!

No wonder France was aroused to greater activity in order to hold its own against its dangerous rival.

Belgium has made equally great exertions, and its entire population is gradually acquiring a knowledge of drawing and technology.

Germany is progressing rapidly in the same direction. The royal school of art at Nuremberg is of European celebrity, and its influence upon industry immense.

Munich and Dresden have each called into existence a great school of industrial art, and Frankfort-on-the-Main is making a grand effort in the same direction, to which the Baroness of Rothschild made a munificent donation of 200,000 marks.

Austria is emulating in this race for art industrial opportunities for its people, and Vienna alone has the following institutes:

1. Academy of Plastic Arts.

2. School of Fine Arts Applied to Industry.

3. School of Design and of Modelling for Art and Industry.

4. Public School of Design and Industry.

5. The Schools for Masons and Stone-cutters.

6. The School of Design for Manufacturing and Spinning.

7. The School of Design for Carpenters.

These institutions, and societies, and museums devoted to similar objects, have visibly improved the architectural and industrial aspects of the metropolis of Austria.

Italy has no great general schools of art but fosters schools for especial art industries. They are as follows:

Florence.—The School of Sculpture in Wood, founded 1868.

Savona.—School of Art and Manufacture for Furniture and Porcelain, founded 1871.

Serravezza.—School of Design and of Sculpture Applied to Ornamentation, founded 1869.

Sesto Florentino.—School of Art and Manufacture for Decorative and Ceramic art, founded 1873.

Venice.—School of Arts Applied to Industry, founded 1873.

There are classes in ornamental design in about forty different towns, thirteen Academies of Fine

Arts in so many different towns, beside half a dozen of Colleges and Royal Institutes of Fine Arts and many institutions but partly devoted to Art, with art and industrial museums at Florence, Turin, Rome and Milan. With so many helps we need not wonder if Italy, as ever, excels in fine work.

Spain has eleven societies devoted to the Fine Arts and at Madrid a conservatory for Arts and Trades with a number of schools for especial industries.

These facts sufficiently establish the general conviction that the interests of the age call for the introduction of the art element in our schools, a necessity Massachusetts first recognized by a legislative act in May, 1870, which made drawing an integral part of the common school system of every town with 10,000 population and over, and to-day drawing is in a fair way of gaining recognition in the schools of New York, St. Louis, Milwaukee and Cincinnati, as well as in Boston.

Especial schools for art training are promising well in New York City, in the Woman's Art School at the Cooper Union, the Philadelphia School of Design for Women, the Philadelphia Academy of Fine Arts, the National Academy of Design in New York, the Lowell Free School of Industrial Design, the School of Design in the University of

Cincinnati, the Worcester County Free Institute in Massachusetts and the School of Architecture and Design at the University of Michigan.

EDUCATIONAL DRAWING.

Mr. Nichols, the author of Art Education, justly complains of the " bad copies from shockingly drawn prints of Alpine views, portraits of Turks, sultanas, saints and Madonnas, poodle dogs, cats, lions, tigers and other tame and wild animals with which students struggle through a great deal of work, and at the end of it all have actually learned nothing —not one fixed principle, not a rule of art, not the least conception of the laws of perspective and correct drawing, not the faintest shadow of a notion of the art of the design. There is neither use nor beauty in such trifling; it does nothing, be it for art or industry, nor for the elevation and improvement of man. We plead for that solid instruction in the elements of drawing and design which is thoroughly educational, and a boon to every mechanic or artist and to which students in the primary department must, according to Professor Walter W. Smith, devote at least two hours per week, and to accomplish a revolution in the taste, skill and industry of the nation, even three to four hours per week.

6

OUR ART INDUSTRIAL EXPORTS AND IMPORTS.

The fact shown up by Mr. Nichols is certainly very significant, that while 26.7 per cent. of our total imports in 1874 were products of art industry, only 3.97 per cent. of our total exports were products of art industry; and while we imported $158,786,319 art industrial products, we exported but $27,525,049, leaving a difference of $131,261,270, of which our own artisans might have earned their share were they sufficiently trained.

"The American mechanic," says the same author, "has by his inventive faculty filled the world with useful labor saving machines without adding much to the sum of grace and beauty. Whenever art is applied to the simplest, commonest product of labor, there will come order, intelligence, grace and increased value."

OUR FUTURE ART.

Antiquity had its art, so had the Middle Ages theirs, and the modern world is brooding over the coming art, which must be purely human and cosmopolitan, and will be born in the New World of freedom, universality and humanity.

Not through Plato, but through works of high art have the Greeks peopled the world with their

ideals; and even so must our ideal of man and nature express itself through art, which far from
being a trick of hand belonging to the earlier
ages is the most God like act of all sympathetic
souls who catch the spirit in matter and translate
it back into it again, and thus create high art in
which the ideal and the real like body and soul
blend as it were into one being.

The style, genius and art of a nation are its life
preserving power. They develop its individuality,
assign it the proper place among the nations, and
connect it with the whole of humanity and all past
as well as present civilizations. What delights us
to-day as beauty in high art meets us to-morrow as
high achievement in State or literature.

If severe or scientific, high, beautiful and de-
clining art are natural cycles in the civilization of
every new and energetic race under a new sky and
surroundings, as Winkelman illustrates from the art
history of the past, then, certainly, art can not fail
to develop also among us, and shed its luster upon
this great nation.

America, the asylum of the nations, the cradle
of liberty, manhood and an altogether new humanity, the garden of childhood, with its orderly
and prosperous homes in which men, women and
children nourished and cultured in duty's appointed ways constitute the happy family—the

foundation of a great State—America which bids
the shackles fall from the manacled slave, gives
wealth to the poor, affluence to the needy and
power to the weak of but yesterday; America
where poverty, suffering, wrong endured, and even
the transgressor's pains stir with divine pity innumerable hearts attuned to almost superhuman love,
the power of which as if by heavenly magic
changes darkness into light, poverty into riches,
vice into virtue, disease into health, weakness into
strength, deformity into beauty, sadness into joy
and despair into hopefulness—does such a land not
furnish high art with motives, new, varied and
great, and promise to inspire works of art before
which those of the past will pale away?

America, with its boundless expanse, stretching
from pole to pole, and from ocean to ocean, with
its heaven-high mountains, and long winding rivers,
with the vegetable forms and animal life of all
climes, with the wealth of its prairies, forests and
mines, and industries; with a population unequaled
in energy, enterprise, endurance, virtue, intelligence,
invention and generous impulse; such a land and
such a population can not but develop the highest
art.

It is certainly untrue that democracy is unfavorable to art. Art flourished first in republican
Greece; it flourished next in the free Italian States

and in Holland before it flourished in France, Germany or England.

We are said to be a cold, common sense, money making people, but no more than the Flemish were, and they developed a school of art which lacked neither genius nor originality. The English are a very realistic people, and produced, perhaps, even on that account, the greatest poet. Why, then, may we not produce the highest painter, and we believe every element does conspire to bring about this consummation ; as national energy, liberty and prosperity cannot long exist without developing the highest national art.

With the worth, the self-possession, and the sweet humility of the coming man of America ; the virtue, freedom, and grace of American womanhood, and the joyous innocence of happy childhood here, growing up in kindergärten to perfect men and women ; with households liking an Eden, schools that are nurseries of all that is manly, useful and beautiful ; with a State that is a beehive, in which all gather honey from flowers growing in the garden of God ; air, light, and even marble must become vocal with the recital of the story of Infinite Love in song, in painting, and in statuary, and thus perpetuate the miracle of the power, wisdom and love of God in the hearts and lives of a beautiful humanity, even by the power of the new gospel of art.

If the well stored larder of the Flanders, as Taine beautifully shows, called out an excellent school of art, what may we not augur for art when heaven and earth shall meet each other in America.

This outlook is stoutly denied, just now, by men into whose open lap America's bounties have hitherto fallen without adequate exertions on their part, and who ungratefully complain of her, because, like the gods, she makes to-day labor the price of her favor, and asks of us to put into the common treasury as much as we take out, that future generations may find as rich a banquet as we were invited to.

Our array of painters and sculptors in the past is a prophecy of our future distinction in this noble field of national glory.

It is a mistake when a philosopher declares the plastic arts trifles. The pre-eminence of the old Greeks is not due as much to their excellent literature as to their high art, by which they have chiselled in marble the divine attributes of man, from childhood to mature man and womanhood; sermons in stone about the perfect life to be read and lived through all time to come.

Feebly, indeed, sees he the eternal verities of things, who is not driven by irresistible power to project them in sensible form; and certainly the highest expression is that which God gave them; and man's wonderful frame expresses the highest thought of God. Verily to infuse the highest intellectual life, and the passions of the stormy soul into marble and bronze, that the eye may see at a glance the adventurous life of a hero, hardly volumes can bring with equal vividness before the mind; if this is weakness it is such as a Dante might well envy. We might begin and finish our argument with the mentioning of the name of the grandly scientific Leonardo Da Vinci, who was a great sculptor, and of whom it is hard to say what he was not great in, was he a trifler? And was the great and stern Michael Angelo, who was all thought, poetry, duty, and patriotism, and the greatest sculptor of modern times, was he another trifler?

Universality, or justice to all relations, is the condition of existence or permanency, and only by acquainting ourselves with the partial attempts of the past, do we avoid old failures. Classic art exclusively cultivated ideal beauty, or perfect form, and perished. Christian art sought exclusively to realize religious emotion, or the passion of the soul, and perished equally. Only that art will endure that will be as universal as nature is herself; and this universality can only be attained through universal art study and culture, so that all men and all times may contribute to the formation of an art as universal as man and nature.

There is a power in art. We know what part it acted in the Church, and even to-day, the carpet under our feet, the tapestry on the wall, the color and design of the stuffs our garments are made of, they all mould us by the persuasive language of their designs and tints; but all this is but a shadow of the future power of art in America.

The American unites, as no other nation, manipulative skill, quick perception, taste, talent, and even genius; he is sufficiently idealistic and realistic to seize upon the soul of things, and heed no less the external niceties of shade and form.

Greece excelled in abstract, or ideal beauty, Italy in the representation of individual beauty, France in elegance of form, the Flemish school in coloring, the German in symbolical representation, England in historical or moral painting; but no nation ever succeeded in fully understanding or imitating the other; only the union of races progressing in our midst brings us into sympathy with all aspects of beauty, and leads to the formation of a great school of art, uniting the excellencies of all; and that is the American destiny, the amalgamation of races, the synthesis of all civilizations, and the highest catholicity—appreciating, enjoying, assimilating and building up into one great structure the elements gathered from all nations.

PART III.

THE KINDERGARTEN AND THE MORALIZATION OF THE MASSES.

THE KINDERGARTEN THE PEOPLE'S COLLEGE.

After ages of darkness men naturally over-rated a little knowledge, and when the present was all vacant they turned to the past, which, however, will not do for us the work of to-day, and thus retards our progress as much as it once assisted it. There is but one way out of this dead sea. We must set to work, our sweet little ones at the age of three or four with the barest elements of what they are to accomplish, that they may not copy but mould, construct and model after the original, Divinity is weaving in their own mind.

The kindergarten alone allowing the child to work in its own way, developes its energy and individuality, both of which our common schools destroy.

We speak of the justice and the public advantage of extending the opportunities of a good Education to all, but do nothing of the kind·in fact, and what we call a public system of Education is but an ill-concealed fraud. That our schools are open to the poor is but a cruel lie. To get but through the grammar school requires steady attendance to fourteen years of age, and to pass through the high school requires three to four years more. Does any one suppose that the poor can support their children during so long a period with the prospect of having to do that for ever afterward ? We are not fault-finding to no purpose. We repeat it, the college and high school of the masses must precede the primary department with which they for ever leave school. The kindergarten training the senses, feeling, imagination, artistic taste and industrial application of the poor is worth to them and to the world more than the college or high school can ever be worth to the rich. What we ask is reasonable, just, timely, and nothing but our mental and moral lethargy or lack of faith in God and man can interfere with taking little children by the hand to train them in the way from which they should not depart when old.

Industrial nations must be trained in kindergärten. For individuality, the source of originality and success in manufacture, as in everything else, has its only chance of culture in infancy unburdened as yet with the work and performance of other men and of a foreign character. If a nation is to become industrial to a degree that renders not only necessaries but comforts as abundant as air and water, Froebel's principle, that ideas or conceptions have to be accompanied by work, creativeness and the joy of accomplishing solid results by our own skill and invention, must pervade schools of every grade, beginning with the kindergarten.

The people perish for want of everything; how else, then, can they be blessed with plenty of good things unless they are trained to profitable work? Make labor all method and the instrument of instruction, and the men engaged in it will not be without art, science and efficiency.

Labor was the first school of man, and is the best school for the child. We pretend to begin with science and end in complete failure. We must adopt the method of Providence in educating the race, and begin with labor and experience which are sure to lead to science.

But in dwelling upon labor, do we not forget the laborer? Not by any means, for besides cultivating our physical and intellectual powers labor regulates the passions, trains us to self command and to mutual service and sociability.

THE PROBLEM OF RELIGION IN OUR SCHOOLS.

The relation of religion to the school has perplexed many, but like other problems, has its solution. Every one rightly objects to have his son or daughter catechised by differently believing men, but no right minded person will object to a child of three, four or five years being spiritually cultured under the training of a teacher of a truly religious temper, as none but a Bedlamite would consider it decent to dogmatize with infants of that age about the mysteries of religion.

The more dogmatic assertion gives way to a higher spiritual tone of the race, the more infancy becomes the proper period for the culture of the religious element in man.

Religion, like industry, to be in our very bones, to be life and work, and to become ingrained in the race and hereditary, must be cultivated in the formative period of early childhood.

Infancy is the safest period for religious training, when it is sure to extend only to what is vital and practical, *the fatherhood of God and the brotherhood of man, principles simple enough for children and broad enough for angels to stand upon.*

MORAL AND NATIONAL EDUCATION.

If the absence of the industrial element of Education renders our public school system deficient, the absence of the social and moral renders it a crime, as the making of a great and righteous nation, that enriches the world with a new civilization, ought certainly to be its main purpose.

Modern States, says Fichte, the patriot philosopher, justly discarding any jurisdiction in preparing man for heaven, think that they can educate him for earth without religion or morality, by the aid of prisons and the like correctional agencies ; and here is the fatal mistake, for if the State has nothing to do with the heaven hereafter, it is concerned in the Kingdom of heaven here, and in that religion of which a man can not be divested without losing his humanity. But we are not left to the judgment of reason or authority as to what we are to think of our common school system ; it has worked out its results and we may judge it by its fruits. There is fraud in trade, fraud in State and fraud everywhere, until all confidence in man is quite gone and the permanency of all institutions is endangered by corruption and self-seeking.

But the soul of man was not meant by God to perish, and this age is great in its measures. We have put down our late rebellion at a cost of five billions of dollars, and that rebellion was but one of the many that lurk in man undisciplined. When this country wanted railroads it donated, as we have seen, to a few companies land equal to more than half of all the cultivated area of the United States, and when we shall rise to the height of the conception of a National Education, which shall shield the life of a great and rising nation against all dangers, coming from without or from within, we will not reckon the cost, and will only be the richer for it in the end.

The last fifty years have developed the conviction that we must educate the people and the next fifty years will organize that Education, for what we have, is a pretence without power to preserve the individual or to save the nation.

The great advantage of intellectual Education to the individual has caused it to be first organized, industrial Education next in private usefulness has been next thought of, and moral Education mainly concerned in the general good, is lagging far behind. We hardly need say by moral Education we do not mean additional school verbiage, but with Professor Bain, the social training of children in their intercourse with one another and with their teachers, and in their labors and duties which have reference to their future position in society.

We must organize a national Education which shall fit men for their future citizenship or social existence. The public danger requires it, the public wealth is adequate to it, and public opinion will soon insist upon it, as without it our profoundest peace is but a plotting of class against class and a war of all against each and of each against all which sooner or later must end in our common destruction.

A nation like an individual must first care for its material basis of existence, but if to live for nothing else but bodily comfort is low in a man, in a great nation heaven and earth sicken at it and bring it to a speedy end.

A perfect man or woman is a noble conception, but what shall we say of a great nation, every pulsation of which is marked by the life of a great man or city, and the type of such a nation we must develop or we shall altogether cease to exist.

Receiving constantly accessions from all nations only a thoroughly organized national Education can preserve our national character, which unsupported by hereditary bent or traditional leanings cannot develop itself spontaneously.

Whatever Education the Greek and the Roman had was national, and hence the model type of the antique character. With all our boast of civilization and Christianity, our Education is anti-social, anti-national, anti-ideal, and selfish and disintegrating to the very core.

We must be trained to justice, benevolence and prudence, the cardinal virtues of life. We must be trained in truly national institutions to work for the well-being, progress and prosperity of the nation ; for co-operation, mutual esteem, and an affection that elevates and purifies the mind ; we must be

trained for sympathy and kindness, and for self-for-
getfulness and self-sacrifice.

It is strange, but nevertheless true, man or his
purely human relations are still left out in the
school as well as in the State of to-day, and hence
the barbarism of war, and of much of our present
legislation. Through the double neglect of man's
moral nature and his self-subsisting power he often
falls; when a cruel code entirely crushes and dis-
honors him by caging him like a brute, and by the
treatment of keepers who goad him on to madness
and torture life out of him, and this penal inquisi-
tion surpasses in the number of its victims and in
cruelty Torquemata in his best days, and that in
this blessed land of freedom, which is still waiting
for the statesman who cares for the elevation of
man and his country rather than for place and
power.

Yet, we must not despair; it is but yesterday
that we had slavery, not a hundred years back and
England visited with capital punishment fifty to
sixty offences, used the torture, and had a hundred
and thirty ships engaged in the slave trade, what
wonder that, with such an Education, we have not
yet risen to the full heighth of the moral law.

It is not for us to develop here the system
according to which every incident in the school is
to be turned into a moral act by which the practice

of one or another of the social virtues is to be rendered habitual. Neither have we space for fully illustrating the interdependence of mental and physical hygiene; how every vice and every virtue or moral disposition acts and reacts upon the health and vitality of the body ; and how, therefore, moral training by infusing vigor into feeble natures lessens the army of physically defective men.

PESTALOZZI'S LIVING ILLUSTRATION OF EDUCATION.

Education must not mean spelling and ciphering, but a saving of the perishing masses. Let us get at the heart of the master and hear him, that we may catch the spirit of the genuine Educator of the century, for upon his bounty we all live; hear Pestalozzi : "I was from morning till evening, almost alone in the midst of my children. Everything which was done for their body or soul proceeded from my hand. Every assistance, every help in time of need, every teaching which they received came immediately from me. My hand lay in their hand, my eye rested on their eye, my tears flowed with theirs, and my laughter accompanied theirs. They were out of the world, they were out of Stanz; they were with me, and I was with them. Their soup was mine, their drink was mine. I had nothing. I had no housekeeper, no friend, no servants around me; I had them alone. Were they well, I stood in their midst; were they ill, I was at their side. I slept in the middle of them. I was the last who went to bed at night, the first who rose in the morning. Even in bed I prayed and talked with them until they were asleep—they wished it to be so."

Do we detract from this man by saying he had but just a drop of the infinite love which will still raise an army, whose hearts will be equally engaged in the work of saving the masses? They will come; here is the field for reformers, and here are the gates of heaven.

STATE AND SCHOOL IGNORING MORAL EDUCATION.

The infinite play of the moral forces, and the ever new arising exigencies of life are such that no amount of individual skill or social organization will ever secure the happiness of man and society, without that proper spiritual temper that always adapts itself to the Divine Will expressed in the external law of the soul and of things, and which disposition can only be cultivated in the early days of childhood.

If the State, therefore, has a right to provide for art and industrial Education, which are contributory to the general welfare, it is certainly not less called upon to provide for the moral Education of the

people, which is equally, if not more productive of
the public weal. While the Church has lost her
coercive power, and the moral scope of man has
increased with the rising issues of a new civilization,
the wholesome influence of home has been weakened through modern factory life. State and
school, in their madness, ignorance or selfishness
intensify these disorganizing tendencies, by practically ignoring the importance of the moral Education of the people, and men in their folly are sur-
prised at the masses, who, unconcerned about the
profitableness of their work to capital, however
high their wages may be, clamor for still higher
ones, and not infrequently set aside every consideration of economy, prudence, foresight, temperance,
and self-improvement. Not less destructive of the
public weal is the neglect of moral culture among
the capitalistic class, which is avaricious, cruel,
haughty and oppressive; however slim the wages
of the poor may be, puts them still lower, and enters
with its equals into a murderous competition ending in universal bankruptcy and ruin.

This demoralization will complete its work of
destruction unless Education regain its old meaning of severe moral training. This is no novelty;
the pages of Plato, Plutarch, Seneca, Montaigne,
and other sages, teem with this lesson, and the
great characters of antiquity show the superiority

of this Education over the parrot work of our schools. Many before us have insisted upon the propriety of making moral science a common school study. But this does not give strength to the will, is only so much more verbiage, and adds hypocrisy to moral turpitude. Whoever cares for the preservation of the race, the State, and the individual, through the moral rectitude of man in the whirlwind of modern private and public life, must first, and last, and ever insist upon the nationalization of the kindergarten, which does not mean teaching but training in morals as well as in art and industry. Education in the kindergarten can be nothing but training, and once rightly started it will continue to be *practical and organic* in all higher grades, which the new Education must be.

OVERWORKED MOTHERS.

The kindergarten is indispensable for the moralization of the masses. For when a poor mother is annoyed, hampered and disturbed in her work of a thousand kinds, so that she has to commence and recommence three times each before she can finish it, by children of three, four, and five years, she is bound to become an incorrigible scold, passionate and half mad, souring the temper of her poor children and training them into quarrelsomeness, stubbornness, passion and madness, and when such a character is formed in infancy for life, we believe, with Horace Mann, that the cultivation of the intellect is only arming meanness with power.

SYSTEMS OF PHILOSOPHY AND MORAL TRAINING.

There is not a moral principle or disposition but predominated in one or another of the sages of the world by whom it was made the foundation of the whole duty of man. The history of morals, therefore, far from being an exclusively speculative study, is of practical import to the moral disciplinarian, who, according to the temper and disposition of the individual he is to subject to moral training, will act upon the principle that morality is based upon justice, benevolence, love, ideal perfection, the absolute good, reason, knowledge and the supreme good, unity, harmony, order and beauty, wisdom and intelligence, the moral order of the universe, conformity to absolute law—and God, universal law, freedom and energy or independence and power, conscience and duty, moral sense and intuition, self activity and development or progress, the nature, fitness or truth of things, sympathy, the greatest happiness, the highest utility, loyalty and obedience, temperance and moderation, repose and supreme happiness, truth, beauty and goodness—as there is not one of these principles but it has been advanced by a philosopher who not only discoursed upon virtue but practiced it, and there is not an individual but virtue can be rendered natural and agreeable to him, if among the various aspects under which morality has been considered that one is taken which mostly accords with his natural bent of mind.

THE CHEMISTRY OF THE PASSIONS.

Hate, malice, revenge, ingratitude, falsehood, dishonesty, lying, selfishness, ambition, strife, violence, cruelty, avarice, lust, brutality, meanness, intemperence and indolence, as also truthfulness, honesty, generosity, contentment, love, gratitude, spirituality, nobleness, industry, thrift and temperance, in short, every vice and virtue of the future man must be traced in the child; the first to be checked, the second to be cultivated, as the young plant is to be trained and trimmed if it is to grow up into a beautiful tree.

We do understand the chemistry of the passions, and there is no excuse for not making our schools laboratories for the creation of a desirable character. There is not a passion but may overturn the State, and not a virtue but may make it great; one vice has often slain many men, as one virtue has often been the making of many. And yet we do much for intellectual development and nothing for moral advancement, though the way to the head is through the heart, and if we were better we would be wiser, and know more to the purpose. Character, says Wendell Phillips, controls the world more than genius. Every one can not have especial gifts, but every one may be great in and through goodness.

Are we not individually, and is not the State as a whole more interested in the moral goodness than in the intellectual greatness of every member of society? Does not self interest stimulate the intellect at every step and in every moment, and should not public schools stimulate our moral faculties for the public and our own ultimate good?

UNIVERSAL INFANT MORAL TRAINING SAVING THE NATION.

We know no greater nor more comprehensive reform than the kindergarten with moral training for its basis. We believe in the multiplication table, but the Ten Commandments and the Golden Rule are of higher authority, and must be wrought into the hearts of the young at the very threshold of life. And we are bold to say, without fear of contradiction, the price may be great, but must be paid, and at no other can this government be preserved, than universal infant moral training in the public nurseries of the nation.

Kindergärten exercising every sense and faculty

of the future nation to the perfection of art, correct by their ideal tendency the deadening materialism of an age of commercial values; for, in studying and developing the minds of others, we acquaint ourselves with the powers, individuality, and dignity of our own.

Froebel's kindergarten is eminently æsthetic and preparing for art life and industry. It is serene and joyous, reconciling the spirit with the flesh, and not less ethical than æsthetic.

As long as Education is hardly half understood the recognition of its importance can be but dim; when it will mould us in our childhood to beautiful men and women, it will bless us in the family and bless us as a nation, and bless the giver as well as those to whom it is given. A hundred years and more we have been talking about Education—it is time we get the thing itself, for the life even of nations not properly improved is but short.

The kindergärtener must be a constant visitor of the families whose children visit the school, lest the home blast the work of the kindergarten; and whoever has no call for a missionary has no call for a kindergärtener.

The nation may refuse now ten millions of dollars for the moralization of the masses and their greater industrial effectiveness through the kindergarten; but, then, it will, in less than a quarter of a century, increase the budget of the War Department by one hundred millions for the demoralization and lessening the productiveness of the nation by a standing army of a quarter of a million of soldiers.

"WHERE IS THY BROTHER?"

How many a man born into the world with a right and title to a glorious humanity, hardly taken from the breast, associates with all that is vile in the gutters, until he expires, after many a misdeed, a beast more than a man. The brutal features of the neglected dead are a fearful reproach to the living. And "Where is thy brother?" "Where is thy brother?" a voice calls over and over to us. In vain is all evasion. For as much as we have neglected his early training his blood, and the blood he has shed, are on our skirt.

The gallows, which to our shame still exist, bear in our country daily witness to this story.

We may number the stars in heaven, but who can count the men who are, Orestes-like, lashed through life by the furies into madness on account of sins they would never have committed had their actions been under the control of habits formed by correct early training in the kindergarten?

THE PEACE OF GOD.

The peace of God lies upon the smiling face of nature, and under proper infant training the child

7

of man would grow up to be a happy inhabitant of this Eden, but under the present neglect of early training, the seeds in the soul, meant to bear rich harvests, grow into bitter fruit; passions wild and strong cloud the mind, until a man betrays his unsuspecting friend, and all is war and treason; and all the elements and fiends join in battle against young and old, sparing neither mother nor babe, until carnage blunts the sword, and flames find nothing to feed upon. What escapes the war famine kills, and the pest comes gleaning in the rear. Is this a fancy picture? The last fifty years have been the most peaceable in the world's history, and who can point at one that was not a year of war?

Oh, for a voice strong enough to be heard all over this unhappy earth, and also gentle, to persuade men to help plant all over the land kindergärten for training men from early childhood up, for love and contentment and the gentle arts of peace.

THE TYPE OF THE SUCCESSFUL MAN.

Look at Leonardo Da Vinci's great work, and say, is not the betrayer rather than the Master the very type of the successful man of the day? The world pretends to worship the one and lives the life of the other. Alas, our ideals are but idle pictures on the wall.

THE MASSES AND OUR CIVILIZATION.

The condition of the masses is the gauge of the civilization of an age or country. Judge, then, our own day, in which want of freedom, knowledge and happiness drive the masses into mutiny. Or shall they bear their brutal condition with stolid indifference?

It is plain the masses cannot prosper without an Education or training to skill and virtue, but we deny it to them on the ground of expense, and to pacify our conscience, or as a make belief, give them the veriest husks of Education, the verbiage of the schools on which they starve. What an economy! We save a penny and lose a dollar. Train the people in kindergärten and in the higher schools to virtue, art and industry, and the drinking bill of the nation will fall off every generation a hundred millions of dollars, and in five generations our gains will be equal to the interest on a capital of $10,000,000,000 at five per cent, and this calculation is true to the letter; not to speak of the millions of women whose hearts are agonizing to-day; the millions of abandoned orphans, and as many fallen women and brutalized men, all victims just of the one evil of drunkenness; while it is most sad to consider that a host of other evils equally destructive, as want, selfishness, idleness, etc., etc., beset us to-day, each of which would succumb to an Education of the masses, which is not one in name, but in very deed, training them to virtue, art and industry.

We repeat it, once, when the whole family lived and worked together in the same room, the children grew up to the moral stature of the parents, as the vine does on the oak. In our civilization the father is taken away from the home ; the domestic details of an extended household, and the social duties of woman's enlarged sphere, deprive the children of the mother's attention, even in affluent families, and their moral training must therefore be attended to by the kindergarten, which, however, will do the work of the mother much better, as it is planned for the purpose, and under our modern system of division of labor everything is done more perfectly.

Does not such an Education cost less than the burning down of our metropolitan towns after the fashion of the Paris Commune, and the loss of fifty thousand men cut down in the very prime of industrial productiveness, not to speak of the infernal crop that must follow such plowing up of the lowest strata of the selfish heart of man ?

THE PROTECTION OF CHILDHOOD.

In the first and rudest state of society the whole family cowed before the brute power of man ; in the second, just closing, man bowed to love and beauty in woman; in the third, just ushering in, man and woman are bowing together before the future of humanity which they behold in the child they are moulding for great and holy purposes. And hence those characteristic institutions for protecting children against ill-treatment springing up all over the country; witness the societies for the prevention of cruelty to children in Boston, New York, Rochester, Newburg, Buffalo, Cleveland San Francisco, Portsmouth, Philadelphia, Cincinnati, Albany, Chicago, etc.

KINDERGARTEN TRAINING AND THE INDUSTRIES.

Unite art, science and manufacture, and you give us the markets of the world, was the common cry for these thirty and more years. But the school alone can give us this union by training in the kindergarten the tiny little fingers to manipulative skill, and by educating the shining little eyes of the children to the effects of form and color. We must educate a new race, the old one may linger among us a little longer, but there is no place for it in the future, and what is to be saved from the wreck must be regenerated from within by Race Education.

Changes clashing with institutions, old interests, or the habits of the millions, make slow progress;

the family or the State, though old as civilization, are, therefore, still far from perfect ; and the public school, embracing as it does the whole of life, is all we can expect it to be for an institution not a hundred years old. Still, commerce, art and manu- facture are becoming impatient at the teacher, who forgetting private and public wants, aims at abstract scholarship, while men perish, and the State totters to its foundation. " Make good and productive men," is the cry of the world, which takes no notice of the learned jargon of the schools.

ROMANTIC CHARITY.

Woe to the masses if they are to rely upon that 'romantic charity that is extended to dog and horse," they can and do starve with all of that, which does not heal the broken hearts of their over-worked wives, nor put shoes on the sore feet of their children. The very name of " Prevention of Pauperism " is sacred to us, but all societies ostentatiously devoted to it can do nothing for it. There is but one means for accomplishing it, moral, art and industrial training from infancy up to full maturity of age.

What a pity to see thousands upon thousands of men engaged in picking up and gathering in the poisonous blossoms dropping from a forest of Upas trees that might have been destroyed in the very seed. It is to no purpose that we thus work, things must be watched and controlled in the germ, and before they get the co-operation of the unbounded forces of nature, which ripens all alike, be it good or evil. In the child we must control the man, or the unruly affairs of society rush on to destruction. Still, let every good work go on, even though it take a thousand to save but one. But, Oh, how much more satisfactory to see one save a thousand, which we would by rightly training the children, which means prevention instead of hopeless cure.

THE COMING ARCHITECTURE.

Criticising is cheap, and nibbling is the business of mean rodents. Feudalism made the destructiveness of the last century a neçessity; this age asks for the building, art, science, industry and religion must rear, and for which humanity must be fitted by Race Education.

It was a feat of strength and service when men pulled down the old building the cement of which had grown to stone, but when men will not stop asserting their zeal by throwing merely about them the brickbats of the loose dirt pile, and hinder the progress of the new building, it becomes a nuisance good citizens can only frown upon. Let us warm up, and when our hearts will be flesh, the stone

piles we live in to-day will take shape, and address
feelingly the inquisitive eye. We must do away
with mechanical patch work and incongruous architectural ornament, one pasted upon the other.
From deep within and from the holier parts of our
nature our habitations must grow and become an
organic part of ourselves.

Protection, we grant, is the bottom purpose of
the house we live in, as of the shell of animals; but
should this protection not first of all extend to the
weakest in the family and to the tenderest and
holiest of interests and relations? Is there no
other coldness than that of our bodily extremities?
Is there nothing that chills young hearts for life?
Are we only to be protected from outward injury,
is there not much in poor households that crushes
dear neglected childhood for life? Fie! shame
upon our age and civilization; houses are not built
with any thought to sweet childhood, and yet
houses are meant for protection. We find a place
in them for everything, for smoking, billiard
rooms and what not, but there is no provision
for the tenderest plant in the household, holy
childhood.

We are dreamers! But our dreams are of God,
of the race and of those dear little seraphim God
ever blesses us with, and will mould the architecture of the future for the nurture and protection

of holy childhood and the realization of its divine possibilities.

Barracks beside poison exhaling gutters with con-taminating surroundings, will give way to houses with double hollow roofs, the receptacles of sweet and tender herbs and flowers, mounted by a rotun-do the inner walls of which will be covered with carvings and paintings, speaking to the souls of the children and lifting them up to where they come from—to God and the height of human destiny, and we shall have new harvests of St. Johns, Fen-elons and Newtons. Winding balusters will lead around and upward the paneled and sculptured walls, and from the straight line to the complete architectural design, animal and human form, the graded teaching shall be on the partly slated wall for the children's imitation and amuse-ment.

When the month of May, or moving time comes, the children needing most protection will be first remembered, and mothers will not mind mounting many stairs, and the rotundo will be first of all considered. Many a house in other respects indif-ferently provided will fetch a higher rent. " This rotundo will fetch out our Carolina's sweet little soul; she is of more importance than all of us put together; my husband is a tolerably good man, I usually try to do the best I know, but Carolina has

more in her, I am sure, than either of us has realized, and that must be brought out."

These cupolas with their spires, as we shall see
them when we hurry through the street, will point
us to heaven and to the future, they will speak to
us of childhood and of peace, they will speak to
us not of Greece or the darkness of the Middle
Ages, but of the blessing God has vouched us in
our own day and civilization.

After many a thousand years—for God can not
grant such a people less—we shall pass away too,
and our rotundo exhumed by a new race will become the monumental spelling book of a new civilization, mounting upon our wings to heights beyond the reach of the sublimest imagination of the
present man.

DYING FROM WANT OF AIR.

God has made a beautiful world and given us
this earth, with air, water, green fields and whatever else is wanted for life and health in great pro-
fusion. And yet His little ones pine away by
thousands and tens of thousands in our large cities.
Poor mothers, anxiously watching, are seeing with
broken hearts death coming on by inches in the pale
cheek of their dear children, never, never kissed by
the fresh breezes of heaven. Ye who call yourselves sons and daughters of God, have you hearts?

then look at this picture, and when you turn from it, turn to God and to duty—plant kindergärten, that dear, dear little ones may not be dying for want of air, God's cheapest and most universal gift. Oh, stop, stop, we pray you, the murder of innocents going on in our midst!

EDUCATION MUST GRAPPLE WITH THE PROBLEM.

The teacher, whom the great Channing puts above the statesman or even the religious teacher, must save us, and none but teachers who stand so high and whose work is of a nature to be sacred above everything else, are called to the work and can save us; they must be teachers as Pestalozzi was, and must press humanity to their bosom with the love a mother does her babe.

No, no, Education has not risen to the height of the dangers menacing the race in the metropolitan civilization of the great cities of the age we are living in. It has not risen to the height of the work that is laid upon this generation. It has not risen to the height of the problems of the day, grappling with crime and fraud in high as well as in low places. It has not risen to the height of the moral conceptions of the better men of the race. It has not risen to the height of our duty towards the masses for whose perdition we have to answer.

LIGHTEN THE BURDEN OF MOTHERS.

Shall we never study how to lighten the burden of mothers upon whom more is laid than they have strength to bear? whose bodies bow and whose hearts are breaking until anguish brings them inch by inch nearer the dreaded mad house, which is— Oh, shame! their first relief upon earth. Reason thus leaves many every year before their sands have run down, and hundreds of thousands half maddened, madden their poor children and fill them with passion and an unmanageable spirit, morally ruined for life and eternity. Does not this fill the heavens with lamentations, and does not God hear, and will the All Father not help! You may trust He will. You ask when? Whenever you say you are ready for His help, the help will be offered freely and effectively.

Open the kindergarten and the little children will be taken care of, and when they come home the spirit of the kindergarten will enter the house with them and bless father, mother, and all.

Ring it into the ears of your rulers; you have no choice between public plunderers, but you want the mothers of your children relieved of duties they can not possibly perform and which belong to the teacher trained in the modern means and methods of the kindergarten and not to a mother running from the wash tub to the baby and from the baby to the dinner and from the dinner to mending and from mending to house cleaning until late at night worn out with hard work, care, anxicty and trouble she falls exhausted upon her bed to be, perhaps, disturbed every hour in the night by a restless baby, which, dragged out as she is, she cannot properly supply with its natural food.

Let workmen cry out for kindergärten for their poor children who to day linger in the gutters where their mothers are often obliged to drive them to get rid of them. Let them cry for it until the very heavens reverberate it and they will get them. Every good man in the land will support them to the full extent of their need. But, if workmen care more for the rights of liquor dealers to poison the unwary on every corner of the street than for wife and children, then their salvation is, indeed, very far off.

Republics are most apt to suffer from revolution and unstable government, especially, when these rapid changes are accelerated by the restlessness of the age ; statesmanship will then strive to nurse stability and a conservative spirit by fostering tenacious habits through early moral training in national infant schools.

THE KINDERGARTEN AND INDUSTRIAL EDUCATION.

The out of date hum drum schools of the day may give us defaulting accountants, belles glittering in the parlor, without taste, and good for nothing else, or socialists and public debaters without practical wisdom or inspiring love for humanity, but what is all learning without a hand or soul? God has given us angels in innocence, children of whom every one has infinite capabilities, and all we study is to find low-priced bunglers, for lessoning them, forgetting the words of Burke that the best Education is the cheapest defence of nations.

How little do we consult the interest of the masses and our own future peace when a great and noble city, that is earnestly feeling about to solve the problem of industrial Education throws her vote against kindergärten.

"Ever since the days of Locke," Miss Blow, of St. Louis, says, "thinkers and philanthropists have been trying to solve the problem of educating skilled laborers, and many have been the experiments of schools for the working classes, nearly all of which have failed, because built on a wrong foundation. The truth which Froebel plainly saw, was that the schools should strive, not to turn out good shoemakers, bookbinders, or watchmakers; not, in fact, to teach any special trade, but to give such preparatory training and practice as would make all technical processes simple. Upon this basis he organized the kindergarten gifts and occupations, and, taken together they represent every

kind of technical activity, from the mere agglomer-
ating of raw material to the delicate processes of
plastic art."

Mr. Thos. Richeson, formerly President of the
St. Louis Chamber of Commerce, and now President of the School Board, speaks with double authority when he says: "The influence of the kindergarten will be felt on all subsequent education.
The early impulse given to mechanical skill and
taste, in regard to form and design, in the kindergarten, reinforced by a thorough course of instruction in industrial drawing in the primary and grammar schools, is sufficient to work a revolution in
the manufactures of the country, and cause our
goods to obtain the preference in foreign as well as
domestic markets."

Yes, Froebel; gifts in the kindergarten, industrial drawing in our common schools, together with
the Russian system of exercise in small and machine
tools, in mechanic halls connected with them, solve
the entire problem of technical Education, and
answer all objections which could be raised against
introducing a hundred trades into our system of
Education. The cry of expense is purely hypocriti-
cal and inimical to the masses, for whose Education
we care not, as a city that expends ten millions for
other purposes, can expend one million more for
the bettering of the condition of the people. Cut

down every other expense, big salaries and sinecures amounting to robbery, and give it to the children of the commonwealth and to the hard-working men, to whom we owe our comforts as well as all else that sustains life.

STREET·CHILDREN.

Can not men, who have a care for the spiritual and moral condition of the people, see in the physiognomy and actions of street children of five and six years of age, the germs which a few years will ripen into those broils and murders, the papers bring us every Monday morning? Verily, we derive but little benefit from our common schools as long as infant schools do not prevent little children from serving upon the pavement an apprenticeship of crime in their most susceptible age.

Little children meet, from crushed mothers and over-worked fathers, with nought but harshness, which, in their conduct with their street-fellows, grows to ruffianism, and later to violence, lawlessness and crime, Church and State vainly endeavor to curb. Let us transfer some of our zeal for arithmetical to moral Education, or let us honestly and openly discard all our care for, or interest in, character, humanity, the State, and all that is good and holy. Our prisons are thronged with criminals, the higher walks of life are crowded with bad men, the picture of the general demoralization held up by the public press disgraces us; is all this not sufficient to convince us of the necessity of instilling through infant schools, in childhood's holy and happy days, those great principles which are to be to our feet a bright and shining lamp through life?

THE ROCK OF EARNEST INFANT MORAL TRAINING.

We are building Latin schools, covering squares, put high school boys in soldiers garb, and exercise them in bloody arms, as if preparing for battle to be given, to whom? To whom? we ask. The answer is too plain to be given. We best train the nation in kindergärten, and the sermon on the mount will be a safer armor than sword or bayonet. The armories we are building up in our midst have more the ominous look of bastiles than of anything else. What does all this mean? Let us stop rearing our common schools upon sand, but build them upon the rock of earnest infant training and moral habits formed for life, and there will be no need for sword or bayonet.

Secure the United States Treasury on Wall Street by endearing the Government to the people by the competency it bestows upon them through an industrial Education; this would be much more worthy of the nation, and in the spirit of our institutions, than converting it into fortifications bristl-

ing with highly-tempered steel bars to the number
of one hundred thousand without, and with deadly
weapons within.

For the art and science of the kindergarten, we
must refer to the works of Froebel, so worthily introduced to the American public by Miss Elizabeth
Peabody, the noble apostle of a system that will
yet bless our country, and which ought to be taught
and practised in every normal college.

INFANT SCHOOLS THE WORLD OVER.

Are we unreasonably pressing Kindergärten?
Certainly not, as they are but improved infant
schools, the growing necessity for which was keenly
felt for the last hundred years, and which were
founded as early as 1767, by the philanthropic
Oberlin in France, and popularized by Miss Edge-
worth in England in 1819.

In 1829 Paris had four infant schools, and in
1848 it had accommodations for 6,000 infants. In
1856 there were in France fifty-six infant schools
and to-day France has 400,000 infants in these
schools. The Spanish Government recognized the
importance of infant schools as early as 1834. In
Italy, the Abbé Aporté observing the perverted
nature and semi-idiotic state in which the children
of the poor entered the primary department, in
consequence of previous neglect, established there

infant schools, but had the fine tact, as our authority, the noble Baron Charles Daru, remarks, to open them first for the higher classes. In 1833 he had four infant schools in operation in Crémona, and Lombardy counted fifty-five infant schools, with over eight hundred children.

Milan had, 1857, 6,000 children in infant schools, of whom 4,000 belonged to the best classes in society. Even in Russia, an Imperial decree issued 1838, recognized the importance of establishing infant schools, and in 1848 St. Petersburg had eighteen infant schools with 2,250 children. And to-day Froebel's kindergarten, or improved infant school, has found a favorable reception in most large cities throughout the civilized world. The State that refuses to embody infant schools in the general system of Education, loudly discards all moral motives and is the actual demoralizer of children who, abused by overworked and exasperated mothers, live half the time in the gutters and become half savage, impervious to any later impressions in the school, save of the multiplication table, and to the effect that if they grab five times five dollars they are the better off by twenty-five dollars than their victim, the sum total of the poor man's common school education.

We are over-anxious for the intellectual Education of the people, while we absolutely do nothing for their moral culture, and Channing said, with as much truth as force, " The exaltation of talent above virtue is the curse of the age."

CRÉCHES OR INFANT NURSERIES.

But even the kindergarten is not the beginning —infant nurseries, in which poor little things of but a few days or weeks are received, are a part of a complete National System of Education. Only when the nation's love will stretch back to our very beginning will we truly love it, and well we may, as we shall then hold from it not only our physical but also moral life. For when the country will bring us up as its children, in public nurseries, if needs be, we shall be brothers indeed, and treat each other as such.

In all our cities there is great need for these nurseries, and the present great infant mortality is greatly due to the neglect of children whose mothers work out.

Motherhood, that should be a source of joy, brings to a poor mother, who has to go out to work, despair, and often leads to infanticide, abandonment, dosing the children with narcotic cordials, leaving them to the charge of incompetent children, who themselves badly want watching, or to the cruelty of strangers, if not to shutting them up between cheerless walls, and converting them through this isolation from the company of men and nature, into semi-idiots.

Paris recognized the necessity of infant nurseries in 1844 and had a number of them in 1847. Vienna had in 1851 seven through the encouragement of the government. Dresden, Gratz in Styria, Pesth and Gross Wardein in Hungary, Prague and Hamburg soon followed. Italy, England, Belgium, Sweden, Denmark, Russia, and even Constantinople have all established infant nurseries. Of course, the first necessity for these infant nurseries arises from poverty, just as our common schools, which, however, were soon found to offer common advantages to all, so the infant nurseries begin now to develop opportunities useful to all, and sink the charitable feature in the great national one. What opportunity there is in these infant nurseries of acquainting mothers with the much needed hygienic and educational advice so necessary for the children's health and moral development and yet so little understood by the generality of mothers.

Are we too sanguine in looking to the wealth and generosity of the metropolis for swelling to a million the ten thousand dollars devoted to the moralization of the masses through the kindergarten by Joseph Seligman, Esq., towards whom our heart goes out in thankfulness, in the name of a grateful people? New York can not be recreant to the great work of humanity, to which her own peace and prosperity prompts her.

Make the art and industrial feature of the kindergarten the key note of all schooling, and man's work will be all grace and loveliness, and he, himself, like all he does, will be all strength and beauty; love, peace, and happiness, will fill every heart and every dwelling, and reconciliation will be written all over the world of man and nature.

America does nothing by halves. Infant nurseries, kinder and school gärten and industrial institutes shall yet as one coherent National System of Education bless the great future nation of America.

My brother reformer, socialist, communist, or however thou mayest call thyself, thou askest for State help, credit, or what not. Should not the weakest and most helpless be first looked after? Let us then begin with training all the children of the State at public expense from very infancy to virtue, industry and general efficiency. The next generation will then most probably need less aid and be more moderate in its demands. Those who have to spare will more willingly share with those who are wanting from no fault of their own, all parties will make an approach towards each other, and our present difficulties will find their solution without strife or contention.

The school teacher must prepare the way for the

reformer, as laws and constitutions cannot save men whose whole temper and disposition is—not to be saved. Let us then train all to industry and, above all, to peace and good will towards one another.

PART IV.

GENERAL INTELLIGENCE INSUFFICIENT.

In former years the promotion of general intelligence among the people was the great desideratum, and schools were organized to meet that want. With the progress of the age the wants of man, of the state, and of the industries have become more numerous and specific; problems become more definite, and especial adaptation to some particular occupation becomes necessary. Men, with no other qualification but general intelligence, do not fit into the industrial system of to-day. They are revolutionary madcaps and firebrands to whom society owes a living, and the spending of many millions per annum to educate the masses up to this sort of intelligence is criminal. We have no right to expend one copper cent out of the wealth of the nation unless we see that copper cent come back again, and that it only can under a strictly industrial Education.

(168)

NATIONS MEASURED BY THEIR INDUSTRY.

The struggle for dynastic, religious and even national wars is now over. Industry is to-day the arena where nations vie with each other, and their life and greatness are measured by their industry. Labor means national wealth, and where labor is not held in universal esteem, says Alexander Humboldt, national wealth soon disappears.

With industry comes progress, liberty and civilization. Industry makes life pleasant, organizes and harmonizes it; it raises the poor and breaks the fetters of nations as of individuals. No nation that stands low industrially can have a high civilization, nor can an enslaved nation rise high industrially.

Rome, and later, the Republic of Venice, could not last long—they had no industry. Little Holland with 600 square miles and three and a half millions population holds by its industry 32,400 square miles and twenty two millions population in America and Asia. And what else gives England her power?

Civilization means labor, progress and development. Not the knowledge of the past, but the creation of the new and the calling into existence that which is coming is civilization.

Industry subjects nature or her raw material to

8

the will of man, develops not only his physical strength but his intellectual resources and enables him to unfold his ideal powers in works of artistic skill.

With wealth and competency come strength and freedom nationally as well as individually.

In their industries nations learn to respect each other and to improve by one another.

It is by its industry that France recuperates so fast after its great defeats and national losses.

INDUSTRY THE LAW OF THE AGE.

Universal industry is the law of this cosmopolitan age, and every institution that will not bend to this law is doomed. This is not an age of almsgiving but of exchange and values and the seeming selfishness of the age is more than compensated by its cosmopolitan mind. A man's goodness is measured by the amount of useful work he does, and the wealth he honestly makes or saves is a public benefaction, while every idle or thriftless man is a public enemy.

Once the mother constantly at work at the whizzing spinning wheel—the very picture of industry—and the father applying himself early and late to his trade, by the joint example of their unwearying industry begot in the young a solidity of character which marked their course through life.

What wonder that with the disappearance of such parental example, the school with its arithmetical tricks makes knaves of us all. This is a serious matter which no amount of words can mend. Through the eye, ear and hand and all the senses busy industry must drop seeds of honesty into the heart. Since industry has vanished from the family hearth and the school has become the home of childhood and youth, the school must become as industrious and doing as the family once was, or we shall never look again upon men as honest as our sires, and we shall perish by reason of our dishonest deeds and through corporations which, as Hobbs says, like a state in the state, or as worms in a living body eat out its entrails.

Our schools force upon children knowledge only looked for in the highest walks of accurate scholarship while they fail to fit them for their own humble sphere in life.

· THE HISTORY OF THINGS VERSUS WORDS.

The philosophy of words, their history, development and connections may teach us something, but the philosophy, history and development of things is vastly more instructive. The masses care not for catching the nice shades and distinctions of words which are but the shadows of things. But the builder, the printer, the paper or glass manufacturer does take an interest in the history and development of building, printing, paper or glass making. And if the changes of words in the course of ages connect us with the past so do things and processes as soon as we behold in them the work of a long line of generations. It is time we turn from the barren study of words to the study of things.

When our schools will be technical and will be provided with industrial libraries and museums, the people will get used to such helps, and every mechanic and artisan will provide himself with a little industrial library and museum, he will learn to take an interest in his trade and study it up in all its relations to past ages and foreign countries.

We shall hear no more of learned professions, as every trade and profession will be learned and will alike be held in honor.

When schools will be centers of trades, provided with the best men, the best tools, collections and helps in particular trades the people will take a great interest in them, and this union of teachers, parents and children will invest them with a power for good unknown in our present schools, which beget only indifference if not positive dislike.

THE LABORER'S STAKE IN THE SOCIAL INTERESTS.

Art industrial Education alone can reconcile all interests by endowing labor with the highest attainable effectiveness. The less the laborer has and consumes, the less interest he has in the laws regulating capital and consumption, and the less is the security of society and the stability of the State and of its laws which are seemingly made against him; and hence the desirableness that every laborer should be a reasonable consumer and have some personal as well as real estate, or a home, that he may have a strong personal motive in studying, defending, developing, and improving the various interests of society in which he has a stake as well as anybody else.

ART INDUSTRIAL LABOR AND COMPETITION.

Art industrial Education will enable us to compete with foreign nations by the higher quality of our fabricates and not through cheap shoddy goods, ruinous alike to the workmen as well as to the reputation of the manufacturer.

In this cosmopolitan age our skill is our only protection, and our claims must be supported by the quality of our work. Let the workmen understand it that their lives, their wives and their children are staked on these schools and institutions which spread art culture and technical skill among them, and that whatever lowers our civilization lowers our standard of art, industry and trade, and consequently sinks them into the ranks of drudging slaves.

The more trades assume the nature of art the less they are subject to the law of wages, or minimum of subsistence. So, art, even of the lower sort, is better paid in Italy than in England, though wages are much higher in the latter country than in the first.

Mechanical work of the same dead level is ruled by the common rate of wages. Stamp a piece of work with an individuality that bespeaks a God-like soul and it will fetch a price refused to slavish work. *Put into your work what nobody can—your own individuality, and you destroy competition and get your own price.* Sink the artisan in the artist and you cease to be the slave of the trade. But this, industrial art culture can only spread and deepen if it is made an integral part of our common school Education.

Only when our art industries will invest things in common use with an art nature will the nation become æsthetic in its tastes; the picture gallery seen once a year affects us but little.

But, alas, there are considerations of a more grave, or rather sad nature which urge upon us an art industrial Education—the condition of woman. The wages of a heavy percentage of women are stated in the Massachusetts Labor Reports to be no higher than $2.50 per week, the working hours of many are as high as 12—14 hours daily, and many find but half the year employment, forcing upon them, as the same official Report adds, the necessity of selling their womanhood for bread to sustain life. Certainly this state of things, being the same in all large cities, loudly calls for the art industrial Education of woman, which would open to her new fields of labor, lessen competition among sales and needle women, remove from others the dangers and temptations of factory life and help women with families to make good earnings at their own hearth.

ART IN CLOTHING.

Some may only see in the sound and fury of Homeric battles something worthy of a university. We take leave to think that there is more art, science, beauty, poetry and civilizing power and influence in clothing than in Homer. The relations of clothing to decency, protection against cold, heat, moisture and other atmospheric influences, or to ornament and the beauty and dignity of the human figure ; the relations of wool, silk, linen and other materials to all these or to color, dust, light, form, cheapness and sanitary considerations, offer all a wide field in scientific and artistic studies of the widest range. The neglect of these studies destroys much of the beauty and poetry of life ; nay, life itself. The art of dressing does not as yet exist, neither as to the beauty and dignity of the human figure, nor as to the preservation of life and health, and we know and assert that a heavy percentage of our mortality is due to this deficiency, especially among women and children whose manner of dressing is singularly suicidal.

The same way every other article of manufacture would gain in use and beauty if made the object of science and art ; but, alas, a thing is held scholarly in proportion to its uselessness or to the lapse of time it has been dead and gone, and thus the present is sacrificed to the past. " Let the dead bury the dead " should be our motto in Education, as in many other things.

Industry, the care, burden and glory of our age, engaging the whole nation and absorbing its entire capital, preserving the life and health of millions and creating the commerce of the world is considered as unworthy of the school and made to give place to all sorts of verbal trash, so little do our rulers and teachers understand the spirit of the age we are living in, or care for what is to become of the rising generation and of the nation.

INDUSTRIAL EDUCATION NO UNCERTAIN EX-
PERIMENT.

Industrial Education is no new or uncertain thing. As early as 1793—1803 nine industrial schools were founded in Berlin, in Prussia, which are in successful operation to this day. The industrial schools at Gand, Liége, Charleroi, Huy and Ververs in Belgium, some of which have been in successful operation for over thirty years, have induced M. Rogier, formerly Minister of the Interior, to found likewise agricultural schools.

Stockholm has a number of industrial schools, and but lately the government has made an effort to organize an industrial school for the accommodation of eight hundred boys and two hundred girls, and a central school for educating teachers for the industrial schools throughout the country. The polytechnic school at Stockholm, besides, offers many advantages to mechanics.

At Florence, in Italy, Count Demidoff has founded, in 1828, an industrial school on the same plan as the one created by him at St. Petersburg which takes care of five hundred children and is still in the best working order.

The English government has carefully examined into the merits of industrial schools and published its results in the reports of 1843, 1844, and 1845. Grants were made 1852, 1856, 1857, 1866 and 1868, at which last date sixty nine industrial schools were sustained by the government.

Wurtemberg had, in 1872, 210 agricultural schools, beside 697 evening agricultural schools for adults. Bavaria had, at the same date, 853 agricultural

8*

schools.   Hessen-Darmstadt, of the size of our common counties, has forty industrial schools.

Austria deserves especial mention.   This great State had much suffered in its finances through internal broils and foreign wars.   The following sketch of its industrial institutions will show the method pursued for its recuperation.

It has established

9 Schools for Textiles.
3   "   "   Lace.
3   "   "   Embroidery.
3   "   "   Straw Plaiting.
27   "   "   Female Industries.
8   "   "   Industrial Design.
3   "   "   Architecture and Machinery.
8   "   "   Turning and Wood Engraving.
1 School   "   Optics.
1   "   "   Shoes.
1   "   "   Glass.
1   "   "   Dyes.
1   "   "   Porcelain.
1   "   "   Watches.
1 Agricultural Academy.
3   "   Colleges.
21   "   High Schools.
7,338   "   Classes connected with common Schools
1,137 Model Gardens connected with common Schools.
4 Schools for Vineyard and Fruit Culture.
4   "   "   Forestry.
452 Schools or Classes for Bee Culture.
299   "   "   "   "   Silk   "
3 Mining Academies.
10 Mining Schools.
2 Schools for Horse Shoeing.
6   "   "   Navigation.

6 Trade Academies.
5 Academies of Fine Arts, Painting, &c.
5   "   " Music.
52 Normal Colleges.
168 Crèches or Infant Nurseries, taking in 17,897 infants
     of workpeople.

These scattered items of industrial Education, in addition to what has been .said before, sufficiently show the universal interest taken in practical Education, and what it may become under the organizing hands of Americans who do nothing on a small scale, especially when the conviction has once taken root that it belongs to popular Education, will do good and pay.

SCHOOL GARDENS.

Garden, fruit, and tree culture, deserve universal attention. American travelers wonder at the great variety of fine fruit in European countries. With the same attention, we might have it just as well. Volumes of ministerial regulations were given during the last sixty years by the Prussian government to its local school authorities, of which the following, already issued, July 2, 1812, may serve as an illustration :

1. Wherever it is practical a nursery shall be connected with every common school ;

2. Proper grounds for the nursery should always be a main consideration in locating schools ;

3. Municipalities should assist in the getting up of the nursery, prepare the soil and fence it; the rest of the work is to be done by the teacher and scholars out of study hours;

4. These nurseries are the property of the school; the teacher has the care over them, and their yield is entirely, or in part, his, according to circumstances;

5. Every teacher whose school has a nursery, if he is competent, is bound to train the youths practically in all appertaining to fruit culture;

6. The teacher should endeavor to meet popular prejudices obstructing this good work, by showing that the poorer soils of sterile regions and colder climates may be made to yield fine fruit sortes;

7. Teachers taking an interest in this cause, and loving it, will cheerfully use their influence with the authorities, for planting the highways and other public places with trees, and for the culture and protection of such trees as are already planted;

8. As youths and adults will be interested in tree culture, malicious trespassers will become rarer; and children who should still be guilty of it, must be severely punished by the school authorities;

9. Teachers who jealously promote tree culture, should, if they possess the otherwise necessary qualifications, get especial promotion to more remunerative school places;

10. Tree culture shall in future form a part of the necessary studies of teachers and of their examinations; they must acquaint themselves with its means, and with men in the vicinity, practically skilled in tree culture ;

11. Superintendents and other school authorities in visiting and in inspecting schools, must not neglect this subject, and pay attention to it in their reports;

12. Every report giving the standing of teachers must especially name those who distinguish themselves by their care bestowed upon this cause, and also those who neglect it.

With untiring energy the government enlightens the local school authorities upon the various advantages of tree culture, which adds to public health as well as wealth, protects crops against violent storms as well as against drouth, beautifies the scenery and increases the love of country as well as the resources and comforts of the family.

With such care have the governments and school authorities of various European countries treated fruit and garden culture for these many years.

Little Bohemia has 1,585 nurseries, and 15,958,-144 fruit trees. Little Moravia produces 662,000 hundred pounds of fruit. Four cantons in Switzerland raised, in 1871, fruit worth 1,350,000 francs, and France provides Englishmen with table-fruit, bringing it annually 17,300,000 francs.

What study and experiment may do for agriculture, the culture of the sugar beet for its sacharine matter, which dates but from this century, may aptly illustrate. . In 1835, Austria imported 540,772 hundred pounds weight of beet sugar, and exported 250 hundred pounds weight. In 1872, it exported 1,303,138 hundred pounds weight, and imported 250 hundred pounds weight. And the whole of Europe produces to-day 18,711,000 hundred weight of beet sugar in 1,663 sugar-houses, of which France alone manufactures 8,000,000 hundred pounds weight.

Egypt has but shortly become a great cotton-raising country, South America is successfully raising the genuine tea-plant of China, the opium plant proves a success in Germany and Bohemia, and indigo in South Hungary. But without multiplying examples of this sort, it is obvious, the few rods available in the vicinity of large cities make garden and fruit culture a valuable help to the masses, and should be taught in our common schools.

Here are the semi-official directions of Austria, for the school gardens of normal institutes for the training of teachers; they should contain :

   1. A selection of the characteristic plants of the country ;

2. All home evergreens and foliage trees, and important wood-shrubs;

3. A seed nursery for fruit, a nursery for the improvement of wild stock, a collection of berry fruits and a nursery for them, plantations of precious fruit trees, dwarf fruit trees, and a trellis for wall fruit and grape vines;

4. An agricultural "experimental garden," agricultural and botanical, with small beds for experimental work of individual pupils;

5. A collection of economical and technical home plants; stalk fruit, hoe fruit, leguminous fodder, aromatic, medicinal, and commercial plants of all kinds;

6. A collection of the chief poisonous home plants;

7. A little kitchen garden with hot-bed or leaf-bed, and beds for planting out;

8. Small beds with flowers, high-bush roses, ornamental shrubs and perennials;

9. A bee-hive in a distant part of the garden; .

10. A large plantation of mulberry trees for silk-worm culture, a large water basin and fountain.

The thousands of school gardens succesfully established in Austria, Sweden, and other countries are a practical success.

Our schools take no notice of the individual or social wants of man. A host of able thinkers have proposed the substitution of our national literature for that of Greece and Rome, while we would to a great degree enforce the substitution of training, life, habit, nature, and observation for books. Education must not be content with reading about the nation, but must make it by the training of our thoughts, passions, feelings, desires and habits, under the lead of national men, in great national institutions. What is wanted is *synthesis*—analysis has far enough advanced. Among the ancients knowledge was concrete, it was life and nature, and hence it was grand, true, and imposing, and a model for all times. As knowledge advanced it became a separate thing ; an abstraction, pale, lifeless, and unreal. We must combine abstract science with life, or the specific modern school with the ambulatory method of the ancients, science and philosophy with nature, or the school with the garden. The word must become flesh again. But the consummation so eagerly wished for by Thomas Elyot (1544), Francis Bacon (1561–1626), John Milton (1644), Samuel Hartlib (1616–1665), Charles Hoole (1620–1666), William Petty (1623–1687), Abraham Cowley (1618–1667), Nathan Decker (1744), John Locke (1693), Adam Smith (1766), John Anderson (1726–1796), George Birkbeck (1799), and by a host of more modern men like Brougham, Playfair, Whitworth, Russell, Spencer, and others, will be brought about by the iron logic Providence has ingrained in the nature of things—by the empty larder and the pest that stalks abroad in the streets of our crowded cities, the one calling for bread and provisions, and the other for trees and alleys, and both for school gardens, and the opportunity for bread and tree culture.

All our schools should be located out of the city and its poisonous atmosphere, and they should have sufficient broad acres for gardens, nurseries, playgrounds, and Saturday and vacations should be spent in field and garden labor.

Forty years ago Mr. Wyse said in his " Reform of Education," "Schools should all have their piece of ground, rooms for different trades, etc. In towns, schools should be placed in the suburbs; wherever most sky, most of the bright and green of nature can be had, there is mercy not to the bodies only of the children but to their minds. Our school associations cast their sunshine or gloom over many long years of after existence. Happiness is the best atmosphere for youthful Education."

The school garden opens a field for observation, experiment, work, an objective knowledge of natural history, science, art, industry and all the æsthetic and social elements which attend gardens, museums, public halls, work shops and schools.

It is humiliating that the United States, which

have for many years been ahead in public school Education, should now fall behind the rest of the civilized countries of the world ; and while Germany, France, Austria, Sweden and even less civilized countries realize all the varied elements of improvements attending the school garden, we, in our lethargy, should look upon it as an ideal which we have not the heart or energy to embody in our public school system, just as other nations did who feel already the regenerating power of this vast measure, the influence of which extends to every phase of life, the æsthetic, social, moral or industrial.

With a little modification of Dr. Seguin's idea we would say, the facilities of the new modes of transportation and quick transit must, through the almost instantaneous transfer of the pupils from the city to the country, make the new idea of teaching from nature practicable, and certainly nothing is so just as to give almost gratuitously to our children the right of travel on all our city roads to and from their place of instruction.

THE SCHOOL GARDEN CITY.

Every large town would then have its School Garden City, with its twenty, fifty, or a hundred thousand children on one spot. What an atmosphere such an army of students and teachers would create! What an opportunity for social and national virtues and inspirations, for the development of a grand humanity and the formation of a great nation! What an opportunity for classifying and organizing children and teachers according to their temper, talent and inclination! Museums, collections, apparatus and opportunities for moral, art, industrial and agricultural training would be afforded on the largest scale.

A cheap meal costing three to four cents, for which every child makes a return by actual work, will be a double lesson of frugality and honest industry, every child should learn during his school years.

Only the School Garden City will, through improved environments, superadded to the physical exercise of an industrial education, check the development of hereditary disease and arrest the deterioration of the human race.

At present, the vice our children imbibe during ten hours in the slums of the city is, during a few brief school hours, glossed over with empty verbiage. In the School Garden City the legions of the future nation's ideal citizens pour in at eight o'clock in the morning, spend the whole day in company with nature, art, science and industry, and return at six o'clock in the evening freighted with lessons of wisdom imbibed from patriot philosophers—with whom to live and work is to be educated—to the bosom of families blessed and strengthened by the hallowed influences carried to them by their dear ones from the sanctuary of the nation.

These things are new! Well, we are promised that there shall be a new heaven and a new earth, for in the old there is little that is of use for great humanity, less beauty and not much more for health, and the making of a new world with its sanitary and otherwise ideal homes, gardens, schools and art industries will busy many hands.

CHILDREN COMPETING WITH PARENTS IN HALF TRADES.

The children of the Republic must get a chance for learning a complete art or trade, as it is neither the interest of the individual nor of the State that forty men should get up just one of the simplest sewing machines in use, and that none of the forty should know the place or function of the trifle he was employed upon about a dozen of years, and consequently be helpless and dependent and virtually a pauper, as he is exposed to be at any time dismissed and replaced by a child of seven years. And what are the results of this fearful competition of children against their fathers? Hovels, groggeries, jails, atheism, madness, revolt, and assassination, with squalid misery ending in the Potter's Field, leaving behind a progeny starting in its descent where its unhappy sire was arrested by the merciful hand of death. O God! who can look into the depth where the fall of that progeny is to lead without crying out for help lest the unfathomable deep make him giddy and he sink into despair for his race! And what for all this? that somebody may die in Paris or London leaving behind in Chicago or New York seven widows and as many lawyers wrangling over his remains and his millions.

OUR SCHOOLS ARE NOT SUITED FOR THE MASSES.

We talk about educating the masses when we have no intention of giving them what deserves the name of Education. Forsooth, it is good enough, though it is neither general nor specific, for what we call the common people. We beg leave to ask for the people a scientific, art industrial, and moral training, one equal in importance and dignity to any of the professions. We do not want smatterers, revolutionists and communists; we want workers and organizers in Church, State, factory and shop. What men, women and children, what a nation and what a State, what institutions, what life, and public spirit and civilization, and peace and prosperity we should have if the mass had each and all a thorough scientific, art industrial and moral training. Such an Education is cheap at any cost. Any thing short of it defrauds the people of their chances in life for a competency and defrauds the State of good and efficient citizens. Only the kindergarten and the industrial common school fit the masses for their future condition and are accessible to them. Our grammar and high schools are no more suited to their wants or accessible to them than our universities, not one in ten of the children of the poor attend them, and 60–70 per cent of the children entering the primary department drop out before they reach the grammar school. We must insist upon industry and art becoming an integral part of the infant, primary and grammar schools, a higher polytechnic grade aids the favored few to the exclusion of the very men who mostly stand in need of help. The propriety of separating general from specific Education is a false dogma. Man must be brought up as an integral being and can not be made of shreds, spending the first ten years of his Education with generalities and then get at things. As the life of the masses is one of labor, to that public Education must adapt itself, and that the more so as labor and practical observation are the foundation of success in almost any vocation.

To day we educate the masses up to the requirement of a decent pauperism, and no more; to do less would disgracefully reflect upon us and upon the State as a whole.

But are not the Hollanders, Belgians, Germans or Chinese industrious, and have they not many poor? Yes, these nations have many industrious drudges; we plead for the welding together of art, science, and labor which insures efficiency, virtue, intelligence, wisdom and skill, a consummation only to be brought about by molding all Education upon Froebel's principle of making men act and think together.

Some men deem labor an evil we have to be rid of, and again they complain of machinery for depriving men of employment. We, on our part, strive for the spiritualization and diversification of labor which will ever be sufficient to employ men, however great our progress in machinery may be.

THE VALUE SKILL ADDS.

The more labor approaches the nature of art the higher the value it adds to the raw material. Beating out lead into a sheet raises its value from 1 to 1.32, while converting it into type raises its value thirty fold. The conversion of copper into common utensils increases its value 4—5 times, making it into the finest hair seives raises its value 53 times. Cast iron worked into nice objects of art gains 150 fold over the value of the raw material, worked into rifled gun barrels it gains 240 fold, into fine knife blades 650 fold, into polished buckles 900 fold. Hemp worked into heavy cables gains four fold, worked into linen 5—10 fold. Silk and wool gain but little through labor, but cotton may be raised in value 40 fold. Steel worked into most delicate spiral watch springs gains million times in value or 400 fold its weight in gold.

NEW TASTES, WANTS, AND EMPLOYMENTS.

Industrialism is not the materialization of man, but the spiritualization of nature, and the realization of what is in man in the external world. Every new want employs a new faculty, finds work for additional hands, and food for more mouths, educates more children, and spreads intelligence, thrift and happiness among men, which is the security of the State, and the making of civilization ; and hence the creation of new wants through the cultivation of taste, and the development of skill by which to supply these new wants and tastes, are worthy ends of public Education. The great Colbert said the fashions were for France a greater source of wealth than the gold mines of the New World were for Spain, and he accordingly made France set the fashions for Europe ; she does more in the line of fashionable art manual industries than any other

country, and to this, and her small properties or
homes, owned by the masses of the population, she
owes her exceptional prosperity.

COMFORTS AS PLENTY AS SNOW FLAKES.

We seek for salvation upon earth, as Rev. Dr.
Pullman forcibly calls it, or a shower of articles
of industry as thick as snow flakes in a stormy winter's day, and that can only be consumated when
Education will take hold upon every child in its
very infancy, and train it to social virtue, art, and
industry, and invention will be cultivated as the
highest of arts for the good of mankind. Yes, invention, the source of so many modern comforts,
must be left no more to hap-hazard. It must become a marked department of study, as it is the
art of arts. It is crude to think that invention, requiring genius can not be systematized and cultivated. Success in any department, or at least in
many, requires genius, which, however, must be
aided by cultivation.

PERSISTENCE ALONE WILL SECURE INDUSTRIAL EDUCATION.

Persistence has wrested from the men in power
the present opportunities of popular Education, and
it is again persistence, and nothing but that, which
will wrest from them the moral and industrial training of the masses. There is no excuse for ignoring

9

industrial Education in an industrial age, but self-ishness is blind to the wants of the masses and to its own future interests which depend upon the general weal.

We boast of our purely intellectual Education, spread it and make it compulsory, and yet it is as sterile as the snow-capped Himalaya, in the light and brightness of which the lost traveler perishes.

Men may have no reason to be dissatisfied with their own condition, and have no wish for a change in our Education, or in any thing else. But let them think on the condition of their children in the general overthrow, when the masses, who have good reason to be dissatisfied, will bring down the social fabric.

THE PROPER MEN WILL COME FORWARD.

No wonder an educator in high position called upon the great dead. To make mankind master the forces of society and of the universe, may task the inflexible spirit of Moses, the love of Jesus, the mind of Paul, the faith of Luther, the science of Newton, and the wisdom of Franklin, but we are no wizards, and cannot summon to the work, the great men of the past; we do call upon the pro-phetic and apostolic men and women of the day, to come forward and help in the work of reducing to order the confused elements of our tumultuous metropolitan life, so full of power, danger, and temptation, by the simple means of an early, earnest, systematic, practical, moral, industrial, and art training. But have we such men and women? Yes; still, they will only come forward for doing the work of God and the race, and not for teaching what to-day are the tricks of the school, and to-morrow the tricks of the street and the exchange.

WORK THE ONLY SOCIAL PANACEA.

Specific remedies for all evils when vicious tendencies are allowed to develop unchecked, children grow up in idleness, and Heaven's laws are daily broken, we have none to offer. A purely intellectual Education, condemned by men like Cousin and Horace Mann, like other forms of one-sided systems of Education, fill the world with misery no amount of tinkering will mend.

Universal industrial Education is the only possible preventive of pauperism, and nothing but early moral training and the consecration of the individual to the whole of humanity and to art and its aspirations through Race Education can take out of industrialism the deadly sting of selfish materialism.

Public charities are only a confession of public misery put in uniform, but not relieved, and no amount of exposure will ever correct them, as we shall never bestow conscientious care upon one as long as we are indifferent about the misery our present system inflicts upon the ninety-nine. Alas, the poor, the orphan, the fallen, and the insane, we under feed, over work, abuse them, yoke them with crime, ill-treat them in sickness, and finally, bury them unceremoniously in an unrecognizable pauper's grave when dead.

Our charities are a burden to the rich without doing good to the poor, the creation of refined taste and artistic skill is the only mode we can conceive of for procuring with employment a competency for the million.

The distribution of grain, bread, money, or land ; the cancelling of debts, the decimation of slaves— the old condition of the masses—and the exposure of newly born children, are some of the aspects under which public misery, and its relief appear already in antiquity.

Formerly, ambitious men went to school to learn how to rule by force of intellect, to day the masses go to school for the sake of their own self-preservation. This, certainly, is a more natural and broader basis, which, in fact, includes the whole of man, and, certainly, it is morally preferable to seek for usefulness than dominion. The school ought to hold up to us the world and its ideal ; and art and industrial schools are more apt to do this than mere grammar schools.

THE VERDICT AGAINST THE OLD EDUCATION.

Do we stand alone in our verdict of the inadequacy of the old Education? Not by any means. Germany, thorough in scholarship and abreast in Education with the most advanced nations, recognizes the necessity of reorganizing Education upon the basis we give it, and which is essentially the same Pestalozzi and Froebel advanced, *the Education through labor for labor*, which while it develops the power of man provides for his subsistence. We crave no novelties. If we maintain Latin and Greek are no fit foundation for modern civilization we have Schleiernmacher — than whom none was more schooled in Plato—and the like authorities on our side, if we ask for an industrial Education for the masses, so does Fichte, the philosopher, and if we speak of technical pursuits upon universities so does Leibnitz.

If we are to educate man or to aid the proper order of his development we must, of course, know him and understand the nature of his faculties, but we ought not to discuss eternally the elementary facts of the psychological nature of man and neglect the practical work of Education, the great social desideratum of the industrial age we are living in.

OUR SCHOOLS NOT UP TO LIFE.

We have entered upon a new life full of vast interests, values and responsibilities. Most of us unable to cope with the forces of the day and the age, or not educated up to the stubborn reality of the things that surround us on every hand, are crushed and succumb to want, disease, insanity, crime, suicide, in short, physical, mental, moral and financial bankruptcy.

We are born as ignorant to day as men were a thousand years ago, and yet after a few years of boyish life we are expected to control mechanical and social forces which have been going on growing and intensifying for many ages, and of which we know little or nothing. It is clear there is but one way of getting broke to our work in life and that is—doing it. Is it a wonder that the masses taught upon school benches how to swim drown as soon as they are thrown into the water?

A NATIONAL UNIVERSITY IN THE SPIRIT OF THE AGE.

A national university has long and often been discussed, an institution to which the whole country could look up to, as every country has, and as is in the spirit of Washington and the fathers of the Republic, who meant the government to lead in Education, and it will be done. Let live men see to it that the National University of the United States be organized in the spirit of the day and not in the spirit of the Middle Ages.

Scholastic acumen had its day and mission. This age is moved by other forces. We want a university which shall embrace every human activity, one that provides for every human want from the highest to the lowest, a university where from the shoemaker and tailor to the musician and painter every mechanic, artisan and artist can acquire that nice insight and knowledge that only the master minds in a trade or profession possess and which often redounds to the prosperity of a nation's industry.

A true university must embrace the entire science of human life, its industry, art, domestic economy, science, commerce, government, political economy, Education, hygiene and every thing else. Colleges exclusively devoted to the languages, opinions and imaginations of the past are out of joint with our age. Latin, Greek and Sanscrit must content themselves with as much time and attention of the rising generation as are in proportion with their use in private or public life.

Let the Congress of the United States engraft industrial Education upon the common schools of the District of Columbia, and make it thereby a model for every State in the Union. The National Government has no right to dictate institutions to the States, but it may create a model government in the District of Columbia, which to know is to adopt, and where it wisely must abstain from driving the nation, it may lead it.

The great National University of the arts and industries should be associated with a United States Museum, furnished upon the principle illustrated by the great international exhibitions of the world, a museum that shall be the world in miniature, giving us an intimate and systematic acquaintance with the raw materials used in the industries, showing their applications for food, clothing, building or other technical purposes, the various stages of their conversion or manufacture into articles of use ; the history of every article of industry during past ages, as also its ethnological elements. Every piece of important machinery should be exhibited at work, the costumes of nations, their houses and habits and institutions, in short, whatever appertains to man and his activities, physical, moral and social should be arranged in the most instructive manner; every art and every science should be brought as a living and useful fact before the visitor, and acquaint him with the workings of the world in which he is to be an actor.

THE WORLD'S FAIRS AND NATIONAL MUSEUMS.

Since the first general exhibition in 1756—1757, under the auspices of the Society for the Promotion of Arts, Manufactures and Commerce at London, these fairs have increased in number and importance, the world over, until the interest, taken in them by governments, exhibitors, and visitors, as is manifest from the following figures, betokens the spirit of the age which plainly calls for museums that shall add permanence to the manifold advanvantages accruing from the present only too fleeting world's fairs.

London... 1851, at a cost of $1,464,000. visited by 6,170,000 spectators.
New York..1853, " " 500,000, " 600,000 "
Paris.......1855, " " 4,000,000, " 4,533,466 "
London.....1862, " " 2,300,000, " 6,211,103 "
Paris... ...1867, " " 4,596,763, " 9,300,000 "
Vienna.....1873, " " 9,850,000, " 7,254,867 "
Phil'a......1876, " " 8,500,000, " 9,910,966 "

What a sermon in favor of these world's fairs! And yet the hurry in which they were got up did not allow a sufficiently judicious and systematic arrangement, nor did the shortness of the time they lasted, or the throng, give opportunities for proper study.

Success requires that every world's fair excel in cost and grandeur every one of its predecessors, but as it is worse than folly to lavish the treasures of almost a kingdom on a mere spasmodic effort, our

9*

*world's fairs must be more than that. They must
initiate the establishment of National Universities
and Museums of arts and industries, and mark new
epochs in art industrial Education, commerce, manufacturing, and in the civilization and whole condition of the population of a country.*

With this great purpose in view the whole management of a world's exhibition, from the site and
structure to the internal arrangement, changes and
takes its inspiration from the more solid nature of
a permanent institution.

Our past museums entirely devoted to high art
had little attraction for the masses, and high art
there, isolated and at great distance from common
callings, was narrow in its range and influence; our
future museums, modeled after our most improved
international fairs, where all the arts of life, low as
well as high, find a place side by side, will draw the
masses, they will instruct and inspire with progress and improvement in whatever field of production they may labor.

The very fact of organizing a National Museum
of the industries, arts and sciences will give an im-
petus to the activities of the nation nothing else
can, and New York, Boston, Philadelphia, Chicago,
St. Louis, San Francisco and Cincinnati will soon
vie with each other in the establishment of grand
Industrial and Art Museums, which will soon be

followed on a smaller scale in every town and county, until at last, wherever there stands a school house there will be an industrial collection and a work room.

An American Academy of Arts and Industries, which will vie in its regenerating influence upon the arts and manufactures of America with the London Society of Arts, and its bearing upon the manufactures of Great Britain, must complete the trio of the National Art and Industrial University and Museum.

England, ever anxious for the promotion of her manufactures, has spent in the last twenty five years as many millions of dollars on the Kensington Museum, which by its choice collection in the industrial arts, its art teaching and publications, has increased English trade more than ten times the above outlay.

The Art Industrial Museum of Vienna is but ten years old, and its influence upon the manufacturing interests and commerce of that Empire is already decidedly felt.

In England artists, manufacturers, men of science, capitalists, statesmen and the court vied with one another for the last thirty years to advance the manufactures and commerce of the nation by making art, science and industry the end of Education, and the most sober and solid public men of

England are daily more and more elaborating the new Education with its industrial universities, colleges and academies which must take the place of scholastic routine.

The Kensington Museum would soon be outstript by an Art and Industrial Museum to which every American would point as to the pride of the New World and the work of the Government of the United States.

A National Industrial University, Museum and Academy will bring the nation a return equal to the investment in the first ten years, in the second they will pay for themselves more than ten fold, and the yield will increase with the growth of our population and the armies of highly skilled and artistic workmen such opportunities will furnish the nation.

The Metropolis of the nation, first in capital, manufacture, and population, offers the greatest opportunity, needs most the influence, and will best extend the advantages of a National Industrial University to every part of the country. The preparations for the coming World's Fair in 1883, should, therefore, all look toward the establishment of the great National University of the United States and the industrial regeneration of our entire system of Education, as the permanent result of the many, many millions our World's Fair must cost to outstrip everything of the sort in the past, as it has to, if it is to be an undoubted success.

MODERN LIFE AND THE SCHOOL.

Look at our improved means of locomotion and intercommunication by railroads, steamboats and telegraphs, the great movement of populations settling the two continents of America and Australia, the opening of Asia to the traffic of the world, the public press bringing daily information from every quarter of the globe, the spread of scientific and useful discoveries and inventions, our free religious and political institutions, what is there about the age that is not great in its cosmopolitan tendencies; and then look at the feeble method, narrow range and small aim of the schools, and say if thou canst forbear blushing for it? The generous spirit of the age demands that we look through the individual to the nation and to the race, and that we rear him through an early social, industrial, art and science training for useful action.

PART V.

THE DEFECTS OF THE PRESENT EDUCATION.

ENERGY, INDIVIDUALITY AND SCHOOL ROUTINE.

IF the preservation of the race is the end of Education, and the removal of pauperism is the great purpose in schooling the masses, then energy and individuality—essential to every success—must be chiefly aimed at. The red tape drill system of our common schools, therefore, which wipes out every trace of energy or character, in teacher and pupil, must be considered pernicious, while the very fitness of industrial art culture for developing in man energy and individuality proves it the very best system for training the masses.

How difficult is the reformation of old institutions upheld by class interest and prejudice. All Education should be objective is the new inspiration. Alas, what ought to be the spirit and method of the new Education is made into an additional study called *Object Lessons*, and the old verbal cramming remains the same as ever in all the studies, so rare is the capacity for applying new edu-

cational methods, or even for grasping their bearings upon the future welfare of the individual, the
State and the race.

We know no more practical aim of public Education than the cultivation of self reliance, skill, energy, originality and taste, that we may fit the
masses for every sphere and contingency in life.

Energy and individuality being the first requi-
sites of a self-supporting, free citizen, the much
vaunted graded schools of our large cities destroying both these qualities, we may well apprehend
much harm for the country from the present public
school system.

The welfare of the people is the highest object
of the State. It can not find employment for all
its citizens, but can qualify them by a thorough industrial training, to employ themselves honestly by
their own skill and energy, sustain themselves, preserve the race and perpetuate the State.

VOICES FROM WITHIN.

When principals of schools declare that they are
turning out worthless machine work, without energy, character, or individuality, reducing all to one
dead level, and training the nation for factory labor,
slavery, and helplessness, it is time that we examine
into this matter.

"Sir," said one of the many principals of the

schools for the million inhabitants of the great metropolis, "I leave every afternoon my school with a broken heart, knowing that I have done no good. The principal or teacher under whom scholars are most efficiently drilled to grind out mechanical answers to stereotyped questions, is the best man. Show goes for everything; thorough work for nothing. My teachers do not consider it their duty to say as much to a boy as ' be good.' "

Another one said : " I know I am destroying the children. Shall I make a sacrifice of myself? What for? If I step out, another one steps in, the system remains the same, and my wife and children lose their bread. The country schools, sir, where the teacher is allowed to have a discriminating mind, and to act upon each case, furnishes the best men of the country, and not the city schools, where red tape takes the place of mind, observation, and conscience."

Still another one said: "I have entered upon my duties with the zeal of a missionary, but my best teachers and myself were hampered by absurd rules and regulations, under which half of the children would be thrown out of the school. To make of children men, goes for nothing. Drilling and cramming is what is required."

" Think of it, sir," said another one, " a boy excelling in one study is bound to stay in its lower grade because he has not an equal talent for another; and knowledge, which ought to be food for the mind, is thus turned by our 'graded system' into an intellectual emetic."

Another one said: "Sir, a few years ago, I was young; the school has made me gray, and I am breaking down. To build up the community through the schoolroom is a chimera. Our system allows us to do little or no good. The individuality of the children is not at all taken into consideration, neither has the individuality of the teacher any scope. The teachers, by their drill and assistance, for the sake of making a deceptive show in the examination, destroy in the boys all self-reliance and manliness."

Another one: "Our whole school system is a degrading police supervision, which condemns itself. Principals and teachers whose judgment is not to be relied upon, ought not to be trusted with such responsibility."

Still another one: "We are reducing all the children to one dead level, making of them a perfect mush."

And another one: "Sir, no one who is not engaged in our public schools knows what they are; they were much better twenty years ago, as the system did not grind us to powder—all, principals, teachers, and children."

THE BALANCE OF INTELLECT AND EMOTION.

Nations and individuals, as well as whole epochs, have suffered from want of balance between the intellect and the emotions; witness Spain, Loyola, or the Middle Ages, with their civil wars, orders, and crusades, all traceable to their exclusive emotional life.

Protestantism in this age of science suffers from a one-sided intellectual culture, which, being purely analytical, gnaws away the foundations of the family, the State, the Church, of art, and even of science and invention, as all synthesis becomes impossible without the constructive power of the imagination, which must be animated by a higher feeling, and life itself thus stripped of beauty and pleasure becomes a burden, and men and nations decay.

Philosophy and history proclaim alike the necessity of cultivating together the emotions and the intellect, and as in our day the latter entirely predominates, we must favor the first by the introduction, of universal art culture. Industrial art Education looking at the same time to the beautiful as well as to the useful, fulfills the canon of a harmonious Education of the whole man, and balances the intellect and the emotions.

Schiller, in his "Æsthetic Education," says:

" The cultivation of the emotions is the most urgent need of the times, as they assimilate knowledge into character, and even lead to the discovery of truth, as the way to the head is through the heart."

The same author says, " Beauty leads the man given up to the senses through form to thought, and the man of abstract thought to the truth of nature."

Love, glory and conquest have in our day given way to morbid greed for gold, and this passion slays now as many as war ever did ; the exercise of our noble nature through art culture alone, can turn us from our passion for money-making in its maniacal aspects.

THE UNITY OF IMPRESSION, REASON AND ACTION.

Mankind are not to be made all painters or tailors, nor arithmetical machines, and the most especial technical training is not more defective than a purely intellectual Education, which leaves undeveloped the æsthetic faculty and the will, the most effective faculty in a world of competition and resistance, man is to shape to his use and to impress with his individuality. We emphasize the importance of these faculties, as their general neglect is productive of wide-spread discomfort, pauperism, drunkenness, crime, and insanity, and general deterioration.

We equally condemn every Education which neglects the culture of the unity of impression, of reason, and of action, which forms the basis of the beautiful, the true, and the good, and conditions the æsthetic, intellectual and moral Education, or the harmonious development of the perfect man.

CRAMMING EASIER THAN CULTIVATING THE FEELINGS.

We all know if we acted up to but one of the many noble axioms the memory furnishes us with, we would be the best and the happiest men. But we lack the power to make our knowledge available, and even here is the rub. We satisfy ourselves with the easier task of teaching by rote trite speeches, rather than train the feelings and emotions, a difficult matter which makes no show, though by fortifying the will, it may in an emergency, spare us disgrace or even save our life, and hence we insist upon an Education which does not exhaust itself in teaching how to talk about matters of which we know nothing, but which does attend to the cultivation of our feelings and emotions, which, of all things, are to a large extent, the man.

ÆSTHETIC CULTURE SHOULD PRECEDE THE INTELLECTUAL.

We lay stress upon Education ; this is right. But our Education is one sided, and commences at the wrong end, inasmuch as it is altogether intellectual, while the first function of man is feeling, and our senses are the avenues to knowledge, wherefore æsthetic culture, or the training of our feelings, ought to precede intellectual culture; and that the more so, as the third and most important faculty of man, the will, depends more upon feeling than upon thought. Correct feeling is the condition of right knowledge. Beside, it is not enough to know things, we must be trained for their healthful enjoyment—the lack of which is the cause of much sinning; and æsthetic culture, although left out in the popular scheme of Education, and underrated even by great thinkers, is the school for this culture. That the laboring masses, who have not one hour in twenty-four which they can call their own, can, with their state of mind, give their young children this training does hardly deserve refutation.

A LITTLE GRAMMAR NO FURNITURE FOR LIFE.

Were this world made by a pedagogue a little grammar would be sufficient furniture for life, but made by Infinite Power, man, amidst the allurements of a world of beauty and flowers, and the destruction of dark and stormy billows and fiercer passions, like the deer in the woods beset on all sides, he falls thousandfold a prey to incessant temptations and attacks, and mars beauteous nature by the tragedy of his life; when trained in feeling and in action, the paragon of all creation, he might have made the forces of nature, her beauty and endless variety contributory to his greatness, power, and glory.

THE SOUL FREEZES IN THE REGION OF PURE THOUGHT.

The one-sided cultivation of the intellect is bearing its bitter fruits. Love passes for weakness and might for right. We are becoming heartless and Godless. The little we can see or hold in the palm of our hand passes for all, and the infinite regions our inner sense or feeling is to reveal to us are lost to hackneyed reason. As the deep mysteries of being can only be reached by our inmost feeling, by which we are related to the Great All, this inner feeling must be cultivated by art. In the region of pure science our soul is bound to freeze in deadly isolation from the Great All.

THE IMPEACHMENT OF THE PRESENT EDUCATION.

We impeach the present system of Education for failing to atune the spiritual temper of the race to the nature of a God-made world.

We impeach it for failing to cultivate a helpful and co-operative temper among men.

We impeach it for failing to form virtuous habits.

We impeach it for not fashioning the minds of men in their very infancy into obedience to the Ten Commandments and the Golden Rule.

We impeach it for neglecting altogether our æsthetic culture.

We impeach it for not cultivating habits of observation and activity.

We impeach it for the want of industrial training and hence, for making life a chance-work, ending too often in private misery and public crime.

We impeach it for leading indirectly to idleness, pride, tyranny, demagogism, revolt, and final anarchy, ending in the destruction of the State.

We impeach it for the premature death of hundreds of thousands of infants in the abodes of misery ; for the weakness and imbecility which desolate the homes of the poor ; for the crimes that fill our jails and penitentiaries ; the insanity that stocks our asylums, or rather cities of the insane ; for the drunkard's grave ; the house of shame ; and for much of other wrongs, as Education is chiefly answerable for what we are, by what it has made, or has neglected to make, of us, in the first and most susceptible days of childhood.

BARREN LEXICOGRAPHICAL SAY SOS.

We fully realize the place of Greece in the civilization of the race, but men like Winkelman, Lessing,.

and C. O. Müller, very Greeks in culture, complain of the dry as dust method which exhausts itself in barren lexicographical say sos, without caring for the ideas or feelings of the Ancients, or for what they said or did. Linguistic lore connects us with all nations and ages, and makes the thought and experience of mankind the property of each, but tens of thousands of youths must not be robbed of the fruit of our own civilization for what hardly deserves the name of the husks of another.

Let colleges raise their standard for entering or graduating; the severer the training the better the men it will furnish us; we only cry out against the classical fraud, as Professor Bain characterizes the present course, that spoils men for useful labor by the tens of thousands, and makes them miserable for life, without giving us one leader who finds in great services rendered humanity a sweet reward for a life of self-denial.

MENTAL POWER THE RESIDUE OF SENSE-IMPRESSIONS.

Morell, a most competent judge of the culture of the age, most severely blames, in his late lectures upon the subject of Education, our building upon the Middle Ages, which followed the Romans, who were in their turn imitators of the Greeks. Our mental power, says he, is partly he-

reditary, and, to a large extent, the residue of accumulated sense-impressions, and hence we ought
to strive after the largest experience. Even so the
art-sense grows by feeding on the beauty of harmony, form, and color, and hence the importance
of leading the child to nature and enriching it with
sense-impressions in every department of knowledge.

WE IMPROVE IDIOTS AND DETERIORATE SOUND MEN.

For one successful man ten are failures; life,
therefore, is made a lottery, for which it is a thing
too sacred. This waste of human life is criminal.
While we train by judicious treatment an idiot into
a useful member of society, we bring up men of
sound bodies and minds in a manner that they are
sure to become burdens to themselves and a public
danger — a crime against society, to be paid for
dearly in the end.

The time is not distant when the altogether nominal nature of our present system of Education will
be universally condemned. Our Education is all
books, which are the memory of the race. But
man is something beside memory or the shadow
of the past. Our Education makes good histor-
ians, but poor heroes: good talkers and poor act-
ors. Action first—knowledge, to deserve the name,

10

must come by induction afterwards. The kindergarten is not an addition to our present system, but a complete revolution of every part of it; properly beginning at the commencement of the child's career and fully developing at every succeeding step.

Every idle, suffering, or criminal member of the body politic is a demonstration of the falsity of the present system of Education, and every line in this volume sustains the impeachment.

Train men to virtue and to action and every one of them will become useful and honorable, make the State great and the world beautiful, and reflect credit upon his Maker and all. The present fraudulent system, turning all into words, wind, poverty, leanness, vice, crime, communism, incendiarism, poor, mad-houses, prisons, gallows, and fusillades must perish, or the State and all else will, as we can and ought to see by the glaring light of the commune-lighted cities, and is loudly heralded by tramps as numerous as grasshoppers everywhere.

THE WORK OF THE NEW CIVILIZATION.

Socrates was as wise and good a man as the race will ever produce. Plato was as spiritual and refined a philosopher, Sophocles as perfect a tragic poet, and Thucydides as great a historic writer as the world will perhaps ever have. Not individual distinction here or there, but the saving and elevating of the masses by methods which reach all and reach them through life, is the work of the new civilization, and a correct early training and art industrial Education alone can accomplish it.

This God-inspired genius or love of the race alone can again create great works of art, purify religion, enlarge the domain of useful science, and save our civilization from perishing by the burning fires of a revolution which the selfishness of the few kindles in the many.

Poetry, religion, philosophy, and science are not, as Positivism teaches, successively displacing each other, but accompany and correct each other more or less at all times, and nothing but a harmonious early training and a universal art industrial Education can keep these equally essential elements of civilization in proper balance.

THE NEW SYNTHETIC SPIRIT AND EDUCATION.

Homogeneity, differentiation, atomism, and at last, organization, are the progressive steps of the world of intellect as well as of the world of matter. Every fact, force, and element of mind, as well as of matter, has to be torn out of its totality to be studied separately, which, however, gives us but shreds and patches of things, a rigorous synthesis must reconstruct into a cosmos.

The spirit of synthesis must, therefore, in our advanced condition, preponderate over the purely analytical and build up the individual, the home, the family, the State, and the nation by creative habits and positive institutions. Our schools are too exclusively analytical, leading to revolution in State and to the unsettling of life and all its boundaries. Only a universal art industrial Education, initiated by systematic early training, can usher in a synthetic civilization.   .

The future synthetic Education will give us the man of action, truth, and character; the present discursive Education gives us the man of words, deceit, and hollowness.

To act sensibly in the present is worth more than the knowing what has transpired through the ages.

The civilization of the masses will remain a failure until we make it mean something more practical than book reading, for which there is little room in life.

The highest truth and excellency are not reached by knowing, but doing and living up to the categorical imperative of " thou shalt and thou sha'nt."

The speculative fancy culture of the few in the past must give way to the realistic civilization of the many in the future. Museums, laboratories, and work-shops must practically illustrate the thoughts and methods of the world in every department of human activity through all times and climes, and, by thus speaking to the people in their own language of facts, make the future civilization of the masses possible.

OUR CIVILIZATION MORE THAN HALF ASIATIC.

The progress of civilization is oddly studied in the slayers and oppressors of the race who retarded civilization instead of being studied in the peaceful workers of society, in employers and employed, in the philanthropic and at the same time business-like treatment—the Ashworths, the Strutts, the Marshalls, the Arkroyds, the Brookses, the Listers, the Salts, the Crossleys, and many other noble manufacturers gave their men by whom they were appreciated.

The past civilization of Europe is more than half Asiatic, resting upon dogmatic cramming with books and authorities, and will never thrive in this young country. In Education, as in government and science, speculation must give way to action. The superstitious awe of the savage for written language clings to us, and we consider all writ holy. Civilization means to us books, and yet all literature is but the shadow of passing things and events. Leonidas and his three hundred Spartans were of vastly more consequence to the Greeks than Herodotus who told the tale; Socrates who lived the life of virtue was of more importance to civilization than Plato, his biographer, just as Jesus stands far above Matthew, and General Washington above Irving.

The natural resources, the material wealth, the machinery, inventions and extended trade of the New World, throwing together all sorts of men; the freedom from the shackles of the past or historical prejudices; the democratic equality of men, and the spirit of freedom pervading our government and laws, tend all to establish here a practical working fraternity of mankind, training and educating the young for useful work rather than for pretentious scholarship that shines only to make the surrounding darkness more painful.

The proper theater of modern civilization, which has for its goal the elevation of man through environments improved by universal art Education is in the United States, which are unsurpassed in wealth, freedom, and enterprise; and here, and nowhere else, the great problem of human destiny will find, in a not distant future, its solution in a great united working brotherhood.

A pauperism preventing Education may be of a low range to an abstractionist, the statesman knows the State is weak in which the masses are poor slaves; hence magnificent Asiatic empires melted away at the approach of the comparatively

few but free Greeks, and the splendid victories at
Thermopylæ, Marathon, and Salamis. It is the
same cause that made the once unconquerable
Rome succumb to barbaric blows.

The time is nearing when means of communication will annihilate the security which springs from
the distance that separates us from Europe and
its vast armies, and then the love of the people for
a government, which like a mother nurses it into
prosperity, will be our only strength and safety.

The spread of wealth brought us freedom ; if the
latter is to be preserved the first must be sustained
by a universal industrial Education.

THE ART OF LIVING.

Education must cultivate the art of living, industry and thrift. The great want of the masses
is capital, which they can only acquire through
skilled labor and thrift, and hence their Education
must be chiefly industrial. The practical good
sense of the age demands that public Education
should raise the productive capacity of labor, increase capital, promote thrift, and by satisfying the
wants of the body stimulate those of the mind.

Intelligent labor alone can provide decent food,
raiment, and shelter for all ; the school, to day,
discourages labor and encourages by half knowledge the crude dreams of communism which asks

of the State what individual exertion alone can achieve.

The world calls for labor, capital, and thrift, and the school mocks the requirements of the day with the tricks of examination shows, until the clamor of the hungry body deadens the cry of the soul, and men curse God and their own day, and end their short life in the prison or asylum, or cut the tender thread of life with violent hand.

The atheism of fashion of the eighteenth century may have been without immediate concern for the State; the atheism of despair of the hungry masses is of a more serious nature if looked at in the light of the Paris Commune, and must be counteracted by the prevention of pauperism through industrial Education.

THE COSMOPOLITAN ASPECT OF LIFE.

The gap between men must be bridged over by improving the temper of all, by a more cosmopolitan aspect of life and a deeper sense of the unity and destiny of the race. The stuff we call history fans in us hate, pride, and jealousy, speaking as it does of nothing but clans and tribes, war and ambition, dominion and slavery.

This must give way to the true history of humanity, or the progress and development of civilization illustrated in the lives and works of men

like St. Vincent de Paul, Fenelon, Howard, Clark-
son, Commenius, Pestalozzi, Joseph Lancaster,
Froebel, John Pounds, Wichern, Girard, Peabody,
Peter Cooper, Garrison, Gerritt Smith, Wendell
Phillips, Channing, Theodore Parker, Mrs. Fry,
Florence Nightingale, and Elizabeth Thompson.

OUR METROPOLITAN CIVILIZATION DEMANDS EARLY MORAL TRAINING.

Antiquity had here and there a Babylon, Tyre,
Sidon, Carthage, Athens, Alexandria, or Rome;
but our civilization is, as Vaughn correctly says,
eminently one of large cities, in which vice and
crime have especial opportunities for escaping detection, developing and spreading by contagion.
The vicious crowding into large centres, make them
seminaries of vice and crime. In large cities, too,
with the opportunities for wealth, pomp, and show,
develop avarice, fraud, deception, and swindle of
every sort, together with indifference, if not contempt, for every thing else than wealth and power.
With the excess of riches and poverty, tyranny,
pride, arrogance, meanness, hate, envy, and strife
fill the State and lead to its destruction. These
deteriorating tendencies of our large cities and
their civilization we have to meet by a conservative early Education and training to moral habits
and social virtues, to industry, and a love of the
10*

true, the good, and the beautiful, to taking pleasure, not in having and ruling, but in doing and serving; and all this has to be done, and can only be done, not by words and precepts, which always come too late and are without force, but by training, as Carlyle says, from the very time that the little chaps can stand upon their feet. At this and no other price can we avert the deterioration arising from the civilization of an age that is eminently one of large cities.

Infant training gives steadiness to principles and habits, resists rapid changes, favors the formation of institutions conservative in their tendencies, and resists the dissolution and early decay arising from the feverish activity and restlessness of our urban civilization.

In the great city, says Paxton Hood, varieties of existence crowd—horror and beauty sit side by side—there every day is the calm and quiet heroism —and there, too, is the unseen, untracked crime. There labor plies its thousand shuttles, and weaves its many hues; there man preys on man, and gambles with affections and hopes and existence, as if all were valueless; there is the devout song and the submissive prayer; and there, too, is the constant plotting, the everlasting scheming, the endeavor to outshine, the petty vanity, the cruel persecution, the helpless, hopeless poverty, lying down to die.

No wonder Aristotle thought a city that has as many as a hundred thousand inhabitants can not subsist. Queen Elizabeth of England had by a royal proclamation interdicted the building of new houses within three miles of London, so as to put a stop to the evils, inconveniences and miseries arising from too much crowding into large cities. So much is clear, we must be better fitted for life in the great cities if our civilization is not to come to a speedy end.

Our great cities and greater life make so many demands upon us, that ninety-nine in a hundred are unequal to the burdens they are to bear. They sink by the wayside, one sooner, another later, while the fewest remain uncrushed, So many fail, are wrecked, suffer; vice, crime, and drunkenness abound; women are broken-hearted, and children are perishing in the gutters, and why, why all this? Simply because *the measure of our schools is not taken from the great life of our great cities;* and unless a God-like training to virtue and a thousand arts and industries prosper the masses, we shall drift into revolution, not here or there, but everywhere.

Only intelligence, industry, law, and order can prosper the commerce of our cities, which in their turn stimulate the progress of science, and make the mind at once comprehensive and robust.

Still, in the absence of a due feeling of our

responsibility, superior knowledge may prove adverse to wisdom, and our greater means may lead to more artificial forms of depravity, and human suffering may become more complicated and hopeless. Such are some of Vaughn's reflections, and which are warnings not to be unheeded in a system of Education that aims at the amelioration of a constantly-growing city population.

The idler, the pleasure-hunter, the rake, the gambler, the swindler find all their place in the large city. Extreme conditions lead there to extreme vices, and men are wont to pay any price for pleasure or for power. We need not repeat here that commerce, wealth, freedom, and civilization are all the offspring of large cities, which have blotted out the distinction between master and slave. But if we do not train the masses the distance between the extremes these very cities are creating will become greater and more galling than those of the slave and the master in the past.

Pass through factories of a thousand kinds, place yourself at the head station of one of our many great railroad lines, study the great marts of the world, visit our police courts, morgues, and prisons, contemplate the pomp and power of wealth and the misery and degradation of abject poverty; study life with its solemnities, grandeurs, successes, calamities, and failures, and then say if our Education is not more a triviality and a mockery of all this than a preparation for it.

OUR GREAT LIFE AND AIMLESS EDUCATION.

Look at the United States with its realized wealth of $30,000,000,000, a clearing house with an annual exchange business of figures so vast, that their mention would be useless, as they transcend all powers of conception, exports and imports equaling about $1,200,000,000, and these ·figures have to be literally doubled and the product has again to be tripled, and again to be doubled, to express the values of the commerce of the world, which all bear upon the operation of every active member of the community, modify it and must be taken into an account ; can we then forbear blushing, that in the presence of these stupendous realities, we allow our public Education to trifle with the work and scope of life which require of us work, work, and again work, and can an Education criminally indifferent to the work, life, and interests of the masses and the elevation of man, lead to anything else but national ruin? We are bewildered by the infinite wealth of nature and our endless resources, and unless a national system of early infant training and art industrial Education is initiated which is more in keeping with the burdens, opportunities and duties of the age, our blessings will turn in our mouths to ashes.

PART VI.

THE NEED OF THE NATION.

WANT of the proper means and conditions of life weakens and deteriorates the human system. It deepens misery by lowering energy and lessening the capacity for useful work until pauperism, crime, and insanity become hereditary.

Raise the productiveness of industry, and as men are supplied with the necessary means of subsistence their energies will be quickened, and with pauperism, crime and insanity will be lessened. Industrial Education is the great need of the nation. It would not only increase the army of usefully employed men, but would make us strong through work; it would train us to industry and order, make us provident, keep active our minds as well as our bodies; it would be a practical school of virtue, as vice springs from idleness, which is always accompanied by ignorance and want.

The noted philanthropist, Frederic Hill, says: "Bad training, drunkenness, and poverty are the chiefest causes of crime, against which the best

(230)

remedies are the cultivation of habits of fore-thought, sobriety, and frugality; the promotion of habits of industry and self-reliance, and the adoption of all other practical means for raising every class of society beyond the sphere of destitution, and into that of comfort and moderate wealth."

The same great thinker insists upon the necessity of training the people in the various industries, which would decrease poverty by adding value to labor, and parents should be made responsible for the crimes of children they have not given those opportunities generously afforded by the State.

Crime results from want of home-training, which is hardly possible without a certain amount of comfort and order, and, hence, the morals of the community require that labor should be valuable, which it only can be where a general system of industrial Education prevails.

The increase of crime among high and low has everywhere prompted the investigation into the causes of crime, the prevention of which must occupy the minds of educators. Culture is too indefinite an aim for a public system of Education costing annually the tax-payers of the land $80,-000,000. Next to the preservation of the race, the preservation of the State through a self-relying, law-abiding, and useful citizenship, or the prevention of pauperism and crime through th · development of skill and virtue, must be the aim of Education.

" By Education," says further Mr. Hill, " is not meant the mere capability of reading and writing, but a systematic development of the different powers of the mind and body, the fostering of good feelings, the cultivation of good principles, and a regular training in good habits. Such an Education necessarily includes industrial occupations, and giving a taste and aptitude for useful employment, so as to prepare the scholar to earn a livelihood without that severe and constant labor by which alone the ignorant and clumsy workman can obtain an honest subsistence, and from which he too often recoils and flies to crime. A good carpenter, shoemaker, or blacksmith is seldom to be found in prison, and still less a good machinist or watchmaker."

An imperfect knowledge of a trade, or a poor trade, will keep the rising generation hovering over the verge of want and crime, into which every next generation will be sure to sink if the effort of rescuing it from its abandonment is not continually renewed. Give the rising generation a perfect knowledge of a remunerative trade, which shall lift it out of struggling poverty into competence and a well-ordered condition, and the next generation, growing up under the moral influences of normal homes, will not be in need of the social quackery of our charitable institutions.

A large, unskilled population, living in crowded tenements in bitter want, calls for a technical training in our schools which would soon rid us of the disease of pauperism, a degrading soup-kitchen charity only aggravates.

Technical training will, by its physical exercise, relieve the nervous system and cultivate simplicity, and thereby counteract the evil tendencies of our present civilization which decidedly increase insanity. Technical Education elevates labor and makes us more industrious, provident, self-supporting, and self-controlling. It prevents drunkenness, idleness, and bad company, and in many other ways prevents crime.

There is hardly an author treating on crime but considers work as its sure prevention. The Massachusetts Board of Charities say : " Exercise is the law of organic existence. Health can not be preserved without it. Work commenced early in life is one of the most effective preventions of dependence and want. Idleness and laziness beget poverty, vice, and crime. Habits thus formed bring the individual to the almshouse, the house of correction, the jail, or the prison. Exercise, industry, occupation of body and mind are powerful antidotes to pauperism, crime, disease, and insanity."

Is it, then, right that we wait until the masses are eaten up by corruption of every sort, and are beyond recovery, before we apply the God-ordained preventative ? When early neglect and a life of ill habits have destroyed body and soul, nothing will, and nothing can, help. We might just as well commence the work of reformation in the grave as in the prison ; we must put every man to his work at school, and in early life, when habits are formed ; and upon this, societies devoted to the prevention of crime must insist. Work comes equally too late with the pauper portion of the community, who come into the world with the laziness of three and four generations in their slender bones. The community at large, the masses, all our children, must be brought up in their school-days to physical as well as to mental work, which is the normal condition of man, and yet the verdict of all is, that our present system of Education cultivates a decided distaste for manual labor.

Reduce the figures of pauperism as much as we may, the poverty of the masses, and the tens of thousands who but shortly belonged to the rich, and to-day suffer want, call for a technical Education. A careful study of the causes of the various forms of defectiveness points to want of industrial Education with its attending poverty and want of hygienic conditions, as to the most common source of these social distempers.

Insanity and idiocy cost the United States to-day directly over $8,000,000 per annum, and indirectly, more than double that—not to speak of the misery it inflicts—fully one-third of which could be prevented by the means of the hygienic conditions which would follow in the wake of industrial Education.

We have seen the cost of the depredations, detection, and detention of the State criminals of the various prisons in the United States amounts to fully $130,000,000, and besides this sum we must bear in mind the vast expense and loss caused by the detection, detention, and pilferings of hundreds of thousands of arrests made annually by the police in the United States. How cheap we could get rid of a large part of all this cost and demoralization if we would bring up the people in our schools to work and industry, or must we wait until these evils eat into the very heart of the nation, and financial ruin and physical and moral decay force upon us the New Education? Is it wise to wait until it may be too late, and we lack the energy and the means to make the change?

A partially theocratic communism may have suited agricultural Judea, equally divided as it was among tribes and families ; the Church organization of charities may have done in the Middle Ages, when almost all the wealth and all the land were in the possession of the Church. Old Rome tried to mitigate pauperism by the public distribution of corn, by which it only aggravated the evil, and England has done very much the same thing by its organized State relief. The present civilization demands that the public Education be in the main organized and conducted for the great work of the prevention of pauperism with all its deteriorating tendencies. This alone justifies taxation for educational purposes, pays richly back what is taken out of the public treasury, and bestows a tangible benefit upon the people. There will always be sporadic cases of want and misery for the exercise of public and private charity. But public Education must prevent pauperism from becoming a public danger, what it decidedly is to-day. One organization for a polite universal Education, and another one for taking fully and completely care of all the burdens of an unchecked pauperism, is more than any nation will, or perhaps can, stand.

Noble impulses are as old as the race ; the cultivation of the intellect does not distinguish our age ; industry has always been insisted upon by the Chinese ; and, according to Herodotus, the

Egyptians punished idleness with death. But the organization of a universal system of Education, based upon the moral, intellectual, and physical nature or wants of man, among which labor stands forth foremost in importance, must lay the foundation to a new civilization, which starts man rightly in the early period of his life, when he is properly enough put under conditions conducive to his development, that he may be least interfered with when he shall have reached his full growth and the age of moral freedom and responsibility.

We know that good taste stands aghast at our declaration, that the prevention of pauperism and crime is the next highest end of Education, the preservation of the race being the first. But we are all one and the same species, and the Education of us all must be based upon the same fundamental principles. The specified lists of thousands of defalcations, amounting to more than $40,000,-000, the annual crop of crime among the higher classes, the industrious metropolitan press brings us the first of the year—not to point to court proceedings—should dispel the notion that the aim of preventing pauperism and crime can be safely dispensed with in the Education of any class, and that work is vulgar, or that it is sufficient for the school to equip men for life with fine words. There never was said a truer word to point out the duty and responsibility of the higher classes than that of the Rev. Wm. Henry Channing: " It is the loafers who are rich that make the loafers who are poor." We do want culture, but such as is based upon work and performance, and not upon words and a puffed-up imagination.

Industrial Education is beginning to be felt as the great need of the nation, men of practical genius are giving it shape, and we hope men of generosity and faith will come forward and give it their support.

NATIONAL TEACHERS' ASSOCIATION.

Hon. A. Newell, the President of the late National Teachers' Association, said, in his admirable address before that distinguished body of educators: "Our public school system can not be regarded as complete until the department of manual labor is added. State Education must teach the children of the people to work, without which they can never become good citizens. Industrial Education will soon be an accomplished fact, like many other things which but shortly were considered 'impracticable.' The many must live by labor, and the school must help them so to live by turning them over to the city workshops, where they would learn to be workers."

The Hon. J. P. Wickersham, State Superintendent of Education of the State of Pennsylvania, said, on the same occasion: "I am not sure but that if half the money expended in the schools of our cities were expended in the erection of shops to teach boys and girls trades, it would be better."

President Runkle, of the Polytechnic Institute of Boston, remarked that young men who commence with learning their trade never come to school to learn the science which underlies their trade, while those who set out with the study of the science hardly ever learn the art or trade, and hence the necessity of combining practice and theory at school. Mr. Runkle explained that in the Russian System of Instruction *the technical operations underlying a number of trades are studied as an elementary art and separate from those trades themselves.* So, for instance, is vise-work an art important to the blacksmith, die-sinker, tool-maker, machinist, gun-smith, boss-finisher, iron mold-maker, jeweller, etc. And vise-work again divides into filing, sawing, tapping, chipping, reaming, thread-cutting, breast-drilling, etc.

Dr. Buchanan, of Ohio, showed the bearing of industrial training on character and intellectual energy, and on the dignity and productiveness of labor, the elevation of our population, the increase of general prosperity, and the solution of the great problem of capital and labor. "The mechanic arts," said he, " are to-day in the same degraded condition the medical profession would be in if instead of having schools, a literature, and public instruction, it blundered along nursing the sick."

MASSACHUSETTS BOARD OF EDUCATION.

The Massachusetts Board of Education shows the possibility of gaining technical and elementary school Education in its Forty-first Annual Report, where all the details of such a course are given, and from which we condense the following statement :

The progress in the mechanic arts, the disappearance of the old apprentice system, and the welfare of the masses, as well as the public peace and the safety of the Republic, demand that our common schools train the heads and hands of the people simultaneously.

President Runkle explains in the mentioned Report, that all existing mechanical operations can be taught as a system of art fundamental to the trades, and that this method forms the only true and philosophical key to all industrial Education. This system distinguishes Instruction Shops which teach exclusively general mechanical operations, or the use of tools, and Construction Shops which teach especial trades.

These ideas have been carried out in the " School

of Mechanic Arts " at Boston in the following Art courses : In *wood*—I. Carpentry and joinery ; II. Wood turning ; III. Pattern-making. In *iron*—I. Vise-work ; II. Forging ; III. Foundry-work ; IV. Machine-tool work. In *textiles*—I. Designing ; II. Pattern-weaving ; III. Dyeing.

Twelve hours per week—three lessons of four hours each—of the student's time are devoted to shop-work, and the balance to drawing and other studies. We can not enter here upon the regulations of the shops, the course of studies or exercises, the methods of examining the work, etc.

The Whittling, or Carving School, at Boston, has been for a long while in successful operation, and so the Industrial School Association. The committee on Report of the Industrial School Association close their Report with the following words : " One such work-school as we have described might furnish four hours' instruction every week for one hundred and ninety-two boys ; or, if evenings were added, for two hundred and eighty-eight boys. This is more than the number of pupils between the ages of thirteen and sixteen commonly found in any one Grammar School. We can not but believe that it would be easy to establish, in connection with all our Grammar Schools for boys, an annex for elementary instruction in the use of the half-dozen universal tools : *i. e.,* the hammer, saw, plane, chisel, file, and square. Three or four hours a week, for one year only, of the Grammar-School course, would be enough to give the boys that intimacy with tools, and that encouragement to the inborn inclination to handicraft, and that guidance in its use, for want of which so many young men now drift into overcrowded and uncongenial occupations, or lapse into idleness or vice."

President Runkle thinks boys are best admitted to technical training at the age of 12–14 years. In cities mechanic art schools located in central parts might combine instruction in manual labor with mental study after a given age. These shops could also be open evenings for the purpose of the manual Education of large numbers who could by no possibility have any other opportunity.

In the district school, a single room fitted up to teach the use of the saw, plane, chisel, and auger, the common wood-working tools, or what seemed best adapted to the locality, would be all that need be done.

The Instruction Schools for the use of tools are the first step; the nature and condition of specific Trade Schools must be left to time and local conditions.

At an expense of a sum no larger than $20,000 can be equipped for the instruction of seven hundred and sixty-eight students to be taken through in a three years' course, beside evening classes in wood shops for: I. Carpentry and joinery; II. Wood-turning; III. Pattern-making; in iron shops for: I. Vise-work; II. Forging; III. Foundry-work; IV. Machine-tool work. The annual expense for the industrial Education of each student does not exceed $10. A shop teaching carpentry and joinery may be furnished—to commence—with $500. The industrial Education of the entire youth of the United States need add no more than 10 per cent. to the cost of our present school system, which breeds wild speculators and hungry communists. The cost of buildings, tools, and machinery, for the Industrial Education of the United States would be less than the capital invested in the school-buildings of the State of New York. But the addition to the public wealth by an annual accession of 200,000 trained men would make the investment the best the nation ever made.

THE WORCESTER FREE INSTITUTE.

The Worcester Free Institute has been on trial for nine years. The students in the Department of Mechanics practice in the school-shop 900 hours in the first, and 500 hours in each of the next three years. In this course the student practices chipping, filing, forging, planing, lathe-work, the use of the milling machine, etc., and is exercised in the fitting and finishing of machinery.

We give in brief the experience of this school. The shop is organized as if for manufacturing, and adapts itself to the school only so far as to give proper variety of work. Construction, perfected as far as possible, is made to serve the nobler purpose of instruction. Mechanical practice forms a constituent part of every week's work throughout the course, and is done in the atmosphere of real business, though without pecuniary return to the student for his labor. Study and work accompanying each other, the school inspires its intelligence into the work of the shop, which in its turn renders practical the learning of the school. The parallel study of science and handicraft gives labor its real dignity. The practice in the shop serves the double purpose of mechanical discipline and of physical exercise, and is a great economy of time and cost. The teaching of handicraft in connection with the school is thought necessary, as few would stop to learn the practical use of tools and machinery after leaving school, and besides, whatever mixes with the discipline of those plastic years from 16–20 years enters into the life and character of the man in a more intimate and organic sense than the contributions of maturer years. The object of the shop is to give a thorough working knowledge of the fundamental processes of mechanism as found in all manufacturing machineshops. The annual salable product of the schoolshop is about $17,000, falling short but $3,000 of the actual expenses of the shop, and this deficit is gradually diminishing. While the school is teaching handicraft, it does not disassociate labor from its producing power. To spend time in learning mechanical processes which are not used, may add to his culture, but not much to his practical fitness for a mechanic's life. Excellence in *con*struction, tested by the demands of the best judges, is an indispensable element in sound *in*struction in the mechanic arts. The country which commands the most energetic and intelligent labor, produces most for a given expenditure of labor. And intelligence in labor has in it the cure of all the ills which now attend labor and its relations to capital. The Worcester Institute has graduated annually about 20 students, and the average age of its entering apprentices is 17 years.

THE DEVELOPING SCHOOL AND MANUAL INSTITUTE.

The American Social Science Association recómmends the plan suggested by Mr. S. P. Ruggles, which is universally endorsed by the press, in contradistinction to the former system of our fathers—

that the youth, whenever he has completed his general education in any of our public or private schools, may enter what may be called a

DEVELOPING SCHOOL,

so established and arranged as to give all the pupils a good general idea of all the different trades, arts, or callings, in order that it may be ascertained by themselves or the superintendent for what kind of business they have the greatest natural genius. Imagine, if you please, one very large room, with a steam-engine and boiler in the middle of it, so that all pupils that have any taste for the management of steam, or steam-engines, could examine every point, and readily understand all about it. Then we would have a carpenter's bench, with a variety of tools used by carpenters, to show how that work was done; then, perhaps, turning-lathes, to show how the wood-turning business was performed; then, with the aid of blackboards, carving-tools, and jig-saws, it might be seen how drawing and carving and jig-sawing were done, by those that have any inclination for that business. We should also have the machine-shop represented by having planing-machines, lathes, upright drills, etc., to represent the machinist business. Foundry work should be shown by having the usual fixtures for sand, and two and three part flasks for moulding, etc.; the casting could be done in soft metals, as lead, zinc, or tin, which could be reused, as the whole art in foundry work consists in the different manner of moulding. We would have a printing-press, type, fixtures, etc., to represent the printing business; mason work, the laying of brick to some extent; stucco work, or the working and the moulding in plaster of Paris could be shown; the whole room being filled with educational problems of instruction, such as three different heights of barometers, the bellows-valve, the gyroscope, the ball on the top of a jet of water, the steam-injecter, etc., etc., all to bring out the thoughts of the youth, enabling the superintendent to ascertain the true bent or natural genius of the individual, so that he could be put to the right manual profession which he is best suited for.

As soon as it should be ascertained what kind of business the pupil is best fitted for by nature, he would be recommended to the Manual Institute where that *trade* should be taught, and be more thoroughly instructed in two years, and become a better mechanic, than in six or seven years under the old system of learning a trade.

We would here like to show the difference between Manual Institutes of all kinds that should be established to teach a trade, art, or calling, and the shops already established for doing work of that particular kind for profit. For example, we will speak of the machine-shop, which, as now arranged, is fitted up with the general tools and fixtures necessary to do a particular class of work, such as locomotive building, or steam-engine building of various sizes, or printing-press machinery, or factory machinery, or tool-making, etc., etc., neither of which would have every variety of tool or fixtures in any one shop for doing every kind of machine work. But when we fit up a machine-shop for the express purpose of *teaching* that trade or art, it should contain, not only planers, lathes, upright drills, gear-cutting machines, etc., for doing work generally, but should contain every tool and appliance of every name and nature that is ever used in any machine-shop, so that the student would become acquainted with every manner of doing work and the management of every kind of tool or device ever used in shops doing any kind of machine work. Also, there should be a very particular selection of the kinds of work to be made at the Manual Institutes, consisting of lathes and planers and other tools that are always kept on sale, large and small work of different kinds, making as great a variety of work as possible for the pupil to practice upon in building, so that he would get a thorough knowledge of all and every part of the machine business ; and each pupil would be taught to make the whole, and put together every machine that was being constructed.

In the Manual Institute the pupil would advance from a lower degree of instruction to a higher as rapidly as his thorough knowledge and good workmanship would justify. The instructor would be paid a satisfactory salary, and not be permitted to make merchandise of the time of the student. All machinery or articles made by the students could be disposed of by being put on sale, and the proceeds appropriated toward defraying the expenses of the " school-shops."

The great and rapid change in the division of labor and the introduction of machinery, and the great variety of appliances for doing all kinds of business, show plainly the importance of changing the system of instruction at the present time. We think it will be admitted that it will be of incalculable advantage to the youth, and would prove in the end to be very economical for the whole community.

It is well known there is no place at the present, nor has there been for some time past, where a boy could " learn a trade."

Every boy, rich or poor, is, we think, as much entitled to be taught a good trade as to have an Education in our public schools. We also believe the proposed plan would be self-supporting in a short time after being once put in successful operation

To recapitulate :

First. There would be great advantage gained by selecting the right youth (by the Developing School) for the right business.

Second. The boys would be *taught* the trade, instead of picking up their knowledge by *mere chance*, as was the case by the former plan ; and not be kept on work which would be most profitable for the master, as it would be his whole object to *teach* the boys, instead of making profit on their work.

Third. The Manual Institute would be much more perfectly fitted up (as described) to *teach* the business than any shop to do work for profit, as all shops heretofore have only been fitted with such tools and appliances as were necessary to do their particular class of work.

Fourth. The kind of work selected to be made by the boys would be both large and small, embracing as great a variety as possible, in order to give them a perfect knowledge of every branch of the business.

Fifth. There would be *good moral discipline* in the Manual Institute, the boys not being mixed up with journeymen and all classes usually found in all shops as generally established.

Sixth. There would be no more expense to the boy while learning the trade and making him a producer, than there was while getting his public-school Education.

Seventh. The worth of the work made by the boys would probably pay current expenses after a very short time.

Mr. Ruggles insists upon keeping entirely apart the school proper from the Developing School and the Manual Institute, into which the children are only to be received after a certain age, or after they have left the grammar school.

The Developing School of S. P. Ruggles is a new and far-reaching thought, with tendencies of remarkable interest to the social student. It is the natural accompaniment of public industrial Education, for a State, with almost infinite means at command, can not act blindly in doing the work of millions, as weak and isolated individuals are wont to do. Or shall the State lavish its resources in teaching men what they will never succeed in, and what will ever be a drag upon them as individuals, and upon the State as a whole? And, hence, we may safely assert, that industrial schools will ever be attended by Developing Schools, equipped for doing the work of a dynamometer, measuring the technical and professional powers and qualities of youth before they are put to what is to constitute their vocation in life.

Every man is an especial organ of society, and

will best perform his own function. But who ever heard of an eye doing the work of the ear, or of an ear doing the work of the eye? As long as every man is not started rightly by the Developing School, and put to his own proper work, society will be out of gear, just as the body is when one or another of its organs is out of order.

Men enter trades without reference to taste, talent, means, climate, soil, natural production, local opportunities, demand, or their own physiological aptitudes and hereditary tendencies, and, hence, they make through life botches and failures, eke out a miserable existence, shift from one thing to another, betake themselves to drinking and gambling, and get into other pitfalls, and into general apathy, and become vagrants and tramps, or get diseased and die prematurely. Upon the concourse of our occupation with the forces of nature within and without us, and with the facilities of time and place, our success and happiness in life depend. We must hitch the infinite forces of nature and society to our own car, and not rush into the battle of life like the general who, in his haste, left behind him the army which was to do the fighting.

Only the Developing School and Manual Institute will remove the ground for the timely complaint of the eminently practical divine, the Rev.

Dr. Hall, of New York, that there is want of a settled purpose in life, a shallowness and lack of development in individual capacity, and an unwillingness among young men to become mechanics, laborers, and farmers.

It is a consideration not unimportant to the race, that we have hitherto counteracted, if not destroyed, the heredity of mechanical genius by the habitual exercise of opposite tendencies. Let the Developing School suit the employment of men to their native bent; and the natural tendencies, which are organic aptitudes, will be deepened by congenial habits of body and mind, and skill and talent will become more and more hereditary.

Drunkenness, vice, crime, pauperism, insanity, and every other deteriorating tendency are hereditary; let us suit men's trades to their talents, three, four, and more generations, in the Developing School, and foster congenial industrial habits in the Manual Institutes of the American system, and we shall thereby co-operate with the Creator, render the upward tendencies of our nature equally hereditary, and improve, with the progress of Art and Civilization, the physiological aptitudes which attend mechanical genius.

Adam Smith observed, already a hundred years ago, and every succeeding philosopher had more and more an opportunity for observing the mischievous tendency of a progressive division of labor, in narrowing the capacity of the individual. This same system of labor overrules to-day every occupation, and a boy has not the slightest chance for learning a trade. So, for instance, with 316,459 artisans and manufacturers in Massachusetts, there are but 1,206 apprentices in the State, or one apprentice to 262 artisans and manufacturers, and in Boston are 51,344 artisans and manufacturers and 371 apprentices, or 138 artisans and manufacturers to one apprentice. This vice, rooted in general conditions beyond the power of the individual, can only be corrected by the State.

But when an evil becomes unbearable, a higher order of things is ready to burst upon us; the travailing pains are the harbingers of the new birth, and what hitherto was mixed up with other functions, is, hence, performed by a new organ, and of course is much more perfectly done: such is the order of nature, and of the social organism.

When the means and conditions of learning a trade can no more be commanded by the individual, a new and separate public organ is shaped with such perfect adjustment to this end, that all haphazard is henceforth precluded, and the function is performed with an accuracy and perfection never anticipated. Everybody's trade or profession is henceforth no more a matter of chance, but the

Developing School gives everybody the trade or profession that is his by nature, and the Manual Institute is fitted to make him a master of every part of his trade.

Only when what is now chance will be brought under the law of nature and reason, the principle of heredity will have its sway in Education. Children with the taint of dipsomania in their blood will not be put to trades which, by their environments, are sure to render this craving irresistible. Children with the taint of consumption in their blood will not be put to indoor trades, like tailoring, shoe-making, watch-making, and the like trades. Children with the homicidal taint will not be put to trades which naturally tend to brutality. And children with the taint of insanity and other nervous disorders will not be put to trades especially wearing upon the nerves. And thus crime, disease, and death will be lessened, the vigor of the human system will be preserved, and its working capacity prolonged, the productive years of men increased, and the public burdens will be lessened, and the general wealth swell.

How many a boy had for want of opportunities for industrial Education to accept the first chance of a trade offered to him, and being misplaced, had his genius smothered, and could do but poorly his work through life. Place a man where he belongs, and drudgery will give way to art, beauty, and invention. Why do men shun work, and run mad with speculation ending in bankruptcy? Because work is no pleasure. And why not? Because men can feel but miserable in doing a kind of work God has not made them for. And this misery and unwillingness for work sharpens the conflict between labor and capital, while Ruggles' Developing School, or the American System, placing men where they belong, transforms mercenary labor into a natural function and pleasant exercise, as men like to do what they can do best. Neither will men hoard to relieve their children from the necessity of labor, when labor will be engaged in as the exercise of natural skill, and an opportunity for technical distinction in an art suited to the talents of the individual. Work will cease to be a slavish task, onerous and burdensome, and no amount of capital a man may become possessed of, will keep him from what is but the natural promptings of his own natural disposition, and the expression of his individuality, and therefore his most rational and enduring happiness.

The Developing School is the egg out of which will be born the future organization of society upon the basis of natural talent. It will put the child where it belongs in the starting of life, and like a plant in a congenial soil, every man will prosper.

God's will, the elements of nature and of society, or the environments and man's freedom, will be made to conspire, and the natural result will be, that production will be doubled, and health of body and mind and, consequently, human happiness will be enhanced. Social problems, with which the world has hitherto grappled in vain, will find their solution in the Developing School originated by the Great American mechanician and inventor, S. P. Ruggles.

The financial crisis may put off, but can not put to rest the problem of technical Education. The old system of apprenticeship is dead, and we must replace it by something new, or we shall make tramps and paupers whose maintenance will cost us more than the mere expense of industrial training. It is certainly cheaper to teach men how they · may take care of themselves than to support them through life.

The Hon. P. Emory Aldrich shows the folly of the cry against the expense of Education. Have we not expended thousands of millions on railroads to which the Government has freely given hundreds of millions of acres? The Commonwealth of Massachusetts has expended nearly or quite $18,000,000 to build four or five miles of railroad under and through one of the mountains of her western border. There are four buildings in the

State of New York, which, before they will be completed, will cost in the aggregate $40,000,000. The same lavishness we meet in every State, and shall we say we have not the means to set the youth of the nation early to work that we may enhance the productiveness of the labor and capital of the land?

What folly, says the same gentleman, to expend millions from the public treasury upon the military and naval schools, wherein a limited number of young men may be instructed in the arts of war, and yet deny to other technical schools, wherein the arts of peaceful industry are taught, all State aid or Government support. Multiply the schools of peaceful industry, fill the land with their light and influence, and you will dispense, to a great extent, with the necessity of military schools and the arts of war.

As we have already remarked, the technical training of 400,000 youths in the United States would hardly add 10 per cent. to the present cost of public Education, while half the product of their labor would soon add daily to the public wealth, at the lowest calculation, $200,000, covering the entire expense of the public school system of the nation. Still, according to another view, the additional cost would be nothing at all, as ten thousand words, or three hours' teaching, being as much as children can daily bear without confusion of mind and injury to their physical system; the present number of teachers and school-buildings will suffice for double the number of pupils, and, hence, school instruction and industrial training combined need not cost more, and may even cost less, than our useless cramming system.

But even if the State is not ready for the universal introduction of industrial Education, the Developing School can be made to do its work with little extra expense, as one or two suffice for a city, the industrial museums of which contain sufficient machines, tools, and instruments, only poorly arranged, and hardly serving a reasonable end, all of which could be arranged in the manner proposed by S. P. Ruggles, so as to assist young men in finding out their peculiar bent and talent, that they may choose correctly their trade, business, or profession, and afford besides constant instruction through the suggestive arrangement of the various parts of the Developing School.

Universal industrial Education changes the whole order of civilization; it is the beginning of a new page in human history. It is a revelation. It sets up work as the equal of thought. It is the recognition of humanity at large, of its wants, its work, and its worth. It will infuse the spirit of humanity into all legislation touching the masses. The co-

ordination of the workshop and the school-house is
the emancipation of labor from present prejudices.

Instead of educating, drawing out, and developing men, and putting them in the way of developing themselves through life, by bringing them in
contact with the means and conditions adapted to
their natural disposition and talent, we smother
and impede their natural growth by putting them
to uncongenial work that constitutes their misery,
and of which they try to rid themselves by wealth
acquired without scrupling at means.

To force work upon men is communistic non-
sense, and will never succeed. Put men to their
proper work and nothing will keep them from it.
Besides, we do best the work we are adapted to,
while the work that is forced upon us is, as a rule,
worthless. When means, climate, soil, talent, health,
heredity, and natural bent, in short, when God, man,
and nature will co-operate in every stroke of work
that is done, and doing will become a pleasure, there
will be such an abundance of the utilities of life that
wealth will no more be an object of greed than air
or water are to-day, and our pleasure will be in doing and not in having, and men will vie with each
other in serving the world, as their work will be
their happiness.

Not a new, arbitrary, and despotic organization
of labor or society, but a new organization of Edu-

cation upon the basis of life, labor, and the natural disposition or talent of man, is wanted, and men put to their own proper work in life may be left free, as their own desire for happiness will be a guarantee for universal order and justice.

Right-living is an art, and can no more be taught by words than any other art. We must go at it at once, and begin with its practice. Education to-day is all theory, but practice must precede theory, and the use of the brush is more apt to make a painter than Newton's theory of colors. Practice is more important than theory, as it will always lead to perfection in executing or art, while theory, in many things, may never rise to the dignity of science, and still less to the truth and reality of life.

THE AMERICAN SOCIAL SCIENCE ASSOCIATION.

Mr. Wendell Phillips, on the Committee on Industrial Education, appointed by the American Association on Social Science, says: "Seven out of ten who come out of our public schools will be obliged to make their living by the work of their hands. Hundreds leave school at fifteen years of age wholly unable to do anything for which any man would be willing or could afford to give them a dollar. The boy who is going to college has two or three more years of Education given him to fit him for his future. Why should not the city extend to the children who prefer some mechanical trade equal favors, parallel advantages, the same amount of training for their future that the college boy has for his? The discrimination against those who prefer to work with their hands is very unjust. Our present school system does a boy rather a harm than a good, as it rather unfits him for the life of labor, which is to be his life."

Rev. Edward E. Hale says: "After intemperance untrained labor is the worst evil, and all our average boys are fit for on leaving the common schools, is to be news-boys, or cash-boys in the great retail shops, or to peddle lozenges."

The Hon. Elizur Wright says: " Our school system is set up wrong end foremost, because children should be taught the use of tools before they learn to read, write, and speak, which is the bottom idea of Froebel's Kindergarten, which is to educate children through work. Ruggles' Developing School gives a boy the mastery of many a tool, and the School Shop teaches him how to do almost everything connected with his trade, whilst, under the old system, he was put to the doing of one thing— the thing most profitable for the boss—over and over forever and forever."

Foremost among the men who have given their best thoughts to the elaboration and popularization of the American system originated by S. P. Ruggles, John Newell, Esq., of Boston, deserves most honorable mention. He made plain in his remarks before the American Association of Social Science, that President Runkle lays mostly stress upon the discipline his system gives, "not caring if the student never touches a tool after he leaves the school;" and naturally so, as the School of Technology was a place for the training of men of science to whom science and not a trade is the end. Mr. Ruggles' system is calculated for youth who wish to ascertain what trade they are most fit for, and want to learn it most perfectly and in the shortest time. The Developing School and Work-shop are intended to replace the old apprentice system, which is irrevocably gone, and will be a vast improvement upon it, as it will instruct a youth just as fast as his talent and progress will allow, and teach him every part of his trade, which, under the present division of labor, is more than he can learn in any single shop.

Mrs. Elizabeth Thompson says : "The best charity is to teach the people how to work most productively, and to elevate labor by placing it on a level with science and making it a part of Education."

THE PRESS ON INDUSTRIAL EDUCATION.

The Boston *Commercial Bulletin* says : "Our existing system does not supply the youths of our cities with the Education which will prepare them to earn a living. Nine-tenths of the failures in life come from the rarity of a man finding his calling. The Developing School provides for this difficulty, and Mr. Ruggles' long experience entitles his opinion as to the necessary change in our educational system to a serious consideration."

The Boston *Post* says : " The impression is almost universal that we must supplement our public school system by industrial training. Our boys to-day on leaving the common school are left for years a burden to their parents, listless seekers for vacant places in stores, or, at the worst, an idle class from which vice and crime are wont to recruit their strength through the always ready agency of temptation."

The Boston *Saturday Evening Express* says : " We have now in the State 300,000 persons who have no practical knowledge in any trade, art, calling, or profession by which to obtain a living, only being useful as a reserve from which a draft can be made for tramps, political bummers, thieves, jail-birds, candidates for all our penal institutions. Nine-tenths of all our criminals arraigned and corrected, are persons who have no technical Education. Let the Developing School of S. P. Ruggles give our boys the chance to select their trade, and the school shop teach them thoroughly in the shortest time to master it, and all will be well."

The Philadelphia *Times* says : " What a terrible satire upon our boasted free school system, nine-tenths of the young criminals sent to the peniten-tiary have enjoyed its advantages, but three-fourths of them have never learned to do an honest stroke of work. Surely there must be something very wrong about a system which thus recruits the great army of idlers and criminals, and it is not wonderful that many thoughtful men believe, though they scarcely dare to speak it aloud, that our public schools are an evil rather than a good."

The Philadelphia *Evening Telegraph* says : " It is evident that to these young men, Education—that is, common and classical Education—is a curse rather than a blessing. Society has developed their mental powers to a point, that they are ' above ' devoting themselves to occupations that they would be perfectly willing to follow were they uneducated ; . . . . society, so far as it does any-thing, actually throws impediments in their way by educating them. Something must be done in the direction of giving technical instruction in all of the common schools, or they will, year after year, grow to be, instead of blessings, curses to us."

PUBLIC ACTION DEMANDED.

The late Report of the Commissioner of Education informs us that the movement to secure industrial art training has made some progress in Philadelphia, and the day is not far distant when there will be engrafted upon the common school system a practical mode of technical study. Public art Education has now become such a necessity that if teachers do not lead in this matter, the manufacturers will soon take the initiation and insist upon drawing being taught in all schools.

The State Report of Rhode Island says: "The subject of class instruction in labor in the various trades and branches of applied arts, is in its infancy. What is feasible and what is not, is a question to be settled only by trial."

At a meeting of the School Commissioners at Utica, N. Y., Feb. 19, 1878, the following resolution was passed:

"*Resolved*, That we recommend study and experiment in the direction of physical labor to the end of devising for our schools some practical system of industrial art which shall stimulate mental action, and give skill in the arts which underlie the trades."

Governor Hartranft, in his message to the Legislature of Pennsylvania, says: "A thorough system of industrial training must embrace the children, the workingmen, and the people. . . . . In addition to the theory, it may be necessary for the State to afford practical training in the mechanical arts. It is not probable that the old system of apprenticeship, which has for various practical reasons fallen into disuse, can ever be generally restored. . . . . Believing that, under these circumstances, no remedy can be found, except through the direct agency of the State, I renew my recommendation contained in the message of 1875, for the establishment of workshops in connection with industrial schools, and beg leave to refer you to the current report of the Superintendent of Public Instruction for the proofs he has collected of the feasibility and advantages of the plan."

"THE SENATE OF THE UNITED STATES.

" *April* 9, 1878.

' Mr. Burnside asked and, by unanimous consent, obtained leave to bring in the following bill, which was read twice and referred to the Committee on Education and Labor :

" *Be it enacted by the Senate and House of Representatives of the United States of America in Congress assembled*, That the school-officers of the District of Columbia shall introduce and sustain industrial expositions of the pupils' handiwork in connection with each public school in their jurisdiction.

" SEC. 2. That these expositions shall consist of all kinds of useful articles made or invented by the pupils, including specimens of wood-work, iron-work, cooking, sewing, knitting, crocheting, and mending; also, farm, orchard, and garden products that are the result of their own industry.

"SEC. 3. That ornamental work be admitted when accompanied by something useful.

"SEC. 4. That the pupils be permitted and encouraged to explain the purpose of each article and the process of its culture or manufacture.

"SEC. 5. That these expositions shall occur as often as once a month during the school-year."

Peter Cooper, the venerable founder of a school of art and industry, South as well as North, says in his open letter addressed to President Hayes: "Let us promote and instruct industry, all over the land, by founding, under national, State, and municipal encouragement, industrial schools of every kind that can advance skill in labor. The rich need the literary and professional school and colleges, and they should have them; but the poor need the industrial school of art and science; and it should be made the duty of the local governments to provide a practical Education for the mass of the people, as the best method of 'guaranteeing to every State a republican form of government.'"

We may study the history of industrial Education at home or abroad; we may listen to the discourse of the teachers of the land in council; the science and ability of the American Social Science Association; the experiments of institutions, and of practical mechanicians and philanthropists; the increasing poverty of the masses; the decay of public health; the decline of private and public virtue and simplicity; the warnings of the truest men and women in the nation, as well as public opinion expressed in our daily journals—all alike proclaim the necessity of educating together the head and hand, and that this is the great need of the nation.

It will not do to say children have no time to study and work at a trade, for the success of the half-time system is too well established, and the Hon. Mr. Newell is right in maintaining that the time given to the tricks of spelling, mental arithmetic, grammar, and geography could be applied to much better purposes. And as to the cost of industrial Education, is it not a noble investment by an annual outlay of fifteen dollars during two years, at most, on each young mechanic, to save him three precious years, enhance his skill and productiveness for life, spread industry, raise labor in intelligence and position, and strike a telling blow at pauperism, drunkenness, vice, crime, disease, insanity, and the whole sickening train of hostile causes which are only too fast undermining the life of this young nation? The quarter of a million it may cost to turn out annually ten thousand skillful mechanics would soon be saved on the police, courts, prisons, and asylums of all sorts, while their industry, at the rate of a dollar a day for each, would produce for the country ten thousand dollars every day. Is this not motive enough to stir us to action? In the name of God and humanity, and our own interests, and the country's future, let us act.

THE NEW ERA AND THE DIVINE LAW OF LABOR.

We are entering upon an epoch as distinct as any of those which mark the past; it comes in a workshop, and work it will until it transforms all; it comes to the masses and to the young, and as it transcends in humbleness, it will transcend in glory.

Slavery, with all its untold horrors, next brigandage, and lastly wholesale hanging, are stages of civilization belonging to the past; to-day a perfidious charity is killing the poor in ten thousand bastiles, covering the land the world over. America, with the practical wisdom and humanity peculiar to it, is ushering in a new era, by a revolution as thorough as it is quiet, by the union of the school and the workshop, which shall supersede poorhouses, jails, mad-houses, and the like institutions characteristic of the past civilization. Only by educating the children of the Republic through

work and to work in the Manual Institutes of the
nation can we hope to establish the reign of the
Divine law of labor.

PAUPERISM EATING UP THE NATIONS.

There is no other way to prevent us from ending in a festering mass of pauperism, crime, disease,
and insanity, but setting all sensibly, kindly, and
practically to work in childhood. To house prop-
. erly to-day our various pauper-classes and defect-
ives, and provide accommodations—which we will
have to do—for the tramps and vagrants in the
United States, would, upon close calculation, require an outlay of $1,000,000,000 on buildings, with
$50,000,000 for recurring annual expenses. How
much cheaper would the industrial Education of the
people be, and how much more would we have to
show for our money. Are we not sufficiently tax-
ridden to feel the force of this argument? Or are
we to pass against pauperism laws of repression
originated in ignorance, selfishness, and pride, at-
tempting substantially to restore the expiring
system of slavery? Everywhere in Europe, almost
all severities, says a writer of unquestioned authority, have been inflicted upon the poor, except
scalping. There is a revolting monotony, we read in
the blue books of England of to-day, in the earlier
history of this policy of repression in all civilized

countries. Without referring to the barbarous
legislation of earlier reigns, we read at the times of
Queen Elizabeth, "all parts of the realm of England and Wales are at present exceedingly
pestered with rogues, vagabonds, and sturdy beggars, by means whereof daily happeneth in the
same realm horrible murders, thefts, and other
great outrages. . . . . It is enacted that these
rogues, and vagabonds, and sturdy beggars are, for
the first offense, to be grievously whipped, and
burned to the gristle of the right ear with a hot
iron of the compass of an inch about; for the
second, they are to be branded felons; for the
third, to suffer death as felons, without benefit of
clergy." In every county of England 300 to 400
vagrants lived by theft and rapine. Threescore
and twelve thousand great and petty thieves and
rogues were hanged in the reign of Henry VIII.
And in the beginning of the reign of Elizabeth
there was not a year wherein 300 to 400 vagabonds
were not eaten up, in one or another county, by
the gallows.

Spain lashed, banished, cropped the ears, enslaved, and put to death mendicants who solicited
alms. France flogged them, put them in the pil-
lory, burned them with a hot iron on the forehead,
and banished them, or made of them galley slaves.
Even under the magnificent Louis XIV. female

beggars were banished, and male beggars flogged, and next time consigned to the horrors of the galleys. Refined Dresden flogged and imprisoned beggars as late as 1790. Hamburg and Switzerland had similar legislation, and Copenhagen condemned men asking charity to solitary confinement in the penitentiary. Such are, by necessity, the means by which the poor, the natural fruit of the old civilization, were kept out of sight.

The number of the poor, says a thoughtful author, is underestimated. It is put in England and Wales at 1,300,000, because as many receive charity on a certain day ; but when we count those who received public charity before or after that day, during that year, we shall find the number of the poor to be fully three times as large, taking out of the public treasury $100,000,000 per annum, a figure which is doubled by what flows from private sources. And even this sum, enormous as it is, it is more than doubled by the cost of crime and police, waste, destruction, pilfering, incendiarism, and cost of intoxicating liquors ; and this may give us a glimpse of the cost of pauperism which is due to the want of industrial Education.

Scotland, with a population of 3,100,000, gives parochial assistance to 350,000 persons ; and London, with a population of 3¼ millions, has 300,000 people receiving parochial relief.

Let us look at the results the want of a universal system of industrial Education has produced in France, and the load of pauperism that beautiful country and great nation is staggering under. In 1866 the following classes got public assistance :

Men appealing to the Bureau of Relief, .	1,303,081
Sick in hospitals, ...	336,130
Lunatics, ...	12,589
Women in childbed, ...	16,132
New-born infants, ...	13,581
Casuals, ...	27,155
Aged and incurables	52,781
Orphaned and abandoned children, . .	45,322
	1,806,771

But even this number has to be more than doubled, and Dean, in his "History of Civilization," states it, on official authority, as 4,000,000, as the number given by us includes but the part relieved.

France expended in 1861 108,441,828 francs upon its poor in 1,557 asylums and hospitals, and yet half the cities of France, and rather more, are unprovided for by public assistance, and according to the best French authorities, misery is hardly relieved, notwithstanding the large sum applied for its alleviation, and had 337,838 vagrant beggars. Paris expended in 1869, 23,806,027 francs for in- and out-door relief to 317,742 persons out of a population of 1,799,880. Its charity department employed 4,349 officials, and 1,989 physicians and surgeons;

100,000 patients were in its hospitals, and 7,000 insane in its asylums, with a yearly increase of 2,500 cases. What an argument, then, France offers against the old Education.

The kingdom of Prussia has over 486,179 paupers, and gives public relief to 4.89 per cent. of its entire population. In 60 of its largest towns, 18.12 per cent. of the population are recipients of public charity ; in 238 towns next in rank, 7.38 per cent. ; and in 672 of the smallest towns 4.91 per cent. are relieved.

Saxony, with 2,337,192 population, has 2,540 poor-houses, and relieves 41,547 poor. Bavaria, with 4,370,977 population, relieves 79,863 poor, and swarms with tramps and beggars as hardly any other country does. Wurtemberg, with a population of 1,400,000, has 1,842 poor-houses, and 16,734 recipients of public charity.

Austria, exclusive of Hungary, relieves 171,768 poor. It has 6,678 poor-houses. It has, besides, in its hospitals for the poor, 212,517 patients, takes care of 68,053 foundlings, 18,824 lying-in mothers, 4,749 insane, etc., etc.

Italy, exclusive of Rome and other districts, counts, in a population of 18,599,029, 1,115,126 poor, upon whom large sums are expended. It has 12,976 hospitals and asylums, in which 861,921,624 francs are invested, and the current expenses of which are 14,945,021 francs.

Let the reader once for all notice the poverty not relieved is not counted in the statistics of public records.

Belgium had in 1868 550,000 poor. Of its 908,-000 families 446,000 are public paupers. It spends on its poor $10,673,792, which, of course, scarcely at all relieves the vast pauperism which would be wiped out if industrial Education was universal and not merely a shred.

Sweden, with a population of 4,114,141, had in 1865 148,000 poor, at a cost of $1,100,000. Denmark had 1,784,741 population, and 74,324 poor relieved. Norway, with 1,720,500 population, had 180,-000 poor relieved. Germany has 900,000 paupers. But these figures are all deceptive; they merely represent the crushed poor who are trodden under-foot as the abject recipients of public charity, while the poor who are nobly struggling against hard fate are fully four or five times as numerous.

And does the present Education yield different results in our country? The State of New York gave from 1868 to 1874 relief to 1,256,955 individuals, which gives an average of 179,565 who received alms annually. In 1872 147,427 applications were made for lodgings at the various police stations of the city of New York. Add to this the tramps the State gave 200,000 lodgings in the same year.

The following table, taken from the official sta-

tistics of the Board of State Charities of Massachusetts, shows the condition the people are drifting to in the Eastern States:

	Wholly and par-tially supported.	*Lodgings giv-en at Boston police stati'ns.*	*Acts of relief to tramps ex-clusive of Bos-ton.*	*Total of State expense.*
1872....	29,066	35,667	33,230	$906,819
1873....	32,738	42,384	45,653	980,404
1874....	41,130	57,014	99,083	1,009,688
1875....	63,237	64,680	137,308	1,172,416
1876....	73,737	60,803	148,936	1,321,011
1877....	82,997	64,419	190,704	1,450,624

Boston has already registered 16,211 families, or
56,738 individuals whose condition is such that
one-half of them are reduced every year to the necessity of applying for public relief, and from observation and comparison we may say that before
the count is completed it will embrace 20,000 families, or 70,000 individuals. This is the best test of
the condition of the masses, to whom our means of
improvement must be adapted, for the tramp and
out-and-out pauper are but the last stage of the
same disease, and beyond the reach of any remedy.

How absurd to judge the condition of the people
by the comparatively few cripples and imbeciles in-
side our pauper institutions; or to take measures
that meet the case of those who take outside public

relief. An effectual prevention of public distress must take notice of, and be adapted to, the great masses which are ever hovering between want and a competency.

As the standard of living, general benevolence, and the disposition and constitution of state and government differ in various countries, the call for public relief will differ, and the statistics of pauperism do not tell the exact story of the condition of the people as they are educated to-day. We must take into consideration the cost of living in our cities, and make an exact study of the average incomes of the masses, and we will be amazed at their trials. We have already noticed the low incomes of the masses in other countries. In Massachusetts the average income in the trades is $482.72 ; the average rent paid by a family is $109.07, and the cost of living is $488.96. Instead of an indispensable surplus for insurance against sickness, old age, death, and the thousand mishaps of life, we have here a deficit growing inevitably, as the years roll on, into pauperism.

How closely must the people border on pauperism, when statistics show us that the number of marriages, of births, of deaths, and of crimes, positively depend upon a few cents more or less in the price of a bushel of wheat or potatoes, or upon the reduction of a few cents in the daily wages of the

people, upon a few weeks' stagnation of commerce,
or upon a few degrees of difference in the temperature of the atmosphere, and the need of a little
more or less fuel. Is not all this evidence that
with general intelligence the school must develop
in the people a higher and more remunerative skill,
and the faculty and the knowledge and the habit
of a wiser economy than they practice to-day? Let
not the man of God say all that is needed is religious training. For as God worketh hitherto, only
he that works too, has God on his side, and the
right use of our powers and means is the fulfillment
of the will of God.

It is often said, that what the schools call ignorance, threatens the perpetuity of our government.
We maintain, general misery threatens it far more,
as it includes every other vice or disorder. A republic with the extremes of wealth and poverty is
a short-lived thing. But there is no reason why a
nation educated to work and to intelligent exertion should perish, as all virtues flow from such an
Education, which is, beside, most conservative in
its tendencies.

The practical teachers of the early and happy days
of Greece and Rome built up the State, the later
grammarians and sophists ruined it, and we are
foolish enough to begin with what they ended, the
spirit of negation that nibbles away every shred of

morals, patriotism, or esteem for anything, until nothing is left for the nation to stand upon.

With scientific exactness we have studied and found everywhere the symptoms of a spreading deterioration of the race. We have studied the various causes of this deterioration, and found them all centered in pauperism, the parent of all possible unhygienic conditions of our physical as well as mental nature ; and, finally, we have seen the fearful compass of pauperism under the old aimless Education, which must be overthrown by one of work and immediate useful results, which alone is sure to prevent pauperism, the source of the maladive deviation from the normal condition and from the very type of the race, among the imbruted stratas of society, whose fall, loss, and total degradation is the sin of the world, and must be wiped out by work, work, and again work, this incessant praying of the whole frame of man, and parent of every grace and blessing to each and to all.

LABOR AND THE MODERN STATE.

Life and nature are positive, and so are workers and observers. Books give us the shadows of things ; they are discursive, mostly negations, rendering us hypercritical and revolutionary. Words can not save the people ; give them bread, clothe them, house them, or make them honest.

Labor, wealth, hygiene, and morality are inseparable. Labor, therefore, is the foundation of the
modern State, and must be made the main object
of public Education. Drawing, mechanics, natural
history, technology, and, finally, the workshop, are
paramount in educating the people.

Much is said about mental training. But the observation and study of the natural history of the place ;
the study of the pursuits of the locality ; its history, character, and institutions, and the observation of the life of the simplest child, are all unequaled in their power of training us for life by
any text-book or set of school lessons.

Industrial work being the foundation of the
modern State, to industrial work the children of the
Republic must be reared in the schools of the nation. This was the secret of the success of the
Greeks, whose educational motto was, the child is
father to the man, and in what the citizen is to
excel he must as a boy be exercised, and, hence, the
law of Solon made the maritime Greeks as well
swim as read at the age of five.

The lack of adaptation of our schools to the wants
of the masses would be without an excuse, were it not
that they are without examples in the past. The
upper ten thousand among the Greeks and Romans
were taken care of by a half a million of slaves, and
looked to the school but for words. B t then

their real business was war, and military exercises formed the main part of their Education. Under feudalism the people did not go to school, neither had they to take care of themselves, as they were taken care of by the lords, of whom they took care. Next came the régime of the small masters, when every hearth was an industrial school. And, until but shortly, slight commercial attainments were a sufficient capital for self-support, and that the school afforded. With the accumulated capital and great industries of to-day, the very existence of the masses is threatened, and Education must become industrial, and save the people from the bitter alternative of starving, stealing, or begging.

But though the greatest and most illustrious men the world has seen, among whom St. Paul is not least, have lived by their trade, European princes are taught trades, and health of body and of soul and of the State, as well as of the individual, demands an Education through work and to work, there is an insuperable objection to it: it conflicts with the inalienable right of every born American, which is, to be brought up for political loafing. We answer, an honest man is the glory of his Maker, to which official honors can add little, but from which they often detract. Political ambition is the bane of the Republic. Work makes the man. Work means duty, and duty is the lesson we need, and Education should inculcate. Endless talk of rights has puffed us up until the bare acknowledgment of a power in the family, in the State, or even in Heaven, is considered an offense to our individual sovereignty ; and this is the feeling of the times and the spirit of the young.

We are told it is the commercial profits that allure away from useful labor. Well, that is just why the children should all be brought up in the common school for work, which, though it relieves them of the temptation of looking after the emoluments, does not unfit them for the performance of the duties of any station, if they have the talent and there is a call for it.

CHANNING ON MANUAL LABOR.

" Manual labor," says Channing, "is a school in which men are placed to get energy of purpose and character, ... a vastly more important endowment than all the teaching of all other schools. Alas, for the man who has not learned to work!" " The universe in which we live was plainly meant by God to stir up thought. Every object, even the simplest in nature and society, every event of life, is made up of various elements, subtly bound together, so that to understand anything we must reduce it to its parts and principles, and examine their relations to one another. . . . . The greatest men have not been book men. Washington, it has often been observed, was no great reader. The learning commonly gathered from books is of less worth than the truth we gain from observation or reflection. Indeed, most of the knowledge from reading is very much a vain show. . . . . What a library is human life. . . . . Every human being is a volume worthy to be studied." " Manual labor . . . fosters a sounder judgment, a keener observation, a more creative imagination, and purer taste than any other vocation. . . . . Not a few of the wisest, grandest spirits have toiled at the work-bench and the plough. A boy might be made, in an institution, a thorough farmer, both in theory and practice, and might, at the same time, learn a trade, and multiply his chances of a comfortable existence."

Almost fifty years ago these words were greeted as an inspiration by men of genius, who made public misery in Europe a study. And shall not we profit by the teachings of our great apostle of the sons of toil ?

THE DREAM OF PHILOSOPHERS.

Huxley pronounces "as the sum and crown of what is to be done for technical Education, the provision of a machinery for winnowing out the capacities and giving them scope. Whatever that might cost, depend upon it the investment would be a good one. I weigh my words when I say that if the nation could purchase a potential Watt, or Davy, or Faraday, at a cost of a hundred thousand pounds down, he would be dirt cheap at the money."

"A large allowance to each man," says Emerson, "to choose his work according to his faculty—to live by his better hand—fills the State with useful and happy laborers."

"God," says Ruskin, "has made us for happiness as well as for work, only we must find, if unhappily our parents and masters have not done it for us, what we are fit for."

What has been but a dream with philosophers has become a reality under the hands of the inspired mechanician and practical and patient thinker, S. P. Ruggles. As Massachusetts has given the country what was in its day the best common school and the first Normal College, so let us hope it will give us to-day the first Developing School and Manual Institute.

THE UNITED STATES LOOKING TO MASSACHUSETTS.

What may we not expect, for the ushering in of the great new era of practical Education in which all the nations will ultimately be blessed, from the noble men and women of Massachusetts, who lead in every work that elevates the masses and builds up the State.

We hope the great women of the country will come forward, as Mrs. Elizabeth Thompson has al ready done, and take pride and pleasure in redeeming mankind by the establishment of a practical training in the place of the old powerless method.

The United States look to-day to Massachusetts, and Massachusetts looks to Boston for the ushering in of a general system of manual Education which will foster private and public virtue and a moderation adding a thousand happy years to the life of the nation. Can Boston, can Massachusetts, falter and give up the lead in such a cause? Judging from the past, we believe it will not.

But our aspiration for Massachusetts, which has made the cause of Education her own, Boston is fast turning into prophecy by the Joint Committee on Public Instruction of the City, consisting of Aldermen Hayden, Slade, and Guild, and Councilmen Pope, Coe, and Wheeler, taking under advice the Developing School, upon the petition of Edward Everett Hale, Wendell Phillips, Thomas C. Amory, S. P. Ruggles, and John Newell.

The remarks of the petitioners were full of force, point, and suggestion, and like the names that graced the occasion, deserve to be made historic.

Thomas C. Amory, Esq., supported the petition, by reminding the Committee that the building and appropriation asked for, have been favorably reported upon by a previous committee. It implies no loss to the treasury. It leads to a diminishing of pauperism and crime, and the outlay is insignificant in comparison with the gain. There is no way to teach the young the useful arts. Apprenticeship has died out, and the workshops recognized in England and Germany as the appropriate substitute, have not yet taken its place. We must educate labor for the mechanic and useful arts, and train skill for its wage, as we do science for its salary. . . . . Our plan matured embraces a council board composed of representatives of the City Council School Board, mechanics, technological, charitable and industrial, and a few other men particularly interested in the subject, workshops, etc. . . . . If diplomas or certificates of proficiency were bestowed on all entitled to be entrusted with work, it might help them, and help skilled labor. . . . . The council and several guilds would carefully scan the progress of invention, dearth, and abundancy of the markets, and the fluctuation of wages, and exert an influence to prevent over-stocking; to build up new industries, to qualify men losing a trade, by substitution of mechanical contrivance, for another; schools for mariners and farm-work would be added. The large bequests would supply every want, and donations are already forthcoming, etc. There are few more precious commodities for a community to produce than men and 'women healthy, strong, and accomplished, to earn their own livelihood, support their dependents, and hive up wealth for the State.

The Rev. Edward Everett Hale said that pauperism was not a chronic necessity in this country, and could be prevented. . . . . The begging class was divided into only two parts—people who never knew anything, and people whose heads have been cultivated at the expense of their hands. If the city would throw the prestige of the system of public Education around the business of making skilled mechanics, it would be found that the number of these paupers would soon be decreased. Good mechanics were always in demand, and he doubted if any really good workmen had found it necessary to ask for relief.

Mr. S. P. Ruggles said it was not to the advantage of manufacturers now to take apprentices, and the great problem was, what are we to do with the army of youths now graduating from the public schools? Are they to become tramps, or what? Mr. Ruggles showed the mistake of supposing that machinery makes lack of work, when, in fact, it is giving more work to artisans, and first-class workmen are more than ever in demand.

The Rev. C. A. Bartol made an earnest plea for the education of the mechanical functions of the brain suffering paralysis from lack of exercise, and interfering with the soundness of the rest by the law of sympathy. The training of the faculties through the hands was especially useful in preventing pauperism. Poverty resulted from the lack of employment for the faculties. The present system of Education was defective in many particulars. Instead of taking recreation in some productive employment, like gardening, students were given gymnasiums.

John Newell, Esq., showed the futility of sending to the great West men who have not learned to do anything worth doing.

Mr. Cole, of the Committee, said in corroboration of the dearth of skilled labor even in the New England States, that of the forty foremen in the mills with which he was connected, not more than five were native born.

Wendell Phillips said it was the duty of the State to see to it that *character, knowledge*, and *skill* were taught to the youth. Children were taken from parents to educate, and how were they returned? They were sent back without any knowledge which would yield them an income of ten cents. Our present system takes the backbone out of youth, and will never make men of the force of a Butler, Theodore Parker, Wade, and others. It is a wonder the American people did not deteriorate through our defective system of Education. The Education of half a century ago was combined with labor, and was superior to the Education of to-day.

Sheriff John M. Clark thought it more necessary to give the general youth of Boston a practical Education than a classical one, and he believed the city would derive benefit from it. It would be vastly better to dispense with a great deal of what is now taught in the public schools, and put in place of it handicraft, the basis of a true and honest life.

Mr. S. F. Gates and Mr. I. M. Blood spoke each of the advantages of universal Industrial Education, and the Committee took under consideration the granting of the appropriation and the building asked for, as the first step toward introducing a system of manual Education, that shall save the children of the Commonwealth from the bitter necessity of starving, begging, or stealing.

These episodes in the new time coming are breaking in upon the logical order of our argument, still we invite them, and may Massachusetts grant to its noblest sons what they ask for her children, and again we shall sin with a gladsome heart by interrupting words by acts. It is not literary work, but work, work for all, we crave, that God's kingdom may come, and never mind our literary sin, but let the sin of the world, crime and pauperism and insanity, be stayed.

The saving of the masses through the reorganization of Education upon the basis of labor, is the watchword of the modern State which rests upon universal production.

There are men, and there are women, who see the star rising in the West, and who, with faith in God, the good and humanity, work with head, heart, and hand to help the coming in of the better day.

THE GREAT REFORMATION WE NEED.

Only work can bring us back to the hardiness of our fathers, and to their stern virtue and simplicity. We all love ingenuity and mechanical invention; the traditions of the harvest-field are fresh in our memories; we all love and honor work; are thoroughly democratic, and love the public school. We have, therefore, every reason to believe that of all countries this will be the first where labor introduced as a universal means of Education will effect the great reformation of which we all feel the need.

Of course we should encourage agriculture and emigration to the West. But our masses come from the surplus populations of the large cities of

Europe with native tendencies for aggregating in large communities. They are often unskilled men, not inclined to great exertion, and, therefore, poor, and, hence, the necessity of making our cities, in which they settle, schools for technical culture and Education, or they will become centers of pauperism, communism, and revolution, recruited from our present schools.

Great cities are the tendency of civilization, and we must turn them into blessings, and we can if we will. It is true we have immense agricultural facilities. Still, it is absurd that, therefore, we should be a purely agricultural people. A nation of fifty millions has men of every sort of talent, and requires opportunities for every sort of culture. Heterogeneity of pursuit is the law of our nature and of civilization. Industry and manufacture stimulate scientific research in every direction, and a thousand trades give scope to the development of every God-given talent which leads to wealth and happiness. Why should we not manufacture everything and be self-sufficient as a nation?

This tying down Education to generalities is against the law of differentiation, the law of God, nature, and society. Education, like everything else, must and will differentiate into specific lines, just as the trunk of a tree does into branches and bear fruit. The world can not always remain a nebulous mass, and it is time we get beyond the fog of general Education, and teach the people to do something specific.

We have a history, government, and a place, and opportunities peculiar to ourselves. So are our tastes and wants, which are best supplied by our own artisans, which keeps alive and develops our own individuality as a nation, which we think as rich and beautiful, to say the least, as any, and worth cultivating.

We have already developed, and will still more develop, new styles and tastes in every art and manufacture, and create new worlds of beauty in which our national spirit will reflect itself, and spread civilization by a thousand things of use and beauty, which shall cultivate the taste, mellow the heart, kindle emotion, call out reflection, and spread comfort, happiness, peace, and good-will among men.

The trifles of art, however, can not save us. Antiquity surpassed us in beauty of form and richness of color. It abounded in imaginings vast in sculpture, architecture, and poetry. It had masters in loftiness of mind and in action. One art it did not know, and all the others could not save it—the God-like love of our race, which discovers the divine nature of man under poverty's rags, and works without ceasing to save and elevate the masses, that none of the angels in disguise, we call brother or sister, may be lost. This art—of all arts the most enduring—must preserve the State, the nation, and the race.

We must rise from the idolatry of the senses to the worship of the heart, from the sensuous delight in the beautiful to the God-like exertion of active life, and rescue the masses from the billows which are rushing in upon them.

Antiquity, the Saracens, the Middle Ages, China, Japan, Persia, and other ages and nations may be our masters in many pretty things, but the art of saving men, women, and children, and making them stand forth in all the perfection of a divine humanity, more than Phidias ever could in marble, or Raphael upon the canvas, this art must become peculiarly our own, and humanity must be, hence, the source of all inspiration and of all action, from the humble artisan to the mighty man of State. The devotion of each to all, and of all to each, and nothing else, can save us from the cruel barbarism with which we are threatened by a materialism as glittering and as cold as ice.

Greece and the materialism in which its sensuous art-culture ended, crumbled away before the moral power of Rome, the depraved empire of which waned before the spiritual dogma of the East. Neither will philosophy and art or political organization avail us, and our worm-eaten commercial

States are bound to go down in revolution and anarchy unless they are regenerated by the preserving efforts of a consummate humanity. A mass of high and low corruption does not form a national unit; there is neither life nor power in it. It can not live, neither ought it.

The questionable idealism of the knowledge and culture of the schools has neither the power nor earnestness to grapple with materialism, the very power of which we must press into the service of humanity, and that we only do when we increase, through industrial training, the productiveness and power for consumption of the masses, which must eventuate in their moral elevation.

Nothing will free us from the low materialism of a shallow empiricism which does not see the things above it and in the far future on the one side, and from the impractical idealism which does not discern the things near and the present on the other hand, of which Buckle complains as the present malady or weakness of the human mind, and bring the millennium of good sense and higher wisdom, but the union of thinking and doing, or letters and industry at school.

INDUSTRY AFFECTING THE CHARACTER.

Industry not only supplies our wants, it develops our understanding, it is the school of mankind, and there is hardly a trait or virtue in human nature but was matured in this school, and the character of men, and ages, and countries, and nations differs as their trades and vocations differ. The hunter, the herdsman, the sailor, the plowman, the tailor, the shoemaker, the mason, the carpenter, the machinist—who does not see how they vary from each other in character? And the technical Education that transforms them all is of a vast moral reach, and touches the very mould and character of whole classes of men who are the constituent parts of the nation.

Establish an industrial system of Education which shall single out for every talent its own proper work as the American system does, and intelligence will be added to strength, and taste to intelligence, and all trades will become arts, and every workman an artist. Beauty and harmony in the works of man will be followed by beauty and harmony in the character of man, and justice and goodness and truth will spread, and the country will be filled with peace and happiness.

THREE STAGES OF INDUSTRIAL EDUCATION.

Froebel, Runkle, and Ruggles indicate the different parts of a complete system of industrial Education. The first gives the child the mastery of the senses; the second, the mastery of the tools; and the third, the mastery of the right trade, which is the *consummation* of the whole. And this division, in fact, is applicable to the whole work of Education.

Stage first. Putting the child into the possession of his senses, æsthetic faculties, reason and moral nature by cultivating the physical powers, mechanical skill in the use of the hands, the sense of symmetry and harmony, a quick judgment of number, measure, and size, readiness of invention, and the social habits of polite life, in a natural, spontaneous, and methodical manner.

Stage second. Putting the boy or girl into the possession of the tools: which are, for the senses and their technical employment, the hammer, chisel, saw, file, etc.; for the æsthetic faculties, drawing, the theory of colors; for the reason, the theoretical studies or pure sciences; and finally, for the moral faculties, correct moral notions or ideas.

Stage third. Putting the youth into the possession of the concrete whole: which is, for the senses and their technical employment, a full and complete trade; for the æsthetic faculties and their practical application, architectural and industrial design and technical ornamentation; for the intellect, the applied sciences; and for the moral faculties, practical ethics, domestic and public economy, politics, etc.

And thus the work of the cultivator of men must be directed, first to the senses, next to the tools, and then to the concrete work of life, the most important and the end of all.

If the advocates of the Russian system mean that a child shall not go to school a year, a month, or a day without using a tool, but that neither shall he leave the school and the workshop until he is a complete workman and can *produce* something that will support him handsomely, this is all right ; but if the public workshop is to set children merely to hammer or file and know nothing in particular, this is sure not to make one tramp less.

A lad wants a trade by which he can make an honest living, and such as Ruggles proposes and practical men declare feasible. A boy's ability in the use of a half-dozen of tools does not alter the fact that manufacturers will not be troubled with teaching him the particulars of twenty different operations in the make-up of an article, which is cheapest produced by so many individuals, though for the State and the workmen it would be best if the latter were skilled mechanics and commanded the highest wages. A boy that can use a half a dozen of tools, but is ignorant of a special trade, is exposed to want and to the danger of having to accept for his calling whatever chances, be he fit for it or not.

Or must even stern industry, under the hands of our teachers, evaporate in *hollow generalities* in order to be considered *educational?* It is time we free ourselves from this shallow pedantry. Let the friends of industrial labor remember that the blows of the hammer are as windy as the blows of the tongue when the performance is no more marketable than words. Bread is the cry of the million, and how shall we rid ourselves of pauperism, crime, and crushing taxation?

But has not the teaching of trades great difficulties?

We answer, none which the American people can not overcome, when crime, pauperism, and insanity threaten to eat us up, and the saving of the multitude demands it.

We have industrial schools after a fashion, or say rather shoe-black brigades, technical institutions, and even excellent schools for particular trades, but they are not of a quality nor sufficiently universal to regenerate humanity, and save the masses, and with them the nation.

OUR EDUCATION WITHOUT A FOUNDATION.

We have schools for the diffusion of literary trifles to the neglect of the development of character and working capacity.

Wm. T. Harris, the Superintendent of the Public

Schools of St. Louis, eminent as a thinker and educator, says kindergarten are peculiarly adapted for
an industrial people.   And as ours is an industrial
age, kindergarten are the portals through which
we must pass to a new and better condition of men
and things.   Our present Education is a building
without a foundation.   We neglect to train system-
atically the original activities of children from their
third to their seventh year, and when the period for
forming creative habits has passed, we stuff them
for years with other men's brain labor, and thus we
induce the morbid greed that makes them cry
through life, "give, give!" though they no more
know how to apply what they get, than how to
originate it.   Kindergarten may add to the present
expense of Education, but they are cheap at any
cost, as they will more than double and treble the
creative capacity, the skill, and the talent, as well
as the love of work of the people.   Under the heat
and burden of the day, the innate longing for a better
day has grown into a restless passion, dangerous
to the very existence of society.   Better we plant
kindergarten and organize industrial schools, and
educate the young for work, than let them grow up
in a manner as to be good for nothing else than to
form Jacobin clubs and revolutionary brigades,
which will be the beginning of the end of our greatness and prosperity, and of the Republic itself. Let

the people see that something is done. We may make laws and constitutions on paper, but the kingdom of heaven is a growth; it calls the little children and prepares them for their future glorious citizenship.

We wonder at the grossness of men who mean to make a new society in a day; but are we, who bring up the rising generation, ever talk about Education and development, and have the child, a manifest growth under our hands, any wiser, when we crush the child under piles of books, instead of setting him to work, that he may grow and develop into what he is in future to do and to be?

We may make learned babblers and expert swindlers, but never men, such as the future is bound to have, and will have, under the new order of things—which God is ushering in, in spite of all our blundering—until we dismiss the old parrot style of teaching, and replace it by training through work to work. A cobbler's or tinsmith's useful improvements are more real and valuable than a confused mass of the dreams from Pythagoras down to Schoppenhauer.

We repeat it; the German system, or Froebel's Kindergarten, educating children through work and to work, the Russian system, brought forward by President Runkle of the Technical Institute of Boston, teaching practically the use of a

variety of tools, and the American system of Developing Schools and Manual Institutes, originated
by S. P. Ruggles, in which the proper trade is
chosen and quickly and perfectly taught, both
theoretically as well as practically, far from con-
flicting with each other, form the successive steps
of a complete industrial Education, beginning with
the child, continued with the boy or girl, and completed with the youth.

INDUSTRIAL EDUCATION AND OVER-PRODUCTION.

But the increase of opportunities for industrial
culture meets with a shrug from the general public, who believe that we suffer already to-day from
over-production. There never was a more dangerous mistake afloat. At the close of the Napo-
leonic wars, and some time afterward, a situation
similar to our own caused in England the same
delusion, which James Mill dispelled, by showing
that a great production and a great demand are inseparable, and to complain of the one is to complain of the other, as those who produce one thing
want to exchange it for something else. Of course
we may overstock the market with one thing, but
the abundance of every sort of manufacture can
never lead to want, no more than men who sit
down to a table can suffer on account of the over-
flowing abundance of the good things set before

them. Suffer from over-production! Strange, more than half of the community suffer from want of the bare necessities of life, and not one in ten is provided with the comforts of life, and we are told that we are over-producing. But are not half of our mechanics out of work? We repeat, yes; because the other half of the people can not or will not do anything that could be given in exchange for what the other half would like to do.

THE FUTURE.

With the curse came labor and the exit from Eden. The Developing School, harmonizing labor with man's inclination and talent, removes that curse, and throws open to us again the gates of Paradise. When work was hard and slavish, and therefore shunned and despised, only high profits, rents, and interest were sufficient motives for industrious application and accumulation, and they form a necessary link in the history of labor. But when labor and inclination shall be wedded to each other in the Developing School, production will become immense; rents, profits, and interest will decline; neither will they be wanted as motive powers for exertion; men will labor for pleasure, and not for gain or from necessity.

With shoemakers doing the work of machinists, and machinists doing the work of tailors, and tailors doing the work of painters, the world is moving on to-day just as square pegs would in round holes, and hence the endless troubles of labor and capital.

Men will not employ to-day their capital productively, as they can get a high bank dividend, and the men who employ their bank credit, are often ruined by the high interest they pay ; and this financial confusion keeps the State in a constant turmoil, and the masses who are to live by their hand, perish from want of industrial opportunities, for money on security as good as gold, and on demand, is an accommodation for capitalistic speculation, but not for the slow and solid industry of the country.   .

The Education of to-day schools the wits of men of opportunity, and fits them for the work of oppressing the masses, and thus impoverishes the country and initiates a war of classes, ending in anarchy and general ruin. The future Education must enhance the industrial capacity of the lowly millions, and thus lead to universal prosperity and peace.

Industry is fully as important as knowledge, and the opportunity for each should be given. Let the school cultivate our powers for creating and organizing, and the desire for doing and accomplishing will take the place of that for having and getting.

When the stimulus of hoarding will be replaced

by the pleasure of exercising our ingenuity and invention, and thrift and industry will be universal,
and all will be provident and reliable, and universal
credit will be a general good, money will be at
cost, and production will rise to a height never
dreamed of. We will become creative like God
and nature, every pulsation will leave behind it a
monument, and the riches of the world will turn the
wealth of to-day into poverty. It is a slander upon
the name and the wisdom of God, aye; upon common sense and humanity, to believe that pauperism,
insanity, and crime are the concomitants of a progressive civilization ; they are the pains of our
folly and ignorance, and warn us off the barren
ground our schools occupy to-day ; they are the
chastening rod by which Providence educates us
up to a higher level. Give the child, the boy and
the girl, and the youth, the training the German,
the Russian, and the American systems call for,
and pauperism, drunkenness, crime, idiocy, insanity, vagrancy, prostitution, and kindred pests will
cease to mar this country and nation. The Kingdom of God is not impossible. It does not call for
Newtons, but simply for sensible and honest men.
Educate the nation for work, for action, and for
industry, and wealth, and health, and beauty, and
goodness, and truth will cover the land as the waters
cover the sea.

A SUMMARY OF INDUSTRIAL EDUCATION.

After all the question is what must and can be done at once? The answer, to be satisfactory, must be brief and unimpeachable.

1. Drawing from the kindergarten and upward must occupy not two lessons, each thirty minutes a week, but four lessons, each three quarters of an hour, as:

> *a.* Drawing is an excellent means for æsthetic culture, the promotion of a purer taste and more artistic skill;
>
> *b.* Four lessons, of three quarters of an hour each, will, far from being play to children and trifling to parents, form an effectual means to inure the children to intelligent manual application;
>
> *c.* Drawing is the best and most universal aid of modern improved trades;
>
> *d.* The parents naturally will insist upon rendering the success of their children in drawing useful for life through the use of tools and knowledge of machinery, and this leads us to the next step.

2. The Russian system of learning the use of tools is but second in importance to drawing.

> *a.* The Russian system not teaching a specific trade, and being systematic in its methods

and elements is best adapted for the second stage of industrial training;

b. The Russian system familiarizing students with the various uses of tools enables them to turn their hands to almost any mechanical pursuit;

c. The handling of tools affords an opportunity for the physical exercise which should at this period accompany mental labor;

d. The pleasant task of acquiring general technical skill through the exercise of tools attaches youths to these companions of their happiest years.

3. Special industrial training must begin with manual art industries, as:

a. The great social desideratum is to afford occupation to labor displaced by machinery;

b. Art industries fall more in the line of pure art and science, and belong therefore more properly to the school which speeds their progress;

c. Art manual industries are appropriate for both sexes alike, and what woman greatly needs is an opportunity for earning, if necessary, her bread in her own home by art manual industry;

d. The art manual trades requiring hardly any machinery may be connected with our schools with very little expense to the State.

4. The erection of large shops and developing schools is the crowning of the industrial school system, as the kindergarten is the opening of it. But, though in the logical order of things mechanic shops come the last, they are not uncalled for, as :

  a. Boys ought to have an opportunity to learn the larger trades what they hardly can in our great shops, and the complete derangement of the apprentice system of to day;

  b. The well being and independence of the people require that they should completely know their trade, while in our factories they learn but a fraction of a fraction of a trade ;

  c. Practical men know the difficulty already existing of finding a man in a workshop who knows how to construct and fit together the various parts of a somewhat complicated piece of work or machinery. The interest of civilization requires, ·therefore, that we train men at school for this purpose, or like many Asiatic nations, we shall be great in small things and very small in great things. This scheme seems to us to take fully into consideration the nature of the school, the needs of the individual and society, as well as the practibility of the proposed measures.

Expensive and complicated developing schools and manual institutes may be a matter of the future, kindergarten training, design, the use of tools and manual art trades, or photography, engraving in wood and metal, carving, etc., can and ought to be at once introduced. Drawing, photographing, industrial ornamentation, the history of industry and its ethnographical description, commercial, and technological natural history, or the three kingdoms and their uses as raw material, natural philosophy, chemistry applied, colors and their effects, the philosophy of art, gardening, landscape, domestic and political economy, the art of health, Education, cookery, dressing, and house-furnishing, and the philosophy of living as a member of the family, municipality, State and general government, and the race are some of the branches we have to pursue with most practical method and intent under the regime of Race Education.

Every college ought to give to its students an opportunity for the practice in general mechanics or the use of tools, and have Ruggle's motorium, or collection of models of all possible motions, simple or complex, doing the inventor the same service the dictionary does to the literary student, by acquainting him with every possible contrivance for the production, transmission, or conversion, of every sort of motion, and saving him the trouble of re-inventing what has been, perhaps, invented long before him.

Every polytechnic school should give in its machine shops the practical application of the teachings of the lecture room, and train the student to do things as well as to know them.

Every town or section of the country ought to establish schools, especially, for those trades which are the sources of its wealth.

The order traced by us here is the natural evolution of industrial Education. These principles are as broad and as specific as any institution requires, the details of which must be a growth springing out of environments and developing with them.

Almost ready for issue, our work can bring but little of the very recent Report of the more than able Commissioner of Education, John Eaton, Esq., but even that is sufficient to corroborate our worst apprehensions. He places in the very front of his Report the significant reflection, " The experience of the mob violence we have passed through should suffice to bring us to the conviction that our safety is only in the most vigilant use of every instrumentality fitted to assure the training of each child in the land in virtue and intelligence, and in the pursuit of some useful and honorable vocation . . . . Indeed, it may be doubted whether we have sufficiently reflected upon the enormities possible in our communities if the systematic vagrancy of the ignorant, vicious and criminal classes should continue to increase. . . . . In reasoning upon the acts of violence which have occured among us during the great late riots, the educator may well ask what the consequences might have been, had these disturbances been preceded, as they were during the horrors of the French revolution of 1793, by a series of dry seasons and bad crops, and these poor crops themselves injured or destroyed."

The thoughtful Commissioner put wisely on record the words of the Hon. John Hitz: "Does the public school system really make any aggressive movement to drain the stagnant pool and malarial marshes of society? Is it not clearly its duty to do so?—to see to the proper training of those who in the future Republic are likely to constitute an important element of the majority. Or shall this rather be left to the spasmodic efforts of charity, and the effects of this neglect to prevent moral and mental malaria be corrected in reformatories and correctional institutions? . . . Until our system of public instruction shall have inaugurated effectual measures to drain these pestiferous moral and mental pools and marshes of society—thus killing the germs of moral and mental disease, and so removing the cause which mainly fills our houses of correction, crowds the dockets of our police courts, and furnishes candidates in increasing numbers for juvenile reformatories—it will not, in my opinion, have accomplished the full scope of its duty.

Another communication by Elisha Harris, M. D., is worth re-stating. "In the United States," says the writer, "we are proving that the common school system is deficient in regard to the special training of wayward, truant and vicious children— nominally registered as common school pupils, but usually neglected or disobedient, or both. . . . What are now termed industrial schools do not meet the especial want under consideration. . . . Neither do the orphan houses, charitable foundations, juvenile asylums and refuges in our country."

"I am not certain that we can devise a supplementary kind of public school to treat and train on farms, in gardens and in workshops and school chambers the residuary groups of youth that we now term truant, disorderly, wayward and perverse, but not arraigned as offenders. In the State of New York, however, we could, I believe, secure the maintenance of a farm and shop, or industrial school for every city and for every county of 50,000 inhabitants. We should do this to prevent crime and public burdens. . . . . An industrial training school should be a true kindergarten in open fields and spacious workrooms, and not the orphan and semi-imbecile, but unruly and troublesome truants, the mischievous and obviously vicious boys who become now our habitual contrivers and wanton perpetrators of offenses and crimes, should be eliminated from the masses of children, and by ready assent and various modes of legal commitment by parents and lawful guardians, be brought into these industrial homes and training schools."

Considering the squalid homes and miserable parents of half the children of large towns, considering the number of groggeries and annual arrests, say 84,514 in the city of New York, of whom 32,453 have families, with such a parentage, but —we will not bind heavy burdens and grievous to be borne, and lay them on men's shoulders, while we will not move them with one of our fingers— we confess, we dare not say, that we can pass through the irksome tasks of a toiling mother—the father being away from home—whose work is never done until death mercifully overtakes her, and be in a humor of addressing two or three troublesome little children in a tone that shall not wound their spiritual nature. We know of what we affirm. We are within bounds when we say not half the children of the poor can dispense with a careful moral training at school. Mr. Harris is correct in saying, "The public school records will show how vast is the number of truants and untutored among the registered school children."

14

The necessity of having public schools at all was once thought to be not very great. Also, was it thought impossible to make such a provision. With a work or duty the power to perform is given, all we want is faith and courage. It is not enough to contrive a few industrial schools in order to prevent 30,000 men in the United Stares from becoming "wanton perpetrators of offenses and crimes;" but our entire public school system must be regenerated upon the basis of moral and industrial training to save five millions of people from harrowing poverty, two millions from utter misery, one million from hovering between life and death, and a half a million from vagrancy, vice and drunkenness. As long as we do not raise to a higher plane the entire masses, crime will find such a congenial soil in the unhygienic conditions of the poverty stricken millions, that every attempt to check its growth will prove a delusion. If we wish to be spared the sight of open revolt against the laws of man and heaven, as there is no security for the individual or society with such fiendish elements among us, we must promote the well being of the millions— of all—this is the price we have to pay for security. There is one God and one humanity, and not one of us suffers but we suffer all.

Do we ask impossibilities, or propose vagaries? Certainly not; if we insist upon the moralization of the masses in proper infant schools. Belgium has to day 929, and probably more, organized and attended by 97,382 children; the Netherlands have 705, with an attendance of 73,018, Hungary has 200, with five seminaries for the training of teachers for kindergärten; Paris has 113 infant schools, and the like encouragements we meet everywhere.

We insist upon industrial training? Have we not sufficiently illustrated their practicability by their success. Prussia has 45 technical and industrial, 9 building, 31 navigation, 6 forestry, and 81 agricultural schools. Little Wurtemberg has over 50, and Bavaria over 150 industrial schools.

We insist upon school gardens and we have cited thousands and thousands of facts in support of that.

We advocate first and last art industrial training, and hundreds of schools of design emulate each other to day, in Europe, in order to advance the higher industries, and thirty of these institutions prove their great mission among us.

Faithful men will speak to the conscience of the nation until it shakes off its lethagy and breathes into Education the breath of the new industrial life, which will secure the well being of the masses, and make us a truly great people.

THE THREATENING DANGER.

The future of the nation is imperiled by the almost universal degeneracy of the masses, who are sacrificed to pelf. The nation is in danger. The hand of Death is upon it. The enemy is among us. He is in the city and all over the land. Who is not aroused? Who has any other care but how to rid the country of the common enemy of us all?

Pauperism, crime, insanity and a general degeneracy are eating up the masses, while extravagance, general corruption and dishonesty are rendering worthless the upper ten thousand. Let us save the nation from this greatest of foes—degeneracy. Let us live for our children. Let us live for one another, and instead of each warring against all, and all against each, let each be for all, and all for each, and all will be well. How precious is the saving of but one life, how much more so the saving of a whole nation! No, it cannot be; we are not so corrupt as to be indifferent about the nation and all the generations to come.

THE DUTY OF THE NATION.

Not wealth, but the health, strength, virtue, intelligence and character of the nation must be the future care of the republic. The noble sentiments of the nation may be repressed for a while, but will assert themselves again ; and then everybody will be brought up for the race and live for the race ; and his motto will be like Fénélon's : "*I prefer my family to myself, my country to my family, and humanity to my country.*" This spirit will prevail when the State shall foster the Education of the heart and hand as well as that of the head.

Education, like the circulation of the blood, is life and health, when it is directed to every point alike ; rushing to one point it brings death to all.

Neglect physical training, and the frail framework of humanity breaks down under its manifold burdens. Neglect industrial training, and the economical relations of man and the very foundations of civilized life are destroyed. Fail to exercise reason, and the light of the world is put out. Neglect man's moral training, and he becomes a monster. Train him exclusively for industry, and he becomes a machine. Train exclusively his moral faculties, and he is made a slave of habit and a zealot. Train exclusively his intellect, and he is turned into an iceberg or heartless villain. Thus a onesided Education spoils man, and makes of the intended king of the cosmos a maniac, pauper, criminal or villain.

To train all faculties alike and combine general and industrial Education, to develop early through science and art judgment and imagination, and do

this with ease, so as to make the exercise or instruction a pleasure, and thus cause it to be or-
ganically appropriated and to become spontaneous,
automatic and hereditary, are some of the chiefest
problems of Education.

Our main proposition that the individual must
be brought up for the race is supported by reason,
nature and authority.   John W. Draper says in his
Intellectual Development of Europe, "Let man
cast off the clog of individuality, and remember
that he has race connections.   The appearance of
isolation presented by the individual is altogether
illusory.   Each individual man drew his life from
another, and to another man he gives rise, losing
in point of fact his aspect of individuality, when his
race connections are considered.   One epoch in life
is not all life.   Man cannot be separated from his
race."   Again, in his Civil Policy in America,
"We have not been introduced here and do not
continue here for our own personal sake, but that
we may share in the development of a result of a
higher order."

The same high authority coincides with us in
our estimate of ancient languages, in which he sees
neither the depositories of human knowledge nor
instruments for mental training: "This evil . . . .
was imported from England . . . . a remnant of
the sixteenth century, but obsolete in this. . . . .

A mastery of the game of chess improves more the mind than the translating of all the Greek and Latin authors in the world."

Buckle says, the natural sciences are democratic in thought, the classics never took notice of the masses, upon whom they had, therefore, no influence, and, hence, their but partial and short-lived civilizations.

The conviction is deepening that neither is the Pope, God, nor the king the state; we dare to add, neither is the kid-gloved Greek and Latin cotery the nation, an appellation it in vain seeks to rob of the great masses of the working people. And we are supported in this our sentiment by the great philosopher and statesman, John Locke, in his solid work on the Human Understanding, where he contrasts the artificial ignorance and learned gibberish of scholarly disputants and all-knowing doctors with the illiterate and condemned mechanic, whose name is thought a disgrace, but from whom we have received the improvements of the useful arts.

Infant schools are a main feature in Race Eucation, but are discarded in our public school system. Still, J. Willm, an educator of world-wide reputation, has said as many as thirty years ago: "The Education of the people will not be truly provided for until infant schools are established everywhere, and the success of primary instruction itself cannot be obtained without this sacrifice."

We insist upon country homes, and will add to the many authorities already quoted, that of the celebrated Isaac Taylor : " It is in the country, and there only, that the minds of children may be kept in a state of healthful activity and be made acquainted with nature without the impertinent go-between of books. A full half and more of all that ought to be learned in early life may be learned out of door by country-bred children, and how incalculable is the advantage of such a method in respect both of the mind and the body."

We insist upon scientific and industrial Education, which sobers us down to work for bread, and raiment and a little to spare. The vast generalities of the indefinite word-culture of our literary schools stimulate limitless desires and make us strive for the impossible. The insanity of exaggeration renders us madmen all, and the Stock Exchange as well as Bedlam has to be cured of this disease, or we shall never return to a sound financial basis. When the nine millions of families in the country will try on an average to make a thousand dollars a year, all will be well again, but as long as each strives for ten times as much, all will burst and all will break.

Race Education is the most complete union between private and public interests, from the contest between which offenses rise. Solon said: "Yourselves will so well be convinced that obedience to my laws is your interest, that you will not be tempted to break them."

Race Education training us to live and work for the race, trains us for virtue or the public good, and fostering in us devotion to the race nourishes in us a noble passion from which great deeds may spring.

The school, the government and public opinion must educate us to work for the good of all. The fragmentary, finite and unreal in each must be supplemented by our living for humanity, the infinite and the whole. Still each must remain arbiter of his will, and, like a statue, stand on his own pedestal. The straight-jacket of communism precludes all freedom and internal growth and individuality. It may, perchance, do for angels, for whom any system will do, because as we fancy them they can do without any. But it will not do for men, certainly not such as they are in our day—and we deal with the present.

The depth or compass of every power' or function of the mind, be it that of judgment, reason, imagination or will, being but the sum of all former repetitions of the same act, is increased by continued exercise. Göethe's dramatic faculty was formed

in the nursery by constant exercise.   Lessing, when
but a child, buried himself among a pile of books.
And the great Linnæus, the first organizer of the
vegetable kingdom, was quieted in the cradle by a
rose put into his hand.

As energy is the one great virtue including all
others, and man is not to be controlled by every
fleeting fancy, but the will is to be king in him,
Education must be as full of action as life is, and
the young must be kept active, as action is the best
school of energy.

Individuality, next in importance to energy, can
only be preserved, under a uniform system of public
instruction, by the adaptation of schools to the variety of pursuits prevalent in the different sections
of the country.

The industrial virtues, formerly contracted by the
daily example of the father working at the family
hearth, must be inculcated to-day by the school.

The prevention of human deterioration through
the cultivation of health and strength, developing
energy and individuality, does the best for that
spontaneity so much vaunted by the ideal lovers
of the good and the beautiful.

The well-being of the race is no low and materialistic aim ; it is the concrete of every high and noble endeavor, and gives it reality.   This our age
better bow in submission to the law of love as the

one embracing every other law and contingency of human progress and development.

A comprehensive glance at the world of legal and moral offenses or at man's motives and desires, as hunger, thirst, gluttony, drunkenness, sensuality, lust, greed, rapacity, tyranny, corruption, servility, meanness, pride, vanity, arrogance, prejudice, zeal, fanaticism, malice, hate, revenge, cruelty and all the frightful host of human passions, which, like so many disenchained brutes, threaten to lay waste as if it was the world itself, what are they but individual selfishness, monopolizing the world for itself?

What is all law and all government, all science and all religion for, but the one to restrain the individual in favor of the collective whole, and the other to enlighten us about our true position as a part in the great, stupendous whole, in which and through which alone we live and have our being.

Must we wait until every brute of a passion has grown strong and untamable, and law and government, the keeper, step in with the red-hot iron and keep us at bay? Race Education trains the individual early to live for and in harmony with the race. Education must do the work of the government in the nursery and in the school. This is the very alphabet of organizing society, and if the lesson has to be repeated, it is not our fault.

It is time the individual be made secondary to the race; it is the reverse order that gave us Cyrus, Alexander, Cæsar, Attila, Charlemagne, Tamourlane, Charles XII., Bonaparte and the like scourges. It was the same order that called forth the wars of the Popes for universal domination, the crusades and religious persecutions. Even in philosophy this individual selfishness has stifled the knowledge of the truth through the pride of system. It was the same individual pride, selfishness and tyranny that put a yoke and reins on a brother and called him a slave, a word at which the heavens wrapt themselves in mourning.

And to this day what is it that thwarts the intentions of the best-designed institutions, makes prisons hot-beds of scrofula, phthisis, madness, vice and crime, and insane asylums and poor-houses the scenes of shocking barbarity but even this same disregard for the race that stifles philanthropy?

We do not pity the sufferer, be he poor, insane or criminal, but even stoop to coin fortunes from the miseries of such men, which makes us the poorest of them all. Yes, only too often our charities are a mockery of the very miseries for the relief of which they are intended. Or does any one expect jailors and waiters to act up to human considerations to which legislators are strangers, as our penal legislation proves them to be?

There is but one sovereign law of human life and action, and this law, as is in the nature of the case, must be the sovereign law of Education, and the one great universal remedy, or rather preventive of every human ill, and this law and remedy is to live and act for the race. The Education of the race brings us daily nearer the fulfilment of this law, which is and must be the basis of the Education of the individual, as it is the basis of the Education of the race.

The Education of the individual and that of humanity in the great drama of the world's history must become one in aim and purpose. Social science, hygiene and Education must become one and inseparable, and the redemption of the race can only be achieved through the combined work of them all.

Rousseau first taught the educator the necessity of studying the child; may we say, it was our humble endeavor in this essay to show the necessity of making a thorough and faithful study of the normal and abnormal conditions of society, of which the child forms an integral part, and without a perfect knowledge of which the Education of a societory being is impossible?

A vigorous employment of the mind exercises all its faculties, and, hence, earnest students have in all ages made equal progress with all methods, as well as in the absence of any. The knowledge of the laws of the mind is as beautiful as that of the stars and as merely contemplative in many of its results. Still, psychology has its golden applications in Education.

But as the social relations of man are entirely artificial, arbitrary and depending on his will, he cannot, in the absence of the physiological and pathological knowledge of society, but blunder and suffer social deterioration, which ends in physical degeneracy and moral depravity; and thus an acquaintance of teachers and parents with the structure of society will appear, to men who have to deal with the many miseries of mankind, of vastly more practical significance than a theoretical mapping out of the faculties of the human mind.

Race Education, or Hereditary Culture, the highest induction of all past educational thought and experience, embracing the whole of humanity, increases the physical power and moral tone of the race, for where the highest, broadest and deepest humanity is, there is God, as devotion to mankind is devotion to God.

PART VII.

DETERIORATION THROUGH UNHYGIENIC CONDITIONS.

We are writing about hollow eyed poverty with a ragged shirt, a mouldy crust of bread, the crime, insanity and early death it is heir to, and are met by the cry, progress and development, an inanity which did not silence earnest voices, ringing through the ages and warning the masses; for verily life and death are put before us, and whatever may become of us, God can raise himself children out of stones, and the purpose of the universe will in no wise be disturbed by such worms as we are, even though we perish.

Deterioration is taken for the poets' tale of the golden age behind us, and exchanged for the more flattering view of progress while we, dealing with facts, care neither for new theories nor for old tales. We see the masses live under unhygienic conditions which can breed nothing but depravity, disease and insanity, and when we examine the crime

(327)

and death lists of the poor, we find effects just such
as we should expect from such causes, which we
say must be removed. We care not how much
worse men were off in the savage state, or in the
Middle Ages, when war, famine and the black pest
were raging; we compare the condition of the
masses with that of the more favorably situated;
we compare it with man in his God ordained and
normal condition, and until it is not brought up to
this standard, our duty is not done.

It is obvious from every page of this work that
we do not believe in a natural law of deterioration.
But we do maintain that the normal type of the
masses is deteriorating under their unhygienic conditions.

INFANT MORTALITY INDICATING THE GENERAL
CONDITION.

If the general mortality is an indication of the
degree of a nation's well being, the death rate of
infants must be still more so, on account of their
sensitiveness to environments, and must engage the
attention of the social student.

It is a mistake to ascribe a small decrease in
the proportion of infant to general mortality, to
improved sanitary conditions. As, for instance, in
New York city, where the death rate of infants
has fallen in 1869—1878 from 52 per cent. to 48 per

cent. of the general mortality. Is a decrease of mortality natural in years of steadily increasing misery? And is this not against all experience, as well as against all reason? Is it not most unwarrantable to draw any conclusions from the falling off in the number of deaths, where we know next to nothing about the number of births, in which the register is most defective? Is it not more reasonable, and in accord with experience, that years of misery bring with them a decreased birth rate? But we are not left to inferences. A decreased rate of birth is established by the steadily falling off of our natural increase of population.

The fact of deterioration and its causes are plain from the following statement of Dr. Engel, who finds that in Prussia survived of—

		1st year.	*3d year.*
1,000 born, ...	1816–1820	836	757
" "	1820–1830	832	749
" "	1830–1840	823	732
" "	1840–1850	821	726
" "	1850–1858	811	718
" "	1858–1863	800	. . .

This is the average for the entire Prussian monarchy. The great cities in which manufactures are carried on, and the population is crowded, show a considerably more unfavorable proportion. So, for instance, in Könisberg survived of—

		1st year.	3d year.
1,000 born, ...	1819–1823	810	712
" "	1824–1828	778	664
" "	1839–1843	766	649
" "	1844–1848	732	622
" "	1849–1853	739	592
" "	1854–1858	700	567
" "	1859–1864	695	...

That the steadily increasing employment of
women in the factory close, before, and after the
birth of a child, is an important factor in this
growing infant death rate, and the deterioration of
those who just escape death, is evident from the
fact, that in Liegnitz, where textile factories employ many women, but 74 children in 100 survive
the first year; though the average survival in Prussia is 80 in 100, while in the district of Arnberg,
where metal industries prevail, and but very few
women are employed in factories, 86–87 in 100
survive.

Wherever textile industries prevail, infant mortality is the accompanying feature. It is so in Saxony. In the eminently weaving districts of Silesia,
this slaughter of infants is most frightful. In Hirsch-
berg during 1850–1865, only 64–65 in 100 born survived the first year, and in Landhut only 63.

In France the normal infant mortality in healthy
regions during the first year amounts to 11–15 in
100. In the Department of de l'Eure, which has

a textile industry of 658,413 spindles, the infant mortality rises to 25.5 in 100 born. In Montmorency, a town without factory life, the infant mortality of the first year is 12.2 in 100, while in Mühlhausen, noted for its textile industries, it averaged 1861–1868, 36.5 in 100, and this mortality was vastly reduced when a respite from their factory labor was granted to women before and after their delivery. In the Canton of Zurich during 1867–1872, the infant mortality was in the first year 30.9 in 100, while it was in the city of Zurich, 34.4 in 100. The entire mortality in the industrial Cantons of Zurich and St. Gallen, was 33.6 and 31.0 in 1,000 population, while it was in the agricultural Cantons of Grison and Valais, 17.7 and 17.2.

The same influence of the industries of localities upon the general, and especially upon infant, mortality we find in England. Manual art industries must enable woman to add to her family earnings without weakening and destroying her children and deteriorating the race through factory employment, altogether incompatible with her functions as a mother.

The following table of Dr. Thomas B. Curtis, showing the percentage of infant mortality during a period of fifty-four years in the city of Boston, speaks for itself:

YEARS.		Percentage of deaths under one to total deaths.	Percentage of deaths under five to total deaths.
MEAN OF 10 YEARS,	1820–29	8.73	25.69
	1830–39	12.66	35.17
	1840–49	12.16	37.52
	1850–59	23.84	46.49
	1865–74	25.40	41.70
MEAN OF 5 YEARS,	1865–69	23.9	41.3
	1870–74	27.0	42.1
SINGLE YEAR,	1874	28.19	42.99
	1875	25.25	44.34
	1876	24.82	43.04
	1877	24.95	40.94

We may look wherever we may, and evidences of a deterioration increasing with a progressing density of population, calling for redoubled etiological, moral, and sanitary agencies force themselves upon our attention.

An excessive infant mortality being often found in the purest atmosphere, at a height of two thousand feet above the level of the sea, its cause cannot be purely local, but must be traced to an enfeebled constitution, that with the masses results from overwork and underfeeding, especially on the part of the mother, and points, therefore, to anti-natal conditions and a continuous deterioration. It is for this reason that this large infant mortality manifests itself immediately after birth and before environments had an opportunity for developing their power, or to influence of themselves to any considerable degree the young citizen, if he was not strongly predisposed, as the following table shows.

In England, according to the life-table, of 1,000,000 that are born—

46.503	die in the first month.
17,195	" " second "
12,178	" " third "
10,100	" " fourth "
9,550	" " fifth "
9,033	" " sixth "
8,547	" " seventh month.
8,087	" " eighth "
7,657	" " ninth "
7,253	" " tenth "
6,872	" " eleventh "
6,515	" " twelfth "
149,493	" " first year.

In France the record shows that of 1,000,000 children born—

29,123	die in the first week.
22,128	" " second week.
22,236	" " sixteen following days.
73,487	" " first month.

It appears, Dr. Jarvis, whom we follow, continues, that in France, 1 in 34 dies in the first week, 1 in 44 in the second, and the same proportion in the next sixteen days, and 1 in 14 in the first month.

In England, 1 in 21 dies in the first month, 1 in 56 in the second, 1 in 77 in the third, and 1 in 131 in the twelfth.

The same great authority says, in Massachusetts and in England, the reports include a considerable number of deaths, mostly in infancy, under the causes termed " Debility," " Atrophy and Debility," " Inanition," " Premature Birth," all resting upon imperfections of constitutional development of force, and inability to digest food and obtain from it sufficient nutriment for the body.

Important as public hygiene is, excessive rates of mortality, morbidity, and defectiveness of every kind can only be thoroughly reached through Education and Public Economy, or the removal of misery, which, through want of wholesome means of living, proper care and moderation, through over work, mental worry, and a thousand and one more ways deteriorates the race, even under the best atmospheric conditions.

Excessive infant mortality, inflicting through the increased morbidity it implies enfeebled constitutions in multitudes of survivors, is, according to Wappäus, not by any means the natural preventive of over population, which is checked by a decrease in fertility, that is in an inverse ratio to civilization.

DETERIORATION AND LIFE INSURANCE.

If life insurances find lives more favorable than the Carlisle tables indicate, let them remember that those tables are constructed upon general lives, while the lives they take are selected. And, again, if sanitary progress has even given an advantage to the selected lives of to-day over those of former days, this proves nothing against the deterioration of the masses, living in constant misery, and therefore under most unhygienic conditions, and but slightly sharing in the sanitary improvements of the day.

While under the late great sanitary progress rates of mortality have fallen fifty per cent. in institutions under the immediate control of governments, they have, according to a late statement in the Cyclopedia Britannica and Dr. Richardson, since thirty years not at all fallen, and even slightly risen, among the general population. And why? Simply because the deteriorating condition of the masses, and their excessive rates of mortality, counterbalance the improved rates of mortality of those classes who are in a condition to avail themselves of the undoubtedly marvelous modern achievements in sanitary science.

DETERIORATION THROUGH CROWDING AND
PAUPERISM.

Is there any question about the excessive rates
of mortality, morbidity, and insanity of large cities?
Or do city populations not increase beyond proportion in comparison with the country? And are
pauperism, misery and crime not increasing with
the spread of the tenement system of our large
cities? Only willful ignorance can question our
position of the deterioration of the masses under
their present *regime* of pauperism.

How with crowding and pauperism, that deep-
seated and race-destroying disease, phthisis—which
constitutes in the city of New York 35.7 per cent.
of all the deaths of the ages from fifteen to fifty
years—increases among the masses, Elisha Harris'
masterly Report of Vital Statistics of 1875 shows;
according to which, while its deaths are 2.36 in
1,000 population in the better, they are fully 4.12
in 1,000 population in the poorer quarters, aver-
aging these localities separately.

We have seen the rate of mortality rise with the
density of population which implies misery and
squalor. Neither can the position be doubted
that cities increase out of all proportion with the
country, and deterioration is the logical sequence,
as well as the ascertained fact. In France the

increase for every 100 population during 1836–1861 has been :

In towns of 5,000	. . . .	1.18
" " 5,000–10,000	. . .	8.76
" " 10,000–20,000	. . .	41.10
" " 20,000 and over	. . .	60.46

The percentage of the urban population in France was :

1846	24.4
1856	27.3
1866	30.4
1872 . , . - . . .	31.0

The enormous growth of cities is not so much peculiar to our country as to our age and its civilization :

Birmingham Incr'd from 73,670 pop. in 1801 to 190,542 in 1841, to 343,696 in 1871.
Sheffield . " " 14,105 " " 1736 " 112,492 " " " 239,947 " "
Manchester " " 41,032 " " 1734 " 300,000 " " " 480,470 " '
Liverpool " " 5,145 " " 1700 " 264,298 " " " 493,346 " "

While the agricultural population of Norfolk has in thirty years increased one-third, the industrial and urban population of Lancashire has doubled itself.

In Massachusetts, towns with 10,000 and more population contained of the whole population of the State in 1800, 6.8 per cent.; in 1840, 22 per cent.; in 1870, 48·7 per cent.

For further illustration of the increasing density of population in American cities we refer the reader to page 412, Vol. I.

15

The result of this crowding is, that while in the healthy rural districts of England, of 1,000,000 of children born alive, 175,410 die under five years, in the district of Liverpool 460,370 die of the same number during the same time. Again, the ratio of deaths of infants under five years in the healthy English rural districts is 33.48 in 1,000, while it is in Boston, 95.6! which is about three times the natural death ratio—three times the natural ratio of morbidity, defectiveness and deterioration.

The following table will show at a glance the growing density of population in the prominent States of the world:

United States	5	to 1 square kilometer.
Austria	67.9	" " "
France	68.4	" " "
German Empire	75.9	" " "
Japan	82.1	" " "
China	100.6	" " "
Great Britain	101.	" " "
Belgium	181.	" " "

The small density of our own population must not deceive us as to our own dangers from crowding, as over 20 per cent. of our entire population are congregated in fifty cities.

The relation between death rates of all ages and also under five years and density of population, in

a series of English districts, is made manifest from
the following representation :

Death rates of all ages. In 1,000 pop.	Death rates under five years. In 1,000 pop.	Density. Persons to one square mile.
16	37.80	166
19	47.53	186
22	63.06	379
25	82.10	1,718
28.5	95.04	4,499
32	111.90	12,357
30	139.50	65,823

A sudden movement of population into the
great centers of commerce and industry leads to
high rents, to speculative building, crowded dwellings, poor living, drunkenness, vice, and shiftlessness and misery of all sorts. The authorities of
Berlin show the proportion of the different classes
of buildings of that city, from the beginning of this
century down to date, and as this crowding and rise
in rent are common, the following table may serve
to illustrate the general deterioration of the masses
through this universal modern dearth of cheap and
wholesome dwellings.

In the public records of Berlin the dwellings are
divided into classes renting under 30, 31–50, 51–
100, 101–200, 201–300, 301–400, 401–500, 501–1,000,
1,001–1,500, and over 1,500 Prussian dollars. The
following table shows the per cent. each class forms
in the whole:

Under to doll's	1815-16.	1829-30.	1840-41.	1850.	1860.	1870.	1872.
30 "	58.20 per cent.	24.62 per cent.	18.69 per cent.	18.78 per cent.	9.70 per cent.	7.20 per cent.	4.93 per cent.
31-50 "	16.94	29.74 "	31.98 "	33.23 "	26.09 "	21.58 "	16.15 "
51-100 "	13.83	23.32 "	24.52 "	24.56 "	32.15 "	35.74 "	38.30 "
101-200 "	7.58	13.59 "	14.69 "	13.70 "	17.90 "	18.35 "	20.88 "
201-300 "	2.04	4.46 "	4.99 "	4.75 "	6.32 "	6.75 "	7.38 "
301-400 "	0.71	1.82 "	2.20 "	2.14 "	3.01 "	3.45 "	3.99 "
401-500 "	0.31	0.98 "	1.16 "	1.04 "	1.68 "	2.07 "	2.40 "
501-1,000 "	0.31	1.25 "	1.40 "	1.41 "	2.38 "	3.30 "	3.99 "
1,001-1,500 "	0.08	0.22 "	0.37 "	0.31 "	0.77 "	0.69 "	0.84 "
1,501 and over. "	....	....	....	....	....	0.57 "	0.74 "
Total	100.00	100.00	100.00	100.00	100.00	100.00	100.00
Absolute........	40,588	51,817	63,551	79,950	95,876	166,144	173,003

These figures tell volumes. Of 173,003 dwellings, only 4.93 per cent. rent under thirty dollars! For the masses, of course, this means living in dark and damp cellars and dying by inches. With a population, fifty per cent. of whom have an income under two hundred dollars, 78.52 per cent. of the dwellings rent for over fifty dollars. What sudden wealth and what misery does this rise in real estate and house rent reveal! and, as the same movement of population drives everywhere the masses into poorer and poorer quarters, they are bound to deteriorate with their dwellings, which are always the surest indication of their condition and state of civilization. Nothing but the decentralization of our large towns by the means of quick transit and suburban homes can eliminate this worst factor of deterioration—crowding into miserable tenements.

With the spread of the potato culture and its becoming the main article of food among the common people, woman's factory work, the deprivation of infants of the mother's breast, and the crowding of the masses into badly ventilated and lighted damp tenements, scrofula, and, with it, general deterioration, have increased among the masses. What would our horses come to if we worked them ten to fourteen hours a day on cut straw, kept mares in the harness up to the foaling season, or used young colts before the plow? These and kindred things we do in working men, women, and children, and would fain escape the responsibility of the effect of our guilty conduct by stupidly denying the patent fact of the deterioration of the masses.

THE INCREASE OF INSANITY.

As next to phthisis insanity is most indicative of deterioration, we shall briefly, but conclusively, prove the correctness of our position as to its increase.

Dr. J. Mortimer Granville has carried on the inquiry as to the proportion of the insane to the rest of the population in England with a more impartial method than any of his predecessors, taking into account and carefully eliminating all elements disturbing the result, and the net outcome of his labors shows 1861–1871 a steady positive increase of 14.94 per cent. or 1.49 per cent. annual increase.

If Granville investigated the subject of insanity as a rigorous statistician, Dr. Juke pursued the opposite method of an exhaustive investigation into the general causes of insanity; the positive increase of which he overwhelmingly shows, and thus reaches the same result of a steady increase of insanity. Each of these inquirers absolutely refused to be influenced by the other's method, and still their several methods—of the one dealing with statistically-sifted facts, and the other dealing with general causes—terminated in the same result.

SCROFULA AMONG FACTORY PEOPLE.

Scrofula, the most consummate expression of deterioration, prevails, according to the learned August Hirsch, among factory populations.

Coronel, who has made an exhaustive study of the factory population of Holland, says of that at Hilversum, overwork, under feeding, poor clothing and miserable homes have spread scrofula and stinted the growth of the people, which is fast disappearing. Frederic Oesterlen, the great German hygienist, shows that among the well to do classes of the Canton of Genf 8 in 1,000 deaths are of scrofula, while among the general population there are 16 in 1,000, and we must not forget that among the exclusively factory population the proportion is, of course, much greater. Lugol shows the connection of an excessive infant mortality and scrofula among the poor in France, and Alphonso Corradi's researches in Italy lead to the same result.

Coronel, an exact student of the condition of the factory population, observed that at Hilversum, between 1850 and 1859 among the factory population there were 58 more deaths than births.

Among the day laborers there were 19 more births than deaths,
    "   agricultural laborers "   "   70   "   "   "   "
    "   comfortable classes "   "   302   "   "   "   "

According to the same authority, die in the first
five years after birth :

Among the factory population 67 in 100.
   "   "   day laborers   59   "
   "   "   mechanics   52   "

The same author has proven by exact measure-
ments the lower stature of the children of the factory population, a fact sustained by later and repeated observations in England and in the United
States.

PAUPERISM AND DETERIORATION.

Have we not sufficiently established the fact that
poverty—the almost inevitable attendant of unskilled labor—deteriorates the masses and is a
question of life and death with them? The poor,
says Dr. Edward Jarvis, in the Report of the State
Board of Health of Massachusetts, have a lower
bodily health and shorter duration of life than the
well-to-do classes. They engage in the hardest and
most dangerous labors, and all the means that they
have of sustaining and of protecting life—the air
they breathe, the food they eat, and the shelter
and clothing that protect them—are all of a low
character, and hence their life and strength are
less developed and sustained, they have more
sickness, less power to resist its ravages, and sink
earlier beneath its force. The hard necessities and
severe labors of the mother often prevent her from

giving the child the pre-natal opportunity of development; neither can she give after birth the little nurseling the attention needed for the establishment of a sound constitution. Ignorance, filth, misery, and other deteriorating conditions in and around the dwellings of the poor do their work of destruction. Dr. Jarvis illustrates the effects of poverty by the high rates of infant and adult mortality among the poor everywhere — facts with which our readers are sufficiently acquainted.

Night and day do not follow each other in more regular succession than crime, death, and disease attend poverty and low and unremunerative employments. To save and elevate man, we must, therefore, elevate labor, or infuse into it the higher elements of human nature, and hence the redemption of the perishing masses imperatively calls for a universal, moral, economical, and art industrial Education. This is our doctrine, and, with it, we stand or fall.

THE SPREAD OF FACTORY LIFE.

With civilization wants, occupations, inventions, machinery and factories, with conditions more destructive than poison, multiply, the effects of which are the inevitable deterioration of the masses, science and humanity must check, if we are not to sustain an annual preventible mortality of fifty thousand productive men, together with the ex-

15*

pense of a hundred thousand years of sickness—as each death implies two cases of a full year's sickness—not to speak of the pauperism, misery, crime, and all the moral and physical deterioration that such an uncalled for mass of orphanage is sure to entail upon entire generations.

The following figures in Mr. Gastell's Labor Report show the decrease of agricultural life in the advancing industrial States of the world:

Russia	86 per cent.
Italy	77 " "
France	51 " "
Prussia	45 " "
England	12 " "

In 1860 there were in the United States 1,311,-246 hands engaged in manufacture; in 1870, 2,053,-996; an increase of 60 per cent, while our farmers, during the same time, increased but 18 per cent.

The Massachusetts Health Report gives the average life of farmers as 65.13, and that of factory laborers as 35.42 years.

According to Dr. William Farr, if 100 expresses the average mortality of the whole community, the average mortality of

Lawyers is	63	Tool and file makers .	121
Watchmakers	104	Hatters, coppersmiths, &	
Tailors	109	needle manufacturers	123
Wool, cotton and flax		Manufacturing chemists,	
laborers	109	dye and color man'f's.	124
Glass workers	119	Earthware manufactur-	
Plumbers and painters .	120	ers	138

It is evident from this highest statistical authority that in many manufactures life is cut down to
less than half of even its moderate length.
The following table taken from Hirt sufficiently
shows the bearing of the trades upon the deterioration of the race :
Percentage of cases of phthisis in the total number
of sick among workmen exposed to the inhalation
of dust :

Metallic.

Needle polishers	69	Compositors	36.9	Varnishers	25
File cutters	62.2	Watchmakers	36.5	Painters	24.5
Lithographers	48.5	Typefounders	34.9	Printers	21.6
Sieve workers	42.1	Engravers	26.9	Belt makers	19.7
Grinders	40.4	Dyers	25	Tinkers	14.1

Mineral.

Flint workers	80	Porcelain makers	16	Masons	12.9
Grindstone makers	40	Potters	14.7	Diamond cutters	9.
Stonecutters	36.4	Carpenters	14.4	Cement makers	8-10
Plasterers	19				

Vegetable.

Cigar makers	49.1	Fellmongers	23.2	Hatters	15.5
Weavers	32.1	Turners	16.2	Button maker	15.1
Rope makers	25.9				

Ixed.

Glass cutters	35	Glass makers	17.8	Day laborers	15.1

No Dust.

Shoemakers	18.7	Coopers	10.1	Tanners	9.2
Brewers	17.2	Glovers	10	Butchers	7.9

The following official statement of the Massachusetts Bureau of Statistics of Labor, on the nature and tendency of factory labor, made by Dr.

John B. Whitaker, will explain the bearing of manufactures on human life :

1. Accidents and casualties among operatives are painfully numerous.
2. Unnatural working positions often cause round shoulders, curvature of the spine, bow legs, etc.
3. Exhaustion from overwork often follows long hours of labor, great speed of machinery, large number of looms, etc.
4. Work by artificial light, especially in winter months, causes a variety of affections of the eyes.
5. The inhalation of foreign particles works great injury to factory hands working in impure air.
6. Exposure to extremes of temperature works very injuriously to operatives working in hot mills.
7. The haste and irregularity with which operatives have to take their meals is the cause of much dyspepsia.
8. These and other causes predispose operatives to fevers with a greater than usual mortality.
9. Operatives are unusually predisposed to contagious diseases.
10. Women working in factories are predisposed to pelvic diseases, producing difficulty in parturition and a variety of uterine diseases.
11. The factory predisposes by contact and loose conversation to sexual abuse.
12. It predisposes to depression of spirits. Hence the care worn, haggard look of factory people and the commonness of hypochondria and hysteria among factory women.
13. It predisposes to intemperance by the exhaustion following long hours.
14. *There is a progressive deterioration produced in families laboring in factories, their children being puny, sickly, and but partly developed ; every generation growing more and more so.*

15. *The factory produces premature old age by its long hours of labor and close confinement. Very few live to be old who work in a factory.*

16. *Factory labor affects the growth and development of children employed; it saps the very foundations of life; decay manifesting itself in consumption and kindred diseases. A factory child will not, nor can it, develop into a robust adult.*

We have throughout this work shown the effect of factory labor upon phthisis and ratio of mortality, and a whole volume could hardly contain all the figures expressing the many, many years operatives are robbed of in our various factories. Deterioration, then, is the inevitable consequence of increasing factory life, especially when we consider that textile, iron and chemical manufactures and mining are mostly increasing, the very pursuits which bear heaviest upon the mortality rates of workmen.

Let us have a universal art industrial Education, and the workmen will divide their time between the factory and their home art occupations. To day long hours of labor mean the slaughter of workmen in factories, and short hours of labor mean the death of many in groggeries.

The effects of the change of employment under the regime of art industrial Education will be supported by the change from the heavy atmosphere of the factory to the country air and cheerful home of the laborer, and its salubrious suburban location.

CHILDREN'S EMPLOYMENT IN FACTORIES AND DETERIORATION.

If the employment of women in factories is one cause of deterioration, the employment of children in factories is another, and yet as division of labor progresses this evil, causing great suffering and degradation, increases. The following description of factory children has been given before the House of Commons by the celebrated Sadler, in the presence of the great manufacturers of England, who dared not challenge the correctness of the statement. Medical men, he said, describe the consequences of children's factory labor to be, in many cases, languor and debility, sickness, loss of appetite, pulmonary complaints, such as difficulty of breathing, coughs, asthmas and consumptions; struma, the endemia of the factory, and other chronic diseases; while if these more distressing effects are not produced, the muscular power is enfeebled, the growth impeded, and life greatly abridged. Deformity is also a common and distressing result of this over strained and too early labor. The bones, in which the animal, in contradistinction to the earthy, matter is known to prevail in early life are then pliable, and often can not sustain the superincumbent weight of the body for so many hours without injury.   Hence, those of the leg become bent; the arch of the foot, which is composed of several bones of a wedge like form, is pressed down, and its elasticity destroyed, from which arises that disease in the foot common in factory districts.   The spine is often greatly affected, and its processes irregularly protruded, by which great deformity is occasioned. The ligaments also fail by over pressure and tension.   Hence, the hinge joints, of which they are the main support, such as those of the knee and ankle are overstrained, producing the deformity called knock knees and lame ankles, so exceedingly common in mills.   Thus are numbers of children distorted and crippled in early life, and frequently rendered incapable of any active exertion during the rest of their days.   To this catalogue of sufferings must be added, mutilation of limbs or loss of life by frequent accident.   The overworking of these children occasions a weariness and lethargy which it is impossible always to resist; hence, drowsy and exhausted, the poor creatures fall too often among the machinery, which is not, in many instances, sufficiently sheltered, when their muscles are lacerated, their bones broken, or their limbs torn off, in which case they are constantly sent to the infirmaries to be cured, and if crippled for life, they are turned out and maintained at public cost; or they are sometimes killed upon the spot. Their presence bespeaks more a hospital than a factory. They are diseased, stunned, crippled, destroyed, deficient of instruction and moral culture, and full of incurable maladies from early work. Upon examination 47 in 106 were found crippled.

The feebler sex suffers most from this enormous wrong perpetrated on children. Female children are often worked beyond the utmost extent of their physical powers, and often receive permanent injury, the effects of which are felt when they become mothers, the contraction of the pelvis increases then greatly the danger and difficulty of parturition, rendering embryotomy, one of the most distressing operations, necessary.

The Artizan's Report of the Paris Exhibition of 1867 clearly proves that the laws forced from the Parliament of England, and later from the French Chambers, are, to a great extent a dead letter. " I have been," says the reporter, " in all the principal manufacturing districts of my own country, and witnessed the sorrowful spectacle of boys and girls hurrying to their work on cold dark mornings, with careworn faces and stooping figures; but for a sight which is most calculated to move a man of ordinary sensibility to compassion, one must go into the neighborhood of the French silk factories, and watch the melancholy procession of babies (they can be called nothing else), dragging their little limbs slowly away from the place where their tiny energies have been tortured out of them."

No more is the lesson of deterioration from the employment of children in factories out of date with us. For, according to the statement of the Report of the Statistics of Labor of Massachusetts, this barbarous practice of working children ten, eleven, or twelve hours a day in factory and shop dwarfs the growth and intellect of children in the Bay State, and will be but little checked by the existing law so long as children of tender age, more fit for the hospital than the mill, are allowed to have a place in factories.

"The factory," says Oesterlen, "destroys the family completely. . . . . Think of the child locked up at home with a few potatoes or a piece of bread . . . . what care or education . . . . think on a young girl going from factory to factory and from boarding place to boarding place deprived of all parental protection and exposed to temptation. . . . From early childhood at the factory and eternally among machinery and its deafening noise the sense for everything else dies away, and no wonder the official reports of the Canton Zurich describe the children of the factory population as stupid, sluggish and brutal, and the clergy complain of their low, reckless and sensual condition. A poor race grown up in misery at home, in poor houses and among the corrupting influence of adult factory laborers and boarding houses, everywhere cheated and abused, no wonder the demoralization and rate of mortality are the greater the earlier in life factory attendance begins." Such are the words of the greatest medical statistician of the age.

" Miserable," says Coronel, speaking of the working people, " through the tyranny and ignorance of others as well as their own, they are sinning against the laws of life, and become victims of an early death. Nature has no charms for them, they are without health, comfort or peace in life. They know only the dark side of life. From the cradle to the grave their life is one struggle against hard work, sickness, misery and grief."

"The pauperized masses," says another great writer, " are victims of protracted starvation, a starvation that lasts the whole year around and every minute of it. . . . A starvation that does not kill in a day, but that is made up of many deprivations and sufferings, and one that without ceasing destroys the body, weakens the mind, sears the conscience, deteriorates the species, begets disease, drunkenness, envy, indolence, recklessness, unscrupulousness, coarseness, beggary, bestiality and theft." Verily, no one can study the condition of the masses and doubt the deteriorating power of this enemy of God and man—pauperism.

No wonder the excellent Edward Reich, like other social students, sees in an improved economical state of the masses the key to every other improvement, as it would do away with the necessity of wife and children engaging in factory labor, with overwork, under feeding, with many other unhygienic conditions and hindrances to their moral elevation!

Nothing but universal art industrial Education can give to labor that efficiency which alone can materially improve the economical condition of the masses, nothing but high skill in the industrial arts can avert woman's destruction in the factory, and nothing short of compulsory public industrial Education can protect children against the connivance between mean or hungry parents and the cupidity of money making men.

DETERIORATION THROUGH THE SCHOOL.

Education should fit us for life and its work, and lo, its barren word culture makes us helpless, until our schools nursing pauperism become breeders of crime, and our educators become deteriorators. The charge is terrible ; more terrible, however, are the facts which sustain the accusation. We refer to the crime history of the country, which is but the history of our Education.

The absence of trade Education among convicts has been observed before, and the connection between crime and idleness is proverbial, but to Richard Vaux, Esq., of Pennsylvania, belongs the honor to have established the causal relation between the absence of the industrial element in our Education and crime through an array of statistical facts, which leave no doubt on the subject.

He makes the following exhibit of the industrial and educational relations of the convicts of the Eastern State Penitentiary of Pennsylvania:

	Received.	Illiterate.		Could Read and Write.		Unapprenticed.		Apprenticed.	
		NO.	PER CENT.	NO.	PER CENT.	NO.	PER CENT.	NO.	PER CENT.
1850—59	1605	243	15.14	1,115	69.47	1,217	75.42	378	24.18
1860—69	2383	410	17.21	1,677	70.37	1,950	18.83	333	18.17
1870—76	1650	361	21.88	1,235	74.85	1,463	88.66	187	11.30

Mr. Vaux covers many pages with statistics, all showing how much the want of a trade, and how little what we term Education has to do with the perpetration of crime.

But there is one set of observations given by Mr. Vaux, most strikingly illustrating the relation of Industrial Education to crime. He divides the years preceding the committal of crime into three periods: with exceedingly few exceptions, the first shows *no trade;* the second, *unskilled labor;* and the third, immediately preceding the criminal act, *idleness.* Such is the evolution of crime.

The comments of Mr. Vaux are from first to last one cry for industrial Education. " More persons convicted of crimes are educated than those who are illiterate. . . . . There is want of educated mechanics, and lack of employment for scholars who have no trade. . . . . A system that fosters prejudice against mechanical Education works public injury. . . . . Industrial Education is one of the most important preventives of crime. . . . . There is an absolute, imperative necessity for engrafting in the present school system practical trade knowledge."

The opinion of Mr. Vaux, the able President of the Board of Inspectors of the State Penitentiary of the Eastern District of Pennsylvania, formed from the survey of so large a field and covering so many years, is entitled to the most earnest consideration of social students.

THE DOCTRINE OF DETERIORATION.

The doctrine of deterioration, far from being fatalistic, discovers in the dangerous tendencies of some of the conditions of life a necessity for a future etiology of crime and disease, which shall dispense with the old hopeless method of drugging the one and punishing the other. Having for its purpose the prevention of crime, disease and defectiveness in all its forms, it is of a most practical nature, and those who accuse it of being a pessimistic theory, know nothing about it. In all the departments of life and science we have hitherto dealt with isolated, spasmodic, and ready results, torn out of their proper connection, and therefore unintelligible and unmanageable ; phenomena and facts can only be grasped and controlled in their genetic processes, in which deterioration deals with the morbid conditions of the physical and moral life of man.

General deterioration being always preceded by the deterioration of tissue and organs following defective nutrition, often caused by an under feeding accompanying poverty and false economic relations, and manifesting itself not only by striking bodily deformity, but by a feeble will, weak mind, and perverted instincts, or pauperism, insanity and vice and crime, doubly interests the student of the moral relations of man.

DETERIORATION THROUGH HEREDITY AND THE SCHOOL.

Though a deterioration conditioned by heredity has to be checked through life by a hygiene resting on observations on heredity and a preventive medicine not yet sufficiently recognized in all their im-

DETERIORATION AND RACE EDUCATION, with practical Application to the People and Industry. By Samuel Royce. 586 pages. Price, $2.50. Boston: *Lee & Shepard,* Publishers.

New York: *Charles T. Dillingham.*

RECOMMENDATIONS.

From the *New York School Journal.*

" Deterioration and Race Education " has been in preparation for several years, and begins to attract attention. This work is strong in facts, arguments, and erudition, etc., etc.

From the *Popular Science Monthly.*

. . . . In this book Education is considered from a broad, humanitarian point of view, and in connection with the great causes of decay and deterioration. The author has collected a great deal of interesting material, interspersed with valuable observations and reflections, and the volume is pervaded by a reformatory and progressive spirit.

From the *Library Table,* Feb. 16.

The author displays a thorough knowledge of his subject, and his conclusions, no less than the startling array of his facts, deserve the most serious consideration of all who are in any way connected with the promotion or administration of public interests. We recommend the volume for careful perusal as one of the most valuable recent contributions to social and educational science.

From the *Reformer,* Jan. 11.

" Deterioration " is replete with erudition and practical wisdom, bearing testimony of the author's genuine philanthropy, and will make its mark—as none can read it without being thoroughly aroused as to the present appalling condition of the masses ; and what is proposed is moderate and sustained by other social thinkers.

From the *Boston Evening Transcript.*

. . . . The range of this work is comprehensive, and the various topics which incidentally arise in connection with the main subject are ably discussed.

I

2

I sincerely trust that much good will result from the work of "Deterioration and Race Education," and that its suggestions may prove beneficial to our whole nation.

GEORGE H. DREW,
Governor of State of Florida.

I have read "Deterioration and Race Education." This work has been prepared with care and ability, and I think will accomplish much good.

HENRY M. MATHEWS,
Governor of W. Virginia.

I am directed by the Governor to express . . . . his great interest in the subject discussed in the volume of " Deterioration and Race Education," and of his appreciation of the same. . . . .

GEORGE W. BURCHARD,
Private Secretary.

A general knowledge of the subject resulting from the dissemination of the views of the author of " Deterioration," as expressed in this volume, can not fail to have a beneficial influence, and must necessarily tend to the amelioration of the condition of the masses.

W. K. ROGERS,
Sec. to the President of the U. S.

I have examined " Deterioration and Race Education " with much interest. It is impossible not to honor the earnest and sincere spirit in which this book has been written. It is full of needful truths bravely spoken, and I am glad to have had the privilege of perusing it.

HENRY C. POTTER, D.D.,
Of Grace Church, N. Y. City.

"Deterioration and Race Education " is interesting to educated persons, and very valuable to the mass of society. I have read it with pleasure and profit and wish it success.

JOHN W. DRAPER, M.D., LL.D.,
Prof. in the University of New York.

" Deterioration and Race Education" is an able and thoughtful work, evincing erudition, earnestness, and a conscientious desire to advance the cause of public education ; I would recommend my fellow-teachers to study the facts and principles set forth in Prof. Royce's work.

THOS. HUNTER, Ph.D.,
President of the Normal College of New York City.

3

I have read "Deterioration" with interest. There is no doubt about its facts. We must revise our system of public education, and better adapt it to the wants of the times.

J. D. RUNKLE,
President Boston Institute of Technology.

———————

"Deterioration" is one of those books well worth the time required to read it carefully. It is a very, very useful book, and one the knowledge of which should be spread.

COLEMAN SELLERS,
President Franklin Institute, Phila.

———————

"Deterioration" should be carefully read, not only by teachers, but by all who are interested in the education and the welfare of humanity.

BEN HYDE BENTON,
President Polytechnic Institute, New Market, Va.

———————

"Deterioration" follows a line of argument greatly needed at the present time in educational affairs, and is an especially useful book.

HON. JOHN EATON,
Commissioner of Education.

"Deterioration" is full of curious and interesting information, and I sympathize with the philanthropic desires of the author

GEORGE WILLIAM CURTIS.

———————

I have read "Deterioration" with just admiration for its depth, breadth, and vigor. This book is like a hundred-pounder loaded to the muzzle. . . . . I am now nearly seventy-four years old, and perhaps the most encouraging thing I have seen done is this plain-spoken, earnest book ; for truly an evil must be demonstrated before it can be cured. Another thing is encouraging it comes with its sharp thunder-claps, etc., etc.

ELIZUR WRIGHT

———————

"Deterioration and Race Education" is of rare value, full of suggestion, and opening up views that can not fail to attract and interest deeply every student of the social questions of the day. Its contribution toward solving these is of great value, and no one can follow such guidance without placing himself in a position to serve humanity efficiently in most important interests.

WENDELL PHILLIPS.

———————

The studies pursued by the author of "Deterioration" are in a direction very generally neglected, and the information given is just in the lines where it is most needed.

REV. EDWARD E. HALE.

———————

"Deterioration and Race Education" is of great value and importance, diffusing knowledge upon subjects on the due consideration of which depends the welfare, if not the very existence, of our social organization.

O. WENDELL HOLMES.

4

" Deterioration and Race Education " is worthy of the attention of the medical profession, and of men of science in general as well as of humanitarians. It is a work full of suggestion and weighty matter.

Elisha Harris, M.D.

I fully concur in what Dr. Elisha Harris has said. " Deterioration " is a book of great value.

Frank H. Hamilton, M.D.

I concur in the recommendation of Prof. Hamilton, and would especially recommend the work to physicians, teachers, and parents.

R. J. O'Sullivan, M.D.

From the *Methodist*, New York, March, 1878.

The studies in this volume are valuable.

From the *Christian Intelligencer*, N. Y., March 21, 1878.

In this volume, crowded with statistics, facts, and opinions upon sociology, and evidently the product of long and careful preparation, the author presents the subject of " deterioration " of the human race in order to show the necessity of aiming at its " amelioration," etc., etc. The facts which the writer has collected from Government, medical, and sociological authorities are painfully interesting, and of great value for reference.

From the *New Jerusalem Messenger*, N. Y., Sept. 4, 1878.

This book presents a fearful array of facts and statistics as to the deterioration of our race. . . . . Mr. Royce has evidently studied his subject in all its branches. . . . . It is a painful book, but like some other bitter doses it is good for us. It is well that thinking people should know and thoroughly appreciate the dangers which threaten us in this day of our boasted civilization. The book is of deepest interest, and a valuable contribution toward the solution of the Social Problems of our time.

From the *Religio-Philosophical Journal*, Chicago, Sept. 21, 1878.

This is really a good book, one which the reviewer gladly takes up amid the monotony of his task of wading through the unending trash which flows from the press, for a good book does not greet him every day. . . . . It marks the dawn of a new era in Education, and has no equal in the whole range of recent educational literature in the broadness of its views, the profound and exhaustive erudition of its treatment, the freshness of its style and thoughts, and general practical truthfulness. . . . . We cannot quote even the passages of pure gold which almost irresistibly tempt us, for they are so many, it would be impossible. . . . . The book should be read by every youth of the land.

From the *Post*, Boston, August 6, 1878.

In a recent book, entitled " Deterioration and Race Education," by Samuel Royce, the condition of the people and the industrial problem are very intelli-

5

gently presented. . . . . We are disposed to fully agree with the author in his
general conclusions. . . . .

From the *Advertiser*, Boston, August 10, 1878.

. . . . As an earnestly written book by a man who has given much consideration to the topics treated, it is worthy the consideration of educators, and, in
fact, of every class. . . . .

From the *Commonwealth*, Boston, July 20, 1878.

The life of the author of "Deterioration" has evidently been devoted to a
thorough and conscientious investigation of the great social problems of the
age, and the facts he has here brought together, painful and humiliating as
many of them are, cannot be ignored by those who have charge of the Education and government of the people, if they would save future history from repeating the horrors of the past. A book so faithful, true, and far-seeing is a
greater boon to the public than any single invention, however brilliant or
labor-saving, inasmuch as wisdom is better than wealth, and men and women
are of more importance than their physical environments. . . . .

From the *Record*, Philadelphia, August 30, 1878.

. . . . The author touches the root of the great problem of the day, in
attributing the alarming growth of crime and pauperism to the want of an educational system adapted to the needs of the lower classes. . . . . The book is
full of potent matter, set before the reader as a "plain, unvarnished tale," and
all the more valuable for its plainness. . . . . The tables of statistics have been
evidently prepared with great care, and present a startling picture of misery
and crime undreamed of, perhaps, even by those who are most interested in the
relief and improvement of the dangerous classes. Not the least useful part of
the book is a beautifully complete index, a model in its way, and one that we
hope to see imitated in future publications of this character.

From the *Mirror*, Manchester, N. H., August 28, 1878.

. . . . "Deterioration" is well-written and packed full of statistics. . . . .
The facts and arguments of the book are calculated to establish its proposition
of the deterioration of the human race, and the necessity of an ameliorating
Education. . . . . To any one interested in social, industrial, and educational
questions—and they are the most important of the time—this work will be
found valuable.

From the *Farmer's Cabinet*, Amherst, N. H., Aug. 13, 1878.

. . . . The author displays a thorough knowledge of his subject, and his conclusions, backed by a startling array of facts, deserve the most serious consideration of all. We commend it to a most earnest reading.

From the *Kansas Times*, September 1, 1878.

This book is really in the interest of humanity, and answers the great questions of the day. . . . . A book everybody should read.

6

From the *Medical Record*, Atlanta, Ga., September, 1878.

. . . . Whether viewed simply in its bearing upon our civil polity as a people, or from a moral and religious standpoint, this work can not fail to attract the interest of the enlightened reader. We bespeak for it a God-speed and a world-wide circulation.

From the *Educational Monthly*, Parkersburg, W.V., Sept., 1878.

" Deterioration " is well worth the thoughtful perusal of every citizen in the land who has at heart the welfare of his fellow-man. The author has collected a vast amount of interesting material, interspersed with valuable observations and suggestions, which are presented earnestly and with marked ability.

From the *Christian Leader*, Utica, N. Y., Sept. 21, 1878.

Truly a book every one, and especially all engaged in the work of Education, either in the home or in the school, should read ; a most excellent manual for the reformer ; a work crowded with startling facts and wise suggestions. . . . .

From the *Argus and Patriot*, Montpelier, Vt., Sept. 18, 1878.

. . . . The pauperization of the masses and their deterioration, together with the prevention of this double bane through the Kindergarten, the Developing School, the Manual Institute, and Race Education, and a variety of kindred subjects are treated in this volume with much research and matured reflection.

From the *Central School Journal*, Iowa, Sept., 1878.

. . . . " Deterioration " is strong in facts and the main subjects are ably discussed, and best presented to the reader by quoting largely from the author. . . . . We bespeak for Mr. Royce, from our readers, a careful and serious perusal of his work.

From the *Buffalo School Journal*, September, 1878.

This is decidedly the freshest book on the subject of Education which we have perused for many a day. . . . . According to the author our systems of culture lead to deterioration. . . . . It will pay to give this book a careful perusal ; the discussion of the subjects indicates much study and research, and the book is most excellent.

From the *New York Times*, September 22, 1878.

The views of this book are sound and true, and the expression of its ideas is so pithy and striking that they cannot fail to impress the reader. . . . . We agree with the author that there are deteriorating elements at work in modern civilization, and that it must be considered the greatest problem of our age how to counteract them. . . . . On the field of Education our time may fairly be described as a clamor between three different ideals, each presenting itself under various guises ; and the stand which Mr. Samuel Royce takes on this battle-field, in this confusion, is, that he rejects summarily the pretensions of all the combatants. His reason is very simple ; they all educate the mind only, and that which he will have educated is the man, by a process which will be able not only to counteract one of the greatest evils of the age—the deterioration through inheritance—but also to embrace the highest educational ideal which can be conceived—the bringing up of the individual for the sake of the race.

From the *San Francisco Sun and Chronicle*, Sept. 8, 1878.

Mr. Royce has given a book that is valuable, not because it is a plea for the Kindergarten, but for the thoughtful and earnest spirit that pervades it and for the vast amount of facts and inferences contained therein. The title-page bears this motto: "The sacredness of human life increases with civilization," and it forms the key-note of the volume. . . . . The book is filled with material interesting alike to the statistician, the educator, the moralist, and the metaphysical student.

From the *Iowa State Register*, Des Moines, Sept. 21, 1878.

. . . . There is much instruction in this volume to those who are looking ahead to the rising generation, and to their destiny; and all progressionists as well as those who are fearful of a recurring historical lapse in civilization, will find much mental food and many good suggestions in its pages.

From the *Christian Standard*, Cincinnati, O., Sept. 21, 1878.

. . . . The book is thoughtful and timely, and looks in a direction in which there can be but little doubt that our educators will be compelled to walk at no distant day.

From the *Universalist Quarterly*, Boston, October, 1878.

This is a book which we have long desired to see and to possess; a book which gathers up into one body the thousand facts concerning pauperism, insanity, disease, crime, and the physical as well as moral degradation and deterioration of the race, scattered through newspapers, magazines, social science publications, medical works, and Government statistical reports. Mr. Royce would have done a useful and important work, if he had only done this; but his treatment of them, the public use he had put them to, and the manner in which he had made them tell upon his argument for race Education, and the necessity of improving the condition of the dangerous and perishing classes, has added double to their value. . . . . We hope the work will be circulated far and wide, and read of all men and women. Every preacher should have it, and use it in his sermons, that he may be able to instruct his people in the aims and results of social science, and make practical his talk of Human Brotherhood.

From the *New Jerusalem Magazine*, Boston, Mass., October, 1878.

. . . . "Deterioration" is in many things a remarkable book. . . . . The writer has the evils of society much at heart, and does not leave us in doubt as to what will bring about relief. He ought to have the best wishes and support of all Christian people. . . . . The book will be of great use to parents and teachers, and a proper development of its principles will do much to remove the evils which it very graphically depicts.

8

portance, the first years of formative infancy, lived under the eye of the teacher of the infant school, are the most important for the correction of hereditary vicious tendencies of body and mind.

Disregarding in our classification of scholars their peculiar hereditary tendencies, what we teach can hardly be worth to the nation a hundred million dollars per annum, as it can only bring men in conflict with themselves to have intellectual convictions at variance with a feeble will, or an all powerful uncorrected hereditary vicious tendency. As opposite hereditary tendencies require opposite treatment, it is obvious that an indiscriminate subjection of all to the same method must do just as much harm as good.

As infancy is, or ought to be, mainly devoted to the physical and moral development of the child, to the eradication of hereditary vicious tendencies and to the development of virtuous tendencies, it becomes the more important to classify young scholars as much as practicable according to the unquestionable symptoms they present of one or another hereditary tendency. We can only repeat, this early application of the principle of heredity in infancy will relieve us of a later and more troublesome in penary institutions.

THE SACREDNESS OF HUMAN LIFE.

We are boldly told that the sacredness of human life is an unscientific proposition, and that the perishing of the masses is of little account. Then we confess we share the weakness and ignorance of men whose hearts yearn for the masses. Darwin knows and teaches better, and warns against the actual deterioration of our moral nature by neglecting to succor the weak and the feeble on account of future contigencies possibly arising from the law of the survival of the fittest.

What is to become of law, order, society and civilization if the sentiment is to become general that the sacredness of human life is but an empty phrase, and that power is all?

THE PHYSICIAN AND THE STATE.

We do believe, and that with Auguste Compte, that the sacredness of human life increases with civilization, and thereupon prognosticate that the medical profession is to occupy in the future a more influential position in the State. The knowledge, study and observation of man from the cradle to the grave, entitles it to such a position, and it will occupy it with the inevitable widening of sanitary science.

There is hardly a function of the State but rests in the last instance upon the law of human life. The school with its precious treasure of young life, the factory with all its bearings upon the life and health of operatives, the tenements of the poor, the architecture of houses and the regulation of streets and whole towns, and whatever bears on the access of light and air, the provision of pure water, wholesome food, drink, the prevention of epidemic and endemic diseases through a more perfect system of drainage, quarantine regulations, etc., hospitals, prisons, asylums, theaters, churches, and all other public institutions, call for the care of the physician whose influence in the State is indispensable if deterioration is to be timely checked wherever and whenever it appears, by declaring the law of human life supreme, and placing the health of the many before the wealth of the few and the State before the individual.

Whatever weakens, enslaves, or debases man, be it the Church, the State, literature, the stage, **or** any other power misdirected, deteriorates him ; but we must restrict our theme of deterioration to a few causes lying nearer our method of amelioration through early moral training and art industrial Education.

To the theoretical educator with man in his full stature before his eye, a self preserving race Educa-

16

tion may be very commonplace in its ends and means, but let him remember that ideal ends are best attained by practical workings, even as the spiritual ends of creation are secured by the rocky foundations of our solid globe.

We bring this chapter to a close because we will not fatigue by unnecessary figures showing the double rate of still births among the poor, the increased days of sickness accompanying hard work, the greater rate of fatality of disease among operatives, the effect of asylums, reformatories, barracks, prisons and poor-houses on the production of tubercles. Reversions to the primitive or normal type is certainly a great corrective of deterioration, and every atom, no doubt, is full of compensating balances. Thus the mental activity in a dense population, breaking the quiet favorable to the generative process, prevents over population. So Sadler has shown populations of 100, 100–150, 150–200, 200–250, 250–300, 300–350, 500–600 to the square mile, give to 100 marriages 420, 396, 390, 388, 378, 353, 331, 246 births, and with the rising density of population, the rate of birth to each marriage has steadily fallen from 4.65 in 1680 to 3.50 in 1805.

Neither can our corrective of early art industrial training be replaced by evening institutes, which prove in France, England, and among us, a failure, as after the exertion of a full day's work, a young man is, as a rule, unfit for studious application.

PART VIII.

THE REIGN OF TERROR.

THE SCHOOLS FURNISH MUTINY WITH CRIMSON ORATORY.

The prophecy of the seers of all ages that all shall sit down to the common feast will turn into a dangerous communistic madness if we do not bring up every child to bring with him to the feast his own basket.

Have we logic, and can we not reason, but eat on like the ox until the slaughter comes? Away, then, with the twaddle of the schools, that at best can but furnish mutiny with its crimson oratory, and let us without loss of time or dangerous delay furnish the land with kindergärten and schools of industrial arts, that every child may grow up rich in skill and art, and fill our houses with beauty, and they and all may have plenty.

Common schools without bread are no safeguard against communism and cause Bismarck many a sleepless night.

(363)

EDUCATION MUST INDIRECTLY GIVE WORK
TO ALL.

Carlyle utters a great truth when he says " the right to work is the right of the working man, and a man willing to work and unable to find it is, perhaps, the saddest sight under the sun." As life is an inalienable right, work, by which alone life can be sustained, must be an inalienable right.

But no more than Providence does cook for us our breakfast, can the State assign to every one of forty millions of people his daily work. The State, like nature, acts through general laws. It can and must so direct the Education of the people that every one who earnestly applies himself may be able to find his proper work and do it. If the State will not perform this, its proper function and duty, it is bound to perish.

THE CONFLICT IS NEARING.

The conflict is nearing and none takes it to heart. Ambition in Church and State blinds us to the coming destruction in which old men, women, and children will helplessly perish. It is a pity that our young civilization with its recent achievements in art and science should be brought through civil war to so speedy an end. But if the State and the Nation will not teach the children of the million to work and pray, or to keep their little hands busy and their young hearts pure, perish they should, and as sure as there is a God, perish they will.

A dangerous state is better laid bare and mended than made worse by cowardly concealment. There is a fire raging in the hearts of most of the poor against the rich that is impatiently waiting the opportunity for bursting forth and destroying the entire social fabric. The feudal slaves have never so hated the old barons—and we know how at times in France, England and Germany they fell with cruel intent upon their masters and families, bent upon their extermination.

We can hear it in every workmen's meeting, or read it in their organs: "The capitalist has no more brains than we have, and often not as much, he is unscrupulously cunning, and is enriched by our labor that produces all things." Working from the beginning of the year to the end, they witness with despair how wife and children drag out a miserable existence, while the leisurely capitalist has more than plenty, and this contrast works on their mind, until the world over there is mutiny, and naught but mutiny in the hearts of the workmen. And woe to all when the outbreak comes! We believe it to be in the economy of God that some men should have many more comforts than others.

But it is against the will of God that any man who is willing to work or does work should want decent shelter, bread or raiment, and yet this is only too often the case, and can not be much longer borne by the masses.

FUSILADES BRING NO SETTLEMENT.

We are told the slaughter of the Commune has taught the poor of all times a lesson.   But, pray, why should the hungry men of 1890 remember that lesson of 1870 any more than the poor of to-day, or even our students remember that of 1849 under Cavaignac in the streets of Paris, which was almost as fearful as that under Thiers in the streets of Versailles?   But, of course, as long as an evil is not removed, its upshot will be the same in every generation.   How can we expect the desperately poor to be wiser to day than they were twenty years ago, when men of study and leisure show that they are not, inasmuch as they have not found the true remedy for the evil.

To say there is no remedy, the masses must hunger, suffer, live and perish worse than the brute, is merely saying there is no God, the world is a hunting ground, and Nimrod is king.   But would not such a summary preached from the balcony to the howling mob below, make a ghastly bonfire of our large cities?

But you would shoot them down? But what of our love of God, religion, and civilization? To use the sword is to fall by the sword. A hungry man is a desperate man, and a man who sees wife and children hunger is more desperate still. A man who has nothing to lose, and to whom his life hangs like a burden is a dangerous thing.

But if the sword has no lessons for the starving man, neither has grammar school wisdom against communism formed in the brain out of the vapors rising from a hungry stomach.

Rely not upon your musket, it will snap like a reed in the hands of a mad people; your long ranged cannons will bend and twist in the hands of the million, and its folds will crush you like an anaconda; your children will look to you for help, and you will answer their fears with your own great overwhelming despair, like another Laocoon.

LOWERING THE STANDARD OF LIVING.

The press is vocal with recipes of 15 cent dinners for a family of six, as a solution of the social problem, as if Brassey had not settled it long ago by practical observation the world over, that labor is efficient exactly in proportion to the good and wholesome meat the laborer eats, that low wages mean slop for food, trash for work, and loss for profit, or what little gain there may be in it, hardly pays for endless asylums, the curses of the poor, and the wrath of heaven, and the retribution sure to come in a world of compensation.

Lowering the standard of living encourages early and reckless marriages, and the least reverse brings the ever half hungry population face to face with out and out starvation. An elevated standard of living leads to thrift, prudence and industry, while a poor fare leads to improvidence, idleness, drunkenness, grossness, over population, or to licentiousness and a systematic slaughtering of the nation in foundling houses.

GREAT ARMIES UPHOLD THE PEACE OF EUROPE.

It is true the common people live in the Old World on what is next to nothing, but also do they fall at every step a burden to public charities, and hence its tens of thousands of organized institutions, which are but a poorly disguised communism, kept up by four millions of soldiers taken away from the productive forces of the country, and to this system, filling the world with poverty, hunger and hate, we oppose a strictly industrious Education, which trains the people from infancy to win their own bread, and to help bear the burdens of a government which brings them up to a competency, without which neither liberty nor any other manly virtue is possible.

THE SOLUTION PROPER TRAINING AFFORDS.

Let us then educate the people from very infancy in all sorts of profitable work, full of art and fancy, and there will be plenty and to spare for all, and where there are cries of despair and cursing to day there will be joy and gratitude.

Ministers of religion have a great opportunity of doing good by advocating industrial Education as a providential means for improving the condition of mankind, while by swinging the police club in the pulpit and joining in ruffian threats against communists, they render religion as odious to the masses in the New World as it has already been made to them in the Old, especially when to mock man's hunger with admonitions when we refuse him bread, is at variance with the spirit and letter of religion. Let ministers remember the judgment that came down upon them in the days of the French revolution. The masses are trodden down and life is crushed out of them—the stone must be rolled off the grave before the people can be resurrected; let the clergy lend a helping hand in removing the load.

What no one can fail to discern, at least dimly, we are pronouncing clearly in declaring that diversity of employment, created by universal industrial art culture, is the only possible corrective of labor thrown upon the pavement by the invention of daily improved machinery, and nothing else will arrest the wheel of revolution which the madness of the hungry masses has already set in motion and which is sure to bring down with a mighty crash. the whole fabric of modern civilization, burying all beneath its ruins, and making all one scene of blood, fire, smoke and ashes, with here and there a widow wringing her hands and a poor orphan beside the wide grave of State and all.

Let not men say, After me the deluge, for all this is not to come after us, but in our own day. The air is full of imprecations and blood, and the madness of passion, and the shockingly terrible revolution of '89 has not sent before it such clear warning, nor when it did come did it find such quantities of explosive material as the revolution that for a great event is close upon us. The great specific care of the State must be so to educate the people that if our improved machinery can only employ one half of our population in the manufacture of common articles, there is still a demand for a variety of ornamental work that will keep all busy, and also the skill to furnish it.

The scope of every work and enterprise is at first but half understood, and so is the scope and work of the Education of the masses to day. We say it must rescue them from poverty, and while it preserves them it must save the State from revolution and ruin, build up commerce, favor alike labor and capital, encourage thrift, spread comfort, promote good will among all, and these and more blessings can only be secured through early training and art industrial culture.

Tell the financial world how to improve its investments by half a per cent, and, tiptoe, it will hail thee a great man. Study forty years how to improve the condition of the masses, and everybody shrugs his shoulders at your eureka as a matter of small concern. We grant the ten commandments and the sermon on the mount are as good a receipt for that as any other, but we want institutions carrying out their spirit. It would make bad blood if one half of the world knew how easy its condition could be improved by the other, if it was not for the cynical " What do I care? " Train little children to social morality, to art, industry, application and invention, to an intelligent, active and virtuous life, things a poor mother, driven by a thousand duties, cares and labors to madness and despair, cannot, absolutely cannot do, and you make the world an Eden. If we don't, it is because we won't. We care not for the world's weal or woe, and when, in the final catastrophe that is drawing near, our wives and children will perish with us unpitied, it will be God's will ratified by the angels in heaven.

SAVE THE MASSES THE CRY OF THE AGES.

Save the people was the cry of Moses, of the the prophets, of Jesus, and of heaven's spokesmen in every age and nation.

And verily the people need saving in this age of industrialism. With what satisfaction can the people answer to themselves the ever recurring questions, "What am I?" "What am I here for?" and "Where am I going?" by "I am a machine," "My business is to produce values mostly for others, and I am in the end, most likely, going with my family to the poor house"? Do not the heavens cloud themselves at this answer, the earth quake and tremble, and all nature groan with agony, and will not we, in the anguish of remorse, in vain seek a refuge from the judgment that will seek and find us out for the pride in which we have forgotton our own flesh and blood, and put God's own image below the state of the brute?

Labor must become a sacrament, the factory a sanctuary, and the operative an angel ministering to his own family as well as to the world.

THE SYMPTOMS OF THE TIMES.

Say not the danger is far off, for what is not genuine good feeling, but in face of the enemy yielded to intimidation, is spurned as weakness. But is the danger really far off? We are hardly justified in so thinking. This very day and hour, as we are writing these lines—and any day or hour these many years, here or in Europe—the voice coming from the people may teach us differently. Here are the resolutions passed with acclamation on the Boston Common by several thousand workingmen, May 25, 1879, after many speeches made in the same spirit :

THE RESOLUTIONS ADOPTED.

Whereas, The workingmen of California have been sorely oppressed under the scorpion lash of capital and the Coolie labor system, and the capitalists, monopolists and aristocrats have joined issue, lowering free American labor to the depths of misery and degradation, and the people had no alternative to redress their grievances except by the ballot or the bayonet, and they have wisely chosen the former to emancipate themselves from the outrageous, inhuman, barbarous and diabolical tyranny of capital and wealth ; and,

Whereas, The Declaration of Independence explicitly and emphatically states that, "when a long train of abuses. usurpations, pursuing invariably the same object, evinces a design to reduce them under absolute despotism, it is their right, and not only their right, but it is their duty, to throw off such government and to provide new guards for their future security ;" and,

Whereas, The authorities have grossly and deliberately abused the power reposed in them by the people, and made every legal effort to reduce them under absolute despotism by forcing upon them a system of coolie labor, which is diametrically opposed to the thirteenth, four-

teenth and fifteenth amendments to the Constitution of
the United States; therefore, be it

Resolved, That we, the working people of Boston, whose
interests are identical with those of the workingmen of
California, as well as all the other States of the Union, do
hereby, in mass meeting assembled, within the shadow of
Faneuil Hall, with Lexington and Concord on the one
hand, and Bunker Hill on the other, congratulate them
on their recent matchless political success, through the instrumentality of the ballot, over the grinding tyranny of
capital and wealth;

Resolved, That, as the Democratic thieves and Republican robbers have united in arrogating to themselves the
power of legislating for the land sharks and land pirates,
railroad monopolists and bonanza thieves in the interest
of the few to the detriment of the many, irrespective of
the welfare of the whole people;

Resolved, That it is the interest of the workingmen of
Massachusetts to emulate the example set by the workingmen of California, in ousting gilded fraud and substituting
honest toil to legislate in the interest of the whole people;

Resolved, That we recommend and urge the workingmen of Boston and the whole State to support and pat-
ronize only those papers that are conducted in the interest
of labor, and have for their object the abolition of wage
slavery, such as the *Irish World* the *Labor Standard,* and
the *Socialist,* all of which may be seen in the Boston Public Library reading room, and to withdraw their support
from such miserable papers as the *Boston Herald,* which
leaves a deposit of poison wherever it falls.

The general tenor of the addresses of the speakers
was in favor of the abolition of the wage system,
and one or two of the more enthusiastic ones recommended the changing of the Constitution of
Massachusetts, in order that it might conform to

their ideas of conducting matters and things in general. The police drill was stigmatized as a move of the capitalists to frighten the workingmen by a parade of military police, whom, one of the speakers said, reminded him of the *gendarmes* of France.

Even this July 4th about ten thousand workmen gathered under the red flag in New York, as many in Philadelphia, Chicago, and in other places, with the following mottoes on their transparencies, and made addresses and passed resolutions in the same spirit:

"Hunger and Crime are the Children of Capital."

"The Earth belongs to the Laborer."

"Down with White Slavery."

"Down with Republican Thieves and Democratic Robbers."

"Workingmen of all Countries unite Yourselves."

"No more Want for the Producers of all Wealth."

"Arouse, Wage Slaves!"

It is utter and culpable blindness when with such a gigantic propaganda among the millions of stout hearts and hands of the nation, we think that the present order of things can be long maintained; repression would be madness, to educate the masses to the highest degree of effectiveness is the only and best thing that can be done for labor, capital, and the State.

The Socialistic Labor Party is organized in about one hundred and twenty sections, covering all the States, and is under the lead of able men, who, smarting under the monstrous evils of our present system of Education, fire the hearts of their brothers against the present social system, or to use the language of their own platform :

We demand the resources of life—the means of production, public transportation and communication—(land, machinery, railroads, telegraph lines, canals, etc.)—become, as fast as practicable, the common property of the whole people, through the Government, thus to abolish the wages system, and substitute in its stead, co-operative production, with a just distribution of its rewards.

RIFLE DIET.

I am not unmindful of the remedies offered as : " Rifle diet," " Too much freedom," " Use force with these brutal creatures," " Hand grenades," " We want a monarchy," " We must create a class of land owners and small renters," " These vagrants must die."

But, pray, do not we make these vagrants, of whom many native Americans are just what our present Education has made them, and are not we to a great degree responsible for this evil ? This " rifle diet " and " hand grenades " declare God and his Church a lie. There is neither common sense nor religion in it, and France has used it to little purpose for fully a hundred years, only widening by it the breach between labor and capital.

We insist this selfish, rancorous spirit must be

supplanted, in rich as well as in poor, by the all powerful spirit of love and the Golden Rule, in which the whole population must be trained in the kindergärten of the nation. But such an Education, we are told, is costly. We say it is cheap at any cost if compared with the final outcome of the present Education, and such resolutions as we have even considered. The false prophets cry peace, but there is no peace, and the quicker we prepare against the worst by turning front and obeying the high mandate of heaven and of our own better humanity, the better for us.

The late labor riots which may be traced by a trail of destruction through seventeen States of the Union, the details of which fill a large volume, is evidence of the universal discontent and concert of action among workmen. Every strike is a rivulet, and they gather and roll on till they become unmanageable streams, and at last we shall have to confront a war, that having so often sent out its outposts, should not at all surprise us. England had last year six hundred strikes, the United States not less, and so everywhere else, and all this bitterness, the distillation of wrong long endured, when it shall vent itself in a cry that will rent heaven and earth, many shall think the end of all things has come.

We appeal to the common sense of the country,

is it sensible to tell the workmen, " Well, we shall better prepare ; we shall get an army of fifty thousand soldiers, and if you can't starve quietly, if you will not keep still when your wives and children cry for bread, we shall shoot you down " ? Is this a just way of meeting the laborers of the land ? what effect can it possibly have, and does it reach the evil and prevent its recurrence ?

Would it not be more sensible and just to look to it that we so educate the people that there be a greater demand for hand made goods, greater art industrial skill to supply the market, and above all, that the moral and spiritual training of the children be such, that rich as well as poor, and all helpfully stand by each other, each doing the best for the other ? Would not such a course have a better immediate effect, and would it not more touch the root of the evil than powder and ball, which, by the way, may be used with detrimental effect on both sides ?

THE INDICATIONS OF SOCIAL DISTURBANCE.

Discontent, jealousy and strife have never developed that bitterness between the peasant and the noble they have between the operative and the manufacturer. The breach that separates them, and the feeling that animates them are incompatible with a lasting peace. All indications point to social disturbance, which can only be averted by a firm and wise hand guided, in directing the Education of the masses, by a heart deeply exercised by care for the welfare of mankind and the peace of the world.

When the wise and moderate De Tocqueville declared, during a season of perfect calm, from his seat in the French Chambers, "That when the principles and beliefs of the masses so widely diverge from those upon which the government rests, revolution cannot but be imminent," all eyes stared at him in surprise, and what all took for madness, proved in less than six months the madness of the prophet, and Louis Philippe died a refugee on English soil.

We but repeat the language of De Tocqueville. We cannot long go on as we do, with the masses of the land preaching socialism, in a hundred assemblies gathering every week in so many towns all over the land.

There is neither justice nor common sense in men toiling and suffering want. It is incompatible with modern ideas or Christian civilization ; it is not in the nature of man to see wife and children suffer while he is producing wealth for others. The masses are getting restless to a degree that threatens the peace of the world. Dynastic wars are things of the past, so are national, and the most fearful ones—social wars are upon us. Attempts upon the peace of the world are thickening all around us, and can only be warded off by a radical change in the condition of the masses, which can only be effected by a radical change in their Education, which must hence aim at rendering their work effective.

THE GREAT FRENCH AND AMERICAN REVOLUTION.

At and previous to the great French Revolution of '89, the people were crushed with taxes, monopolies and rich corporations; riches and poverty, luxury and want, formed the striking contrast. The cry, "Bread, bread!" opened the revolution, in which all shared at first, to establish a constitutional government, but it soon became a war of the poor against the rich, a civil war, or a war of classes, and this calamity threatens to day the civilized world.

Our revolution of '76 was not for equality, there was no occasion for that—but for freedom from a foreign yoke, which being thrown off, we achieved peace.

THE STRUGGLE FOR EQUALITY, OR WAR OF CLASSES.

The present struggle is for equality, or rather against a most galling inequality, or ceaseless toil, misery and contempt—the inevitable lot of the poor—a war of passion and madness of the poor man against the rich, or of the workingman against the hated capitalist, with whom he imagines to have a long account of injuries to settle. And this passion is fanned by the mad hope of bettering himself by the general overthrow of the present social system, a doctrine preached by enthusiasts, fair apostles and workmen, and spreading with the discontent and misery of the poor.

The indifference of the rich against this madness spreading like fire among the poor all over the civilized world, is another madness, or rather a crime against their wives and children and the State, when justice to themselves as well as to the poor requires that they should so educate the poor as to afford them an opportunity for achieving an equality in point of means, necessary for securing life, liberty and the pursuit of happiness.

The war of classes, steadily approaching everywhere, is of a most dangerous nature, as the party defeated to day is sure to return to the fray to morrow, only the more exasperated, renewing the war thus over and again, until one or the other, and oftener both, parties are destroyed.

If at the great French Revolution there was great misery among the masses, and hence great discontent, coupled with haughty contempt among the rich and luxuriant, if it was an age of great intellectual activity, of cutting loose from all authority in matters of Church, State and social customs, if it was a new era for asserting the rights of man and reorganizing human society, every one of these features, only intensified, marks the age we live in, and the symptoms of a similar storm approaching may be seen everywhere.

AN INSTRUCTIVE CHAPTER OF SOCIAL WAR.

We would warn against conjuring up the demon of social war, the most tyrannical and fearful, which has neither heart, entrails, nor ear for the cries of its victims.

Think on 1792! what bloody intrigues and slaughter of victims crowded into innumerable prisons, old men, women and children. The wisest and the best dispatched under most cruel mockery and the reproach that they were wretches, unworthy the name of man.

Inhuman cruelty spread from town to town, and from province to province, until fury seized upon all, and women became tigers and men devils, and all the land, its wealth and its monuments of art and industry, became the prey of revolutionary flames, and one wide grave swallowed all.

We may well tremble at the name of *social revolution*, in which authority is often in the hands of most abandoned men.

There is not a chapter in history the reading of which is more calculated to stop us in our thoughtless rushing on toward a fearful war of classes than that of the French revolution.

"Debtors," says an eye witness, speaking of the Reign of Terror, "paid their debts by denouncing their creditors; criminals punished by the law denounced their prosecutors and judges; those who had no places denounced those who had; heirs denounced those whose fortunes would descend to them; husbands found it a commodious way of getting rid of their wives, and children denounced their parents."

Think on hired bands of assassins commissioned by a revolutionary authority to penetrate at midnight into your domicile and drag you, your wife and children thence to a dungeon. Think on these assassins maddened with wine, dispatch hundreds of victims whose crime is gold, or virtue, purer even than that, after a mock trial of a few brief moments, hacking them down by hap hazard sabre strokes at the ghastly light of a revolutionary torch. Think on invalids being refused the privilege of being dispatched upon their sick bed, but dragged from their houses and murdered upon the pavement.

What a sight! the courts of the prisons streaming with blood and strewn with the limbs of the murdered victims.

Think on the twenty thousand victims at one time in the prisons of Paris, and over a hundred thousand in the prisons of France ; of course, we refer to revolutionary victims, many heaped pell mell upon rotten straw, exposed to vermin, to rats and mice, which devoured even the very shoes upon their feet.

Think on upward of twelve thousand men and women butchered in the prisons of Paris in the great September slaughter of '92, organized by Danton, and these horrors were, if possible, surpassed in the provinces.

Think on mistakes often made and treated with levity, by which one man was murdered for another, one brother for another, the father for the son, and the mother for the daughter ; thus was sport made of human life.

Young females far advanced in pregnancy ; others who had just become mothers, in a state of weakness and paleness ; others distracted because their children had been torn from their breasts, were daily and nightly precipitated into dungeons.

They were dragged from prison to prison, their hands loaded with irons. Some of them had collars around their necks ; some of them fainted on their entrance, and were carried in the arms of jailors, who laughed at their terrors ; others wept.

The bolts of the prisons were opening and shutting night and day, as many as sixty persons left one day for the scaffold, and the next as many as a hundred.

Entire generations were extirpated in one day. The venerable Malesherbes, venerated all over Europe for his wisdom and virtue, upward of eighty years, was dragged to the scaffold at the head of his whole family. He perished, together with his sister, his daughter, and his son in law, and the daughter and son in law of his daughter.

Fourteen young girls of Verdun were led out together to the scaffold. They disappeared together under the knife of the guillotine. Twenty women from Poicton, the greater part of whom were peasant girls, were also butchered together.

The piercing cries of maternal despair of one of these unfortunate women when the child just sucking was torn from her breast by the executioner, to finish her, were most dreadful. Several of the others died in the cart on the way to the scaffold, but their dead bodies were guillotined.

Think on a father answering to the call of the name of his son, and dying for him.

Think on wives, dying from choice with their husbands, whose death they would not survive, and even so daughters preferring to die with their fathers.

17

Think on poor waiting maids perishing by noble devotion with their innocent mistresses.

Think on old men bowed under the weight of years and loaded with honors for their achievements in art, science and philosophy, condemned by bloody tribunals and butchered by assassins.

Think on charming women, broken hearted mothers, sweet and innocent virgins, ruthlessly murdered by these same revolutionary committees and worthless vagabonds.

Think on the forty-five magistrates of the Parliament of Paris, the thirty-three of the Parliament of Toulouse, or thirty revenue officers, or twenty-five of the first manufacturers of Sedan led forth in gangs to the scaffold.

Think on the generals of the victorious armies sent out against La Vendee, led to the scaffold, like droves of cattle to the slaughter house. Not a single complaint issued from their mouths; they advanced in silence and seemed to avoid looking up toward heaven, lest their countenances should express too much indignation. Men of all colors and principles have thus been launched forward to the scaffold in *batches*.

Think on Bailly, loaded with the honors of a patriot and philosopher, doomed to suffer the most cruel torments, and suffering death in the midst of ignominy, like another Socrates. They spat upon

him, gave him furious blows, in spite of the remon-
strances of his executioner. He was literally covered with mud, and was kept in tortures for three
hours while his scaffold was being erected amidst a
heap of dirt and filth, his hands tied behind his
back, he bore quietly the taunts and outrages of
the multitudes. A chill rain falling down in tor-
rents, he answered calmly to a man who tauntingly
said to him, " You tremble, Bailly," " It is with
cold, my friend."

Think on the slaughter at Nantes. Fusilading
was too unexpeditious a method of butchering
men, massing men and dispatching them with grape
shot satisfied the commissioner no more, he drowned
them, therefore, by the ship load, and thus emptied
five thousand persons into the waves of the Loire.

Think on Lyons, where the executioner pulled
down whole streets by the aid of eight hundred men
ordered from Paris. This destruction was not swift
enough, and so whole portions of the city were un-
dermined and blown up.

Think on the hundreds of thousands slaughtered
in the Vendee, on the millions that perished during
the revolution ; but neither the heart nor the imagination of man is vast enough to realize the agonies
of such numbers ; we may speak of them, but we
hardly know what we say, only individual sufferings touch us, and so we would name Madame

Roland, Madame Desmulines and Charlotte Corday as types of noble women who like them perished by the thousand.

Think on the Convention, the Commune, the Committee of Safety, the Dantons, La Croix, Marats and Robespierre!

Let none say the days of '92 can never again return. Have not the streets of Paris been the scene of carnage in 1848? We thought then Cavaignac had forever throttled the red specter, but we have seen it has risen under the Commune to more fearful proportions! And it will again. Beelzebub can not be thrown out by Beelzebub. Children in whose eyes we see the heavens open and God coming to the race, they alone can put the monster to rest—by right training preserve the child in every one of us, children we must become, and we will only be the wiser for this childhood which is of heaven.

We claim exemption from fanaticism (?) and boast upon our common sense and moderation. But have we so soon forgotton the scenes of horror of our own civil war?

A half a million of brothers falling by each other's hand! What a world of misery and of crime is contained in this line. Think of Libby prison and Andersonville! Thousands and tens of thousands of valiant men, once the pride of their country, starved and thinned down to caricatures of what they once were, hardly recognized by their own mothers, to whom they were returned incurable idiots.

Is it then not criminally jeopardizing our families, the State, and all we hold dear, if by our neglect, the masses are through misery drifting into a state of mind which makes civil war inevitable at no distant day?

WE ARE LIABLE TO THE SAME EXCESSES.

No nation is free from the dangers of fanatacism in times of excitement, in which bloody scenes have been enacted in England, Germany, Poland, and everywhere else.

It was the great and rare devotion to humanity in the days of the French Revolution more than anything else that kindled that enthusiasm which ended in a popular fury which knew no bounds, or in real madness, and this noble but dangerous enthusiasm is as operative to day as ever, and so are the other elements we have seen to have been among the active causes of the great French Revolution, only that time has added new fuel, and the massess know better their power, and how to organize it to victory.

De Tocqueville, speaking of the French Revolution says, " It was a period of generosity, of enthusiasm, of manliness, of greatness—a period of immortal glory upon which men will look back with admiration and respect when all who witnessed it, and we who follow them, shall have long since passed away."

The same author says the enthusiasm of the refined classes coalescing with the roughness of the masses caused the shameful excesses of the French Revolution; what then may we expect from the civil wars close upon us, when the great masses will be entirely under the lead or control of their own men, swayed as they are by the axiom, " By workmen the workmen must be freed "?

But justice requires us to remark, in times of great excitement all men, and even the best, are liable to excesses. If under Robespierre a hundred thousand victims crowded the prisons of France, the Thermidorians kept there twenty-five ·thousand, and the reactionaries or gentlemen were just as active in murdering the patriots as the Jacobins were in murdering the aristocrats. The patriots may at least claim indulgence on account of the heat of passion, or the great public danger that required the arousing of the energies of the nation to repel foreign invasion. But what excuse was there for the timid and decent men who heaped murder upon murder after all danger was over, and the conscience of the nation had been aroused against bloody excesses within?

Like the French Revolution no civil war can be brought to a termination until a half a dozen of parties are overthrown one by another, a process often ending in the disintegration of the nation, and which, therefore, should not be provoked.

OUR CRIMINAL INDIFFERENCE.

Incessant toil, small wages, seeking foreign markets, and the club or ball and powder for the masses, if they dare as much as to mutter, is the policy of the industrial Pharisees, who would exterminate the race to build up fortunes for themselves, as the kings of Egypt did to raise themselves pyramids, which make us to day wonder and shudder. Not the masses, but those who, instead of making their condition bearable, talk of clubbing and shooting them down like dogs, threaten the peace of the world. Once the feudal barons, indignant at the pestiferous vermin of slaves that dared oppose their will, determined to slay them, later kings and emperors, astonished at the insolence of citizens, thought the rebels must be shot down, and to day modern capitalists think the laboring masses must be clubbed down for objecting to see their half famished families perish in filth.

Of course, baron, king, slaveholder and capitalist equally muzzled the Church, declared themselves lords of the earth and of God's children, whom they all equally oppressed.

But if scattered peasants would not stand oppression from old illustrious families for ages in possession of the land, is it likely that a versatile city population will stand to be despised and starved by an upshot of their own making, and that in an age that worships at the altars of the gods of liberty and equality?

Is there nothing that will open the eyes of our leaders, and are we doomed to perish in a civil war that will drench the soil in the blood of innocent men, women and children?

"Already," has long ago warned us, an observer of the times, "we have a revolution slumbering, but gathering power in all our cities, and still we pursue our way with intrepid stupidity, dreaming of Eden in the very midst of a *reign of terror.*"

Another author says, "All the large cities may become, one day or another, the theater of events as tragic as those which have nearly caused the total ruin of Paris." The danger of communism and a reign of terror are acknowledged, and what remedy is offered? Armies! Yes, to eat us up and make us all slaves. But our soldiers are no more the brutes they once were, and will not consent to engage in the trade of fratricides for a quarter of a dollar a day, for verily they cannot be far behind Cossacks who are beginning to fraternize with the people they are called upon to shoot down.

Some stupidly advise us to rely solely upon teaching the people a conservative social philosophy. To such saviours, we would say with Macaulay, " The *rich* man who vindicates the rights of property, should seem very inconclusive to the *poor* man who hears his children cry for bread."

And honest religion will not insult the poor man by addressing him, unless it can first point out to him the way of winning his daily bread.

THE LIBERATION OF THE MASSES THE GIST OF HISTORY.

We cannot and we will not believe that it is the will of God that the great mass of mankind shall live in misery. Yea, if we know and believe anything, we know and believe that it is not the will of God that as much as one of his children should perish. Baron, king, emperor, slave holder and capitalist alike forget the difference between divine sufferance and the will of God. No, no, bitter poverty and slavery are not the will of God, ' nor low, contemptible, torturing cares ; the want of intellectual cultivation—aye, even of mere animal enjoyments ; the self contempt, which is but the echo of the world's verdict—all these, perpetu-

17*

ated from generation to generation, are able at last
to vulgarize and deteriorate the type of the species; and the worst of it is that the soul is vul-
garized in the long run as well as the body.' Let
us not insult Deity; this is the work of man and
not of God. Providence is moving on with unfal-
tering step to blot out the brutalizing system that
has long enough cursed the race, and every century
is a step forward, and they are blind who imagine
they can stop the onward march of history that
more and more lifts up the masses from their misery
and degradation, neither the club of the police, nor
all the powder and iron in the world can do it, for
there is something stronger than that and than
everything else—truth, justice, mercy, humanity,
aye, with bended knee and a humble mind we dare
utter it—*the will of God.* " *Will not one French
Revolution and Reign of Terror suffice us, but must
there be two?   There will be two if needed; there
will be twenty if needed; there will be just as many
as are needed."   We know the blackness of those
days, but with Carlyle we say,* " *God's will must be
done, and if it takes twenty Reigns of Terror."
But why not do the will of God without any?*

THE MASSES MUST SHARE OUR BLESSINGS.

And, pray, what is the remedy? The masses
must be made to participate in all the blessings of

an advanced civilization. And how? By an Education that is not a dead letter and a mockery, but one that shall bless them in body and in soul, sufficiently indicated in these pages, and one that is in perfect harmony with the spirit of the age and the interests of mankind.

Distribution is to day the monopoly of railroad companies, light that of gas companies, fuel that of coal companies, and so everything else is getting into fewer and fewer hands, what else remains for the masses if they are not to drift into a perfect slavery to the few, but to be trained by art industry, to stamp the products of their hand with an individuality altogether their own, and of which nothing can rob them?

Do we want peace? Let us see to it that the masses be put in a position in which they may have a chance for acquiring property. "Who," says Sir T. More, "quarrel more than beggars? Who does more earnestly long for a change than he that is uneasy in his present circumstances? And who run to create confusions with so desperate a boldness as those who, having nothing to lose, hope to gain by them?"

Do we want thrift? Let us see to it that the masses be put in a position in which they may have a chance for acquiring property. As the proverb says, "Make a man the owner of a bare rock, and he will soon make of it a garden; rent him a garden, and he will soon make of it a desert." Do we want cleanliness, virtue, wisdom and self respect? Let us see to it that they may have a chance for acquiring property, for as a rule, a man who is in hopeless poverty with nothing to lose and nothing to gain, with nobody to care about him, will in his turn care for nobody and nothing, but will be a mean, vicious, and dangerous man.

Or, are these truisms which everybody knows and tramples upon? And is Sir James Mackintosh right when he said, " Whatever excellence, whatever freedom is discoverable in governments, has been infused into them by the shock of a revolution, and their subsequent progress has only been the accumulation of abuse . . . . as the natural operation of tranquillity is to strengthen all those who are interested in perpetuating abuse " ?

Alas, men act as if they expected the masses to tear from their brow their Maker's image, to put there the brand of slavery. But by what right? Never, never! not if all the woods were made into police clubs, and Iron Mountain were forged into bayonets! These words may be taken to day as tirades—they will gather meaning with the coming Reign of Terror announcing its approach in the flaming horizon.

THE STRUGGLE FOR HUMAN EMANCIPATION.

The great revolution in the midst of which we are living is unnoticed by small men who have no capacity for measuring great moral events and tendencies. The salvation of the masses is accomplishing itself, and God liveth and worketh in our midst.

The masses are putting on the armor. They are organizing societies grappling with the life problem of the age—their final emancipation.

Gentlemen may see in them mean, miserable drudges. But an immense moral and intellectual activity is working out in them one of the most stupendous purposes of Providence—the redemption of the world.

The agonies, the sufferings, the patience, the steadiness, the self control with which the great masses of mankind have entered upon the struggle of human emancipation, stamps it the most divine act of the centuries.

The details of this great movement of the age lie beyond the scope of our work. There are five volumes before us giving sketches of secret societies which govern the world unseen ; just as many volumes are before us devoted to the work and spread of the trade unions ; here are four volumes, a history of the means and efforts of the maↄses in their struggle for emancipation, and there is another volume, containing a history and description of the labor press devoted to the emancipation of the masses.

THE INTERNATIONAL.

We cannot pass without mentioning the *International*, an organization as logical, as complete, and as effective as any that ever influenced the destiny of mankind, and we challenge contradiction when we say that no human organization has ever, in so short a time, permeated the great masses with principles of utmost reach as the International.

It has educated the masses and familiarized them with ideas which will act as a powerful ferment long after the International will have ceased to exist as an organization. It has at one time numbered as many as three million of members, organized under the General Council of the International Association of Workingmen in every State and country throughout the wide world, and has proved stronger than the most wary and powerful governments it has succeeded to invade and undermine.

The following programme of the questions which the General Council of London addressed to all the sections to be considered at the Congress of Geneva, may indicate the nature and grasp of the ideas spread by this powerful organization :

" *First.* Organization of the International Association; its ends; its means of action.

" *Second.* Workingmen's Societies; their past, their present, their future; stoppage; strikes, means of remedying them; primary and professional instruction.

" *Third.* Work of women and children in factories, from a moral and sanitary point of view.

" *Fourth.* Reduction of working hours; its end, bearing, moral consequences; *obligation of labor for all.*

" *Fifth.* Association; its principles, its application; co-operation as distinguished from association proper.

" *Sixth.* *Relations of capital and labor ;* foreign competition; treaties of commerce.

" *Seventh.* Direct and indirect taxes.

" *Eighth.* International institutions; mutual credit, paper money, weights, measures, coin and language.

" *Ninth.* Necessity of abolishing the Russian influence in Europe by the application of the principle of the right of the people to arrange for themselves, and the re-constitution of Poland upon democratic and social bases.

" *Tenth.* *Standing armies* in their relations with production.

" *Eleventh.* Religious ideas; their influence upon the social, political and intellectual movement.

" *Twelfth.* Establishment of a society for mutual help; aid, moral and material, given to the orphans of the Association.

THE GREAT PROPAGANDA.

Underestimate your opponent and you are beaten. The forces engaged in the emancipation of the masses are of a truly gigantic nature.

Throughout the wide world workingmen are holding regular meetings in which their interests are ably discussed in a socialistic spirit by earnest,

honest, able and well read men of their own order. They hold State, national and international
conventions. They send out speakers, and make
propaganda by the distribution of pamphlets. In
politics they have learned to avoid being used as
tools by either of the parties of the day, pursuing
but one aim, their own elevation. Their publications, discussions and platforms show a vigor and
a logical sequence arresting the attention of any
earnest thinker, who knows that the convictions
of the masses have a greater share in the formation
of the future laws and government of the land than
any or all the political tricks of the hour.

THE CALL FOR THE EMANCIPATION OF THE MASSES.

We would arouse the attention of thinking men
to the struggle for emancipation among the working men. Any self satisfied *gentleman* who rails at
the expression of *emancipation* we would advise to
try and feed, shelter aud clothe his family in Boston, Chicago, New York or St. Louis, pay the
doctor and undertaker—whose bills swell under
such a regime—lay by for slack times and his
orphans, as his days will be neither sweet nor many,
and all this besides many other little family expenses, with a dollar and a half a day, and many,
many a day with nothing at all to do. Yes, such a

life, misery and degradation, call for emancipation, which is coming as sure as there is a God, and as truth and justice are not without a meaning. It is best for us to be honest and face the truth.

The great enigma of the world's history lies at last open before us—it is the elevation of man above the level of brutality, misery and crime. It is the struggle of the kingdom of heaven against all that is dragging the race downward. It is the struggle for the deliverance of the masses from the one man power of king or monopolist, which degrades them into a mere means, chattel or instrument for the sake of building up some high potentate or colossal fortune. It is the struggle for the establishment of a universal democratic republic, with reason, industry, justice and humanity for its foundations. God, who rules the stars in their orbs, controls the mind and will of man, and will establish His kingdom on earth as He has in the heavens.

Once the strong and the cunning seized upon the soil, and freedom seemed to have forever disappeared from the face of the earth. To day monopoly has seized upon capital, the modern instrument of labor. But the spirit that is in man is not to be crushed, and like the Phœnix, the masses rise young and strong from their ashes, and build themselves a future in which hardly the names of their oppressors shall be remembered.

COMMUNISM BECOMING A RELIGIOUS FANATICISM.

Poor men love their wives and children as well as other men do, and see them pine, sicken and die in misery much before their day.   They do, most assuredly, realize their degradation, and believe the hour will come which will bring their emancipation. Every workman says, " We cannot, and we will not stand this slavery much longer."   And the way they pursue to shake off this yoke is most wise, most heroic, and most God like.   They are quietly making propaganda among themselves these many years; they are converting the doctrines of socialism into articles of belief; they are making communism a religion, a faith in which, and by which their wives and children shall live again.   And we think that we will break the power of God's believing and suffering children with a few clubs and muskets.   Let us awake from our infatuation which is as great as the peril by which we are menaced.

Our own selfish little schemes blind us to the eternal powers which play around us, and by which we will ultimately be crushed.   To us humanity is not here to be redeemed, but to work for us, and we are false to the gospel of man's redemption.

OIIN STUART MILL ON COMMUNISM.

What wonder communism is making progress ! John Stuart Mill says in his great work on Politi

cal Economy, " If the choice were to be made between *communism* with all its chances, and the
present state of society with all its sufferings and
injustices; if the institution of private property
necessarily carried with it as a consequence, that
the produce of labor should be apportioned as we
now see it, *almost in an inverse ratio to the labor*
—the largest portions to those who have never
worked at all, the next largest to those whose work
is almost nominal, and so in a descending scale, the
remuneration dwindling as the work grows harder
and more disagreeable, until the most fatiguing and
exhaustive bodily labor cannot count with cer-
tainty on being able to earn even the necessaries of
life ; if this or communism were the alternative, all
the difficulties great or small of communism, would
be but as dust in the balance."

UNIVERSAL COMPETENCY DISARMS COMMUNISM.

Our abrogation of property in man is but formal,
and the difference between once and now is, that
*while the slave could not acquire property because he
was himself the legal property of somebody else, the
poor becomes himself the real property of somebody
else, because he cannot acquire property.*

We have, therefore, either to establish communism in order that all men may have the means of
living indispensable to personal independence, and

render all accumulation of private property impossible, or leaving the rights of property as they are, we must by a proper Education bestow upon all men the power of acquiring and accumulating property.

PROPERTY INSEPARABLE FROM HUMAN NATURE.

We most summarily object to communism which, under the cover of giving property to all, destroys individual property in the end altogether, by giving the property of all to the State, while the essential condition of personal liberty is the right of man freely to dispose over things or property.

Our whole life is a process of interchange between ourselves, and that which is not ourselves; our every breath is sustained by the atmospheric ocean in which we are submersed, and the imponderable forces of the universe, like heaven's angels, come and go, and there would be neither life nor warmth without them in the clod.

This never ending interchange between the within and the without—the very process of life, is the source of the conception of subject and object, from which springs the distinction between mine and thine already observable in early childhood. These most elementary principles of human consciousness naturally enter into the formation of our mental activities, and most of all into our social virtues, which have often a direct relation to property, which brings out their whole force and individuality. Blot out the distinction of mine and thine, and with it the conception of property, and honesty, justice, equity, love, mercy, generosity, benevolence, liberality, prudence, wisdom, temperance, forethought, thrift, economy and a thousand other distinctions lose half their meaning, and hence property, its acquisition and its uses are a school of virtue to ninety-nine men in every hundred.

There was a time when the conception of property was undeveloped, and man's property in himself was a disputable point. Three hundred thousand Greeks could then be kept in bondage by the other ten thousand, and a million of subjects could then be manacled by one Asiatic despot. To day men know they hold their title to themselves from God, and the whole world is not strong enough to hold one man in bondage.

GENERAL POVERTY ASSISTS COMMUNISM.

The conception of property is deepening. Man is beginning to feel that he expands, grows, and develops with property, and that he is scarcely half a man without it, and that the republic must become something else than a motley crew of beggars of whom here and there a few have more than plenty, without, of course, the ability of developing the virtues only a free nation can, and who, therefore, in their souls are but beggarly men like the rest.

Are we who fight communism, the declared enemy of property, to oppose this sound instinct for possession in the people? Never! It is the only valid title by which we defend what we hold as property, and the people shall get it too, but how?

GENERAL EFFECTIVENESS THROUGH INDUSTRIAL EDUCATION.

The products of labor may not be distributed with exact justice. A few dollars, may, perhaps, and most probably are unjustly withheld from each laborer to enrich some capitalists. Still, wrangling over methods of distribution can have no practical result. For, suppose we add ten to twenty per cent. to the wages of the poor man, his condition would hardly be perceptibly improved. But raise the laborer in point of art, skill, industry, energy and morals, so as to improve him most materially as an artizan and as a man, and his income is soon doubled and quadrupled, and hence, to secure to every man his share in property as well as in all the other blessings of civilization the kindergarten system must be honestly carried through every school and grade, and Race Education must arm men for the efficient performance of their part in life, and they will achieve each a name and distinction in addition to property and enjoyment. As we believe men will not always be content to pass as nondescript masses, but will stand out each by himself like a monument, for some signal service or other rendered humanity in the enlargement of science, art, or industry.

We are no contemners of men and institutions. History is not without a meaning. Be it whatever it may, it hides a great future, of which it is the promise. The universal deep belief in the work and office of Education is worth a thousand years of human life and struggle, even if it take another thousand years to give us the right Education.

The soil that rears to day the forest with all the life which peoples it was once all barren rock. Neither will our Education always be the sterile thing it is to day. Already we are turning from words to things, one step more, and from things we shall move on to man.

Not scholars, but men we want, and men the school shall make. We do not want educators talking five hours a day into our children, but we do want them to live, work, and converse ten hours a day with them; this, and nothing else is Education, and we would not give a penny for any other.

This Education costs time, labor and money, we know. But as men increase, and their affairs get entangled, they have under the old system only got along by the expenditure of the treasures of empires upon armies reared for the work of death and destruction. Such is the experience of the world. These treasures we must spend in the new era upon rearing the great masses for life and its work, and for God and humanity.

Men of large interests trembling for their security, think they have already an army of fifty thousand soldiers, and are preparing for making it a hundred thousand, and for doubling it with every decennial, until they bring it up to a half a million. Let it be known, the game is understood, and that the people will not vote a dollar for the army, and we will get an Education deserving the name. It is wrong to plunder the rich, and it is not less so to murder the poor. You want security, educate the masses.

How many a time must we repeat it, it takes ten men to make a pin, more than ten trades the family and its work embrace, and woman, unaided, is to do it all, and educate or make man beside. This is cruel mockery, overtasking woman and underrating man. Oh, let the school do its work, and grant some rest to the unaided mothers of the masses, who, cruelly tied down to their work and

their children do wither by inches, the wronged
and forgotten saints of the race who perish for
want of opportunity to take a breath of fresh air,
or to revive at the sight of a green twig or blade
of grass.

Yes, the world has learned to believe in Education, for a purpose;. it will get it, and the great
and good of the race are but the prophecy of what
it will make of each and all of us. And why not? Is
not all nature, the great and beautiful in star, flower,
rainbow, in mountain, river, forest, or ocean, and
above all, in the human heart and mind, rich beyond nature, is not all this, and even more, the
very Infinite at our command? But, alas, all this we
shut off to day and open the book, the dead letter
of which killeth.

The school must be the miniature of life and the
world, something that can be continued, but not
that must be laid aside or forgotten when we enter
upon our career. Cramming the mind every minute of time with the thoughts of all ages may have
a more ideal look; but, what we want is that the
knowledge of the world put on flesh and bone; let
this be done, and we shall become a new humanity,
with new and better thoughts than the world has
yet known.

Great humanity, what a picture! many wander-
ing about with neither hope nor ambition, nor a

trace of the divine effigy in them, preying upon all and preyed upon by all. There is relief in turning to a minority of men, of greatest skill and industry, to them the world is all right. Between these two extremes God struggles in the masses for the race, great sufferings have shorn them of their strength, but their hands are fairly upon the pillars of the building, which in their blindness they mean to bring down with them dying, some by getting entire possession of the political machine, and others by co-operating with their communistic brothers of Paris, the nihilists of Russia, or the New York mob during the war of the rebellion, or the hungry stalwarts of Pittsburg, Chicago, St. Louis, and every where else the world over.

Here are palatial mansions with leisure for reflection; alas, the occupants are hungering for power and possession, they content themselves to build for great humanity jails, poor-houses and asylums which dole out dry crumbs of bread seasoned with the tears hard treatment wrings out of dull eyes, while the less charitable, putting their own construction upon Malthus and Darwin, say, the gutters are good enough for the brats; their mother hags best betake themselves to the garret until the coroner ferret them out, and a well fed soldiery will soon get even with its lean brothers.

There is nothing in the blue dome of heaven

above or in the green earth beneath, there is nothing that chirps in the air, or cuts the sea, or in the
laughing valley, or upon the top of high mountains
which proclaims a God who meant the world of
mankind to be such as we find it to-day.

What is more plentiful than fresh air? Men
for thousands of years built homes from which they
were at the greatest trouble to keep out the breezes
of heaven, and generation after generation was
swept away by the pest, until the genius of the
nineteenth century gave birth to hygiene, which
rediscovered to us the air that plays all around us,
and said, lo! here it is, take plenty of it, and the
more the better.

It is with our social health the same. God never
made the well being of his creatures dependent
upon things which have to be fetched down from
heaven, or brought up from the sea or the bowels
of the earth. The conditions of our well-being are
within us and around us. Honesty, skill, and industry always paid. Throw open the kindergarten
and the industrial school to every mother's child,
and with the heart pure and the hand skillful and
ready, humanity will be as gladsome as laughing
nature is.

There is no other alternative; either a more effective Education must enable the masses to get by
increased energy and higher forms of productive-

ness a greater share of the comforts and blessings of civilization, and thus prove that the degradation of the masses is not the inseparable attendant of the present social order, or the International is right and the present system of society must be overturned, which it will if we do not energetically seize upon the first alternative, and work it out successfully, which we believe will be accomplished.

THE AGE AND ITS LITERATURE.

If the literature of every age is the copy of the times and our classic period of literature, as Taine shows, is the reflex of the life, splendor, pageantry, and sparkling wit of the court, our democratic literature will be the copy of the life of the masses; its name may be 'conflict,' and of the style of the 'Miserables,' and our government will then be all spasms of revolt and fusilades; or its name may be 'reconciliation,' from the union of all classes, and the blending of art and industry, and, under the inspiration of love, energy, and beauty, the future may have again its Bacons, Shakespeares, and Newtons, and all the land may be peace and happiness.

THIS IS NO WAR OF CLUBS AND PISTOLS.

Old kings, followed by all the dogs of war, have been laid prostrate by Providence, leading in the onward march of humanity, and we are made to believe that God and humanity are in the end to succumb before the Stock Exchange and its club-armed minions. Fool, hast thou not yet learned that this is no war of clubs or pistols, but that we are in the thickest of the fight between the powers of the air, led on by the father of lies, and the host of heaven led on by God, who has girded Himself for the fray like a man of war, and dost thou mean to meet Him with clubs? Art thou blind to the stakes, and dost thou not know that truth and falsehood, justice and tyranny, all heaven and all hell are measuring their forces, and that the children of God are upheld in this fearful combat by the knowledge, that *God alone can remain victor?* But thou canst see naught but clubs as wooden as thine own head. Well, our God is a consuming fire, and will eat them up as a flame consumes dry stubble.

THE NEW ASPECT OF REVOLUTIONS.

Revolution assumes a new aspect on our globe. Knit together by the iron sinews of a great railroad system, and covered with a telegraphic network, endowing it, as it were, with a nervous system and one great brain, making the whole race one man, the solidarity of mankind is turned into a fact, for good or for evil. Hence the agonies of the poor and oppressed of all the earth become the agonies of each, whose force and resistance becomes intensified and multiplied by the force and resistance of all, and revolutions become universal and irresistible. When the judgment comes in one place it will come in all. A revolution in Paris or London will mean revolution in New York and in St. Petersburgh, and the combustible matter here will be ignited by the lightning flash anywhere. It behoves, therefore, governments to prevent public dangers through a wise and effective Education.

THE WRONGS OF THE POOR.

Every page, almost, of our work teems with the wrongs of the poor, which are only tolerated by the sufferance of God, like other forms of evil doing, but we are deaf to the cry of the poor, and their miseries have to be as continually thrust upon our attention as they are incessantly inflicted upon them. Here is a late picture to which the city of New York was sitting, the painter is a divine well known by his pencil:

"Fourteen people asleep in this one room, or trying to get asleep, some on a few handfuls of straw, but more on the bare floor, with neither blanket nor pillow. You say this is exceptional. It is not. Thus sleep, night by night, with no

better comfort, 120,000 families who live in tenement houses of greater or less squalor. There are
a half million people in New York dying by inches
in tenement houses.

" There it is, cuddled up in the cell of the police
station. They come shivering in, tip their torn
hats, and say, 'A night's lodging, sir,' and are
turned into the dreadful dormitories. You can
hardly stand the noxious air long enough to look;
how can they endure it all night, and every night?
Think of it, 140,000 lodgers of this sort every
year in the stàtion houses, and what pathos in the
thought that whole families, turned out of doors
because they

CAN'T PAY THEIR RENT,

must tumble in here for shelter, the respectable
and the reprobate, they who have struggled for decency and good name flung helpless into the loath-
some pool, innocent childhood and vicious old age,
God's poor and Satan's desperadoes. Out of a
population of 1,000,000 people of New York, 300,-
000 people are helped by charity, private or municipal. Hear it, ye Christian Churches, and pour
forth your benefactions ! Hear it, ye ministers of
Christ, and utter words of sympathy for the suffering and thunders of indignation against the sources
of wretchedness ! Hear it, mayoralities and alder-

manic Boards and judicial benches and constabu-
laries! Depend upon it, if we do not heed, and
neither the Courts nor the Churches wake up to their
duty, God will scourge us as the yellow fever never
scourged New Orleans, as the plague never smote
London, as the earthquake never shook Caraccas,
as the fire never whelmed Sodom. In this cluster
of cities 15,000 bare footed, homeless children of
the streets!

"One regiment is made up of bootblacks. They
seem jolly, but they have known sorrows greater
than many an old man. Amid the vilest of temptations, and kicked and cuffed up garrets and down
cellars, they make their two or three dollars a
week, and by fifteen years of natural life are sixty
years old in sin.

"Another regiment of this great battalion of sufferings is made up of the newsboys; the sharpest,
wisest, wittiest lads of the town. For the great
multitude there remain hunger and cold and naked-
ness and early graves or quick prisons.

"But there are other regiments marching on—regiments of rag pickers, regiments of match sellers,
regiments of juvenile thieves, great reserve corps
of darkness and death."

The masses, in Boston, Baltimore, St. Louis,
Cincinnati, Chicago, New Orleans, Louisville, or

any other large city in the Union present pretty much the same picture.

Heart rending cases of starving women and children, and of men ending their misery and making their exit out of a pitiless world by suicide have become a daily occurrence with us.

Our studies about the condition of the masses, their poverty, rates of mortality, insanity and crime, what sages said and educators observed, the march of civilization, the scourges of humanity, the conflict of classes, every line and word in the preceding pages points directly or indirectly to universal industrial Education, but to rise to the full height of our argument we must study the genius of the age we live in, that we may seize its very spirit and speak with authority and power about the demands of the hour and the day.

It may be a pleasure to dream about what has been said and done in the past, but to act our part in the living present is service and duty which the world has a right to ask of us.

My country! my country! what more can I say for thy peace that I have not said? The warning has gone forth; arise and prepare for the great coming event. Oh, where are thy statesmen who study thy greatness and thy safety! Or have we become so small that we cannot grasp the whole country

and its future, and does our own present littleness
obstruct the outlook?

VOICES FROM THE DEEP.

I.

If I could speak with the tongue of angels, I
should assemble around me the workmen of the
world, and say to them: As truly as your and my
Father and the Maker of heaven and earth liveth,
you, too, and your wives and your children shall
live again.

II.

Oh, for the evangelist of the industrial age which
is carrying us in its arms as a mother does her
babe.   Little understood, the forces of the new era
are rushing in upon us, and we are all suffering,
want and fear, and even the prophecy of help is
far from us.   But the messenger is coming, and the
radiance of his countenance is a pledge of the
tenor of his message, which cannot but be in accord with the love and harmony which binds suns
and planets into the mystic dance of the Pleiades.

III.

As true as there is a God He is our Father. The
apostles, of what is falsely called science, may tell
you the weak and the poor must go to the wall
and the strong must use their tiger right. I tell
you, God and His kingdom come to the poor,

whom He will lift up and cause to walk in high places. The ministering angels of God are walking up and down the land, they see your wrongs, and your sufferings are weighed in the balance.

IV.

Not one of your little ones dies from weakness, want or neglect, but a thousand angels hover over it unseen, interceding for you and yours with God and the race. When you are at work, and your wives' tired arms are aching, their temples are bursting with headache, care and anxiety, and their hearts are breaking, God's angels are with them, and when you return from your toil and, finding a bleak, cheerless home, you exchange it for the excitement of the bar room where a thousand demons attach themselves to you, these same angels mourn for you as only angels can. With so much of the love of God shed abroad in human hearts, God's salvation cannot be afar off, and it is not—God's methods are as simple as they are great.

V.

Suffer little children to come, for through them the way to heaven will be made straight to all. Suffer them to come where they belong, to the kindergarten, where their tiny little fingers shall find pleasant exercise, and acquire skill in all sorts of manipulations, where their taste, their inventive powers, and their moral and spiritual nature shall be duly cultivated, and a solid foundation be laid for a deep and universal industrial art culture, embodying the scientific and spiritual laws of the universe of man and nature, which shall hasten the regeneration of the world, and prepare the way for the kingdom of God among men.

VI.

God has given us bones, muscles and sinews, and bodily work must attend mental exercise. Instead of working with dumb bells, ropes and bars, our children must engage in mechanical gymnastics, exercising themselves in the use of a dozen or more of tools, learning to be skillful in mechanical operations, underlying all the common trades, and closing their Education with choosing, on proper trial, the trade they are best adapted to, and of every part of which they will soon be master after such previous training.

VII.

The analytical and constructive, or reflective, active and inventive method of Froebel's early infant training carried by habit into the daily tasks of the artisan masses, and nothing else, can carry us into the front ranks of nations distinguished for their industrial achievements.

VIII.

Through the æsthetic element in the culture of the Greeks have their masses shared in the civilization of their day, and have lifted, by their general high standard of thought, feeling, and action, the élite to an eminence, it has never reached among purely intellectual nations with a sporadic culture, depraved masses and a general low standard. Art must swell the popular wave, upon the crest of which borne the few can touch the clouds.

IX.

Through work and industry Providence has schooled the race; its method is final and will solve the problem pressing for solution.

Driven from the first garden the race has lost God and happiness, and through the kinder and the school garden and its work, its teachings, and its inspirations the race will find God and happiness again.

X.

Sitting in darkness, and hearing cries and lamentations of children, men, and women, the glories of heaven shining in upon us overmatch our senses, and we cry for strength, for the billows of hell and the splendors of heaven are too much for us.

XI.

In the City of God, art armed with love and beauty will infuse a soul into dumb matter, the very pavement will bear us, as it were, upon arms of love, the air will be the breath of the beloved, and God will be the never setting sun, the light and love of all, and the consummation is at hand. Heaven is now and here, and not then and there.

XII.

Here is the City of God, full of the splendor of industry and the glories of art; there the Commune, the city of blood; the first, vocal with love and beauty, and the All Perfect; the second, gleaming with ghastly flames, made hotter by cries of children and curses of men and women; we must choose, for everything is dragging us down, and only by the inner energy of our souls can we rise.

XIII.

Let us not blame God or man for seeming social dissonance. The conditions of being have their limitations, and there is an iron logic of things. Economical relations will finally come under the arbitrament of the law of the moral order of the universe. In the school of life and Providence, as in every other one, some are ahead and some behind, but the forces are in operation which will bring up all to the mark, and eternal harmony and beauty are fully as sure to crown the world of man as the world of nature.

XIV.

The benign heavens above us, the scenery bathed in soft light, the cattle browsing in the field or slaking their thirst in the stream, the divine form and structure of man, the beauty of every flower and atom, like the rainbow in the sky, pledge to the feeling heart the peace, power, and love of God, which will wipe away sorrow's tear from human eyes.

XV.

Is there anything so great, glorious and full of sunshine as man's divine call to bring about this consummation by filling the land, through his own will and power, with joy and gladness? The enchanter's wand is in our hand; we have only to use it, and universal happiness will spring up under its magic power of love.

XVI.

Despair not, we cry into the present tumult of agitated debate. God liveth in the economical relations of the world of man as He does in the realms of nature, and what to our minds leads to disintegration induces organizations more perfect than any in the past.

XVII.

Multitudes of children are perishing, mothers are crushed by burdens too much for their strength, stout-hearted toilers by the millions, seeing the game of life closing in upon them at middle age, strain their vision, if, peradventure, they might descry at the distance the promised land, but their thoughts thicken, gloom settles upon their souls, and hope for their children failing, they die in despair.

XVIII.

The break of morning is preceded by the darkest hour, and out of the thickest cloud the lightning flashes. The heavens are opening, and the City of God is coming down, its foundations garnished with all manner of precious stones, its streets are of pure gold. High art shedding its subduing color over the glories of God, lends them enchantment, as the soft mist does to the landscape.

XIX.

O God, the prophet is as sluggish as the people, and Thy words strike him terribly through the broken hearts of wife and children. Speak through whom Thou pleasest and when Thou pleasest, and let him break in peace the bread of life to those

Thou hast given him. But, forgive—speak—Thy word shall be delivered, and Thy will shall be done ultimately.

XX.

Humbly but perseveringly your friends shall deliver their message, that you and your wives and your children may live again, that peace, purity, and goodness may rule, and every heart be glad, and every soul may shine a bright star in the heavens in which we are dwelling.

XXI.

Men of active bodies and minds, conversant with the ways of the world and sensitive to pain and pleasure have denied themselves the comforts and, to a large extent, the necessaries of life; they have seen their wives and children but half clad; they have seen them suffer and partly die from sheer want, that the good things and the dear life, they gave up with bleeding hearts, might spring up a rich harvest for the million.

These men ask the world to utilize these sacrifices, or before God and His justice they will ask of it an account of their labors and their losses. " We are enthusiasts." Well, with Ruskin we say, " This is another of the devil's words." We may be covered with wounds and bruises, we claim

nothing; we are but a voice from God, every one
may hear in his own heart. Is there not enough
in every body to make him love his neighbor and
his race? Has not every body a thorn in his flesh
that calls for a tender hand to gently pull it out?
Do all the good you can and help us do all the
good we feel we ought to do, and we shall be as
calm as a summer's morning, and contentedly bid
the gentle reader a cordial farewell.

XXII.

We are building for the Infinite
Temples of marble, ivory and gold,
And com'th He to us, we set Him to work,
A slave begrimed with dust and dirt,
A very sanscullot ; but His garments
Hanging loosely and odd on His shoulders,
His glory bursts through the tattered rags.
We followed Him reeling in the street,
Hooted by children and barked at by dogs.
A little further on the police club
Threatened to come down upon His head.
We remember we have seen Him in court,
Not as all shall see Him at last—as Judge,
But jeered at and taken away to prison,
And then let out to work for contractors.
We have seen Him—we are not blaspheming—
In the bruised harlot's bloated face ;
For even there His majesty betray'd Him.
We have seen Him make His home in hovels
Shunned by the meanest of His creatures,
We have seen Him a tramp and an outcast,
A thief and a lepper, the Lord of Glory !
We have seen Him a father, a brother,

A husband, aye, a child, much abused
By His nearest and dearest, because poor.
We have seen Him in grief and loneliness,
Unnoticed by all save the angels,
Who did recognize in Him their Lord,
Bending over His loved little ones,
Stricken by the hand of death, because poor.
We have seen Him a sage, saint and prophet,
Railed and sneered at by all because poor.
When souls familiar with God shall see
Him in all these various disguises
In th' hungry, thirsty, sick, nak'd and in pris'n.
The outcast, thief and harlot shall vanish
Like a mist, and all saints, we shall worship
By living a life full of work and love.

END OF VOLUME II.

INDEX TO VOLUME II.

DETERIORATION AND THE ELEVATION OF MAN THROUGH RACE
EDUCATION. By Samuel Royce. Third revised and enlarged
Edition, in two volumes. Vol. I., 477 pages ; Vol. II., 456
pages. Price, $5.00. Boston : *Lee & Shepard*, Publishers.
New York : *Charles T. Dillingham*.

RECOMMENDATIONS.

From the *New York School Journal*.

"Deterioration and Race Education" has been in preparation for several
years, and begins to attract attention. This work is strong in facts, arguments,
and erudition, etc., etc.

From the *Popular Science Monthly*.

. . . . In this book Education is considered from a broad, humanitarian
point of view, and in connection with the great causes of decay and deterioration. The author has collected a great deal of interesting material, interspersed
with valuable observations and reflections, and the volume is pervaded by a
reformatory and progressive spirit.

From the *Library Table*, Feb. 16.

The author displays a thorough knowledge of his subject, and his conclusions, no less than the startling array of his facts, deserve the most serious consideration of all who are in any way connected with the promotion or administration of public interests. We recommend the volume for careful perusal as
one of the most valuable recent contributions to social and educational science.

From the *Reformer*, Jan. 11.

"Deterioration" is replete with erudition and practical wisdom, bearing testimony of the author's genuine philanthropy, and will make its mark—as none
can read it without being thoroughly aroused as to the present appalling condition of the masses ; and what is proposed is moderate and sustained by other
social thinkers.

From the *Boston Evening Transcript*.

. . . . The range of this work is comprehensive, and the various topics which
incidentally arise in connection with the main subject are ably discussed.

3

I have read "Deterioration" with interest. There is no doubt about its facts. We must revise our system of public education, and better adapt it to the wants of the times.

J. D. RUNKLE,
President Boston Institute of Technology.

"Deterioration" is one of those books well worth the time required to read it carefully. It is a very, very useful book, and one the knowledge of which should be spread.

COLEMAN SELLERS,
President Franklin Institute, Phila.

"Deterioration" should be carefully read, not only by teachers, but by all who are interested in the education and the welfare of humanity.

BEN HYDE BENTON,
President Polytechnic Institute, New Market, Va.

"Deterioration" follows a line of argument greatly needed at the present time in educational affairs, and is an especially useful book.

HON. JOHN EATON,
Commissioner of Education.

"Deterioration" is full of curious and interesting information, and I sympathize with the philanthropic desires of the author.

GEORGE WILLIAM CURTIS.

I have read "Deterioration" with just admiration for its depth, breadth, and vigor. This book is like a hundred-pounder loaded to the muzzle. . . . . I am now nearly seventy-four years old, and perhaps the most encouraging thing I have seen done is this plain-spoken, earnest book; for truly an evil must be demonstrated before it can be cured. Another thing is encouraging it comes with its sharp thunder-claps, etc., etc.

ELIZUR WRIGHT

"Deterioration and Race Education" is of rare value, full of suggestion, and opening up views that can not fail to attract and interest deeply every student of the social questions of the day. Its contribution toward solving these is of great value, and no one can follow such guidance without placing himself in a position to serve humanity efficiently in most important interests.

WENDELL PHILLIPS.

The studies pursued by the author of "Deterioration" are in a direction very generally neglected, and the information given is just in the lines where it is most needed.

REV. EDWARD E. HALE.

"Deterioration and Race Education" is of great value and importance, diffusing knowledge upon subjects on the due consideration of which depends the welfare, if not the very existence, of our social organization.

O. WENDELL HOLMES.

4

"Deterioration and Race Education" is worthy of the attention of the medical profession, and of men of science in general as well as of humanitarians. It is a work full of suggestion and weighty matter.

ELISHA HARRIS, M.D.

I fully concur in what Dr. Elisha Harris has said. "Deterioration" is a book of great value.

FRANK H. HAMILTON, M.D.

I concur in the recommendation of Prof. Hamilton, and would especially recommend the work to physicians, teachers, and parents.

R. J. O'SULLIVAN, M.D.

From the *Methodist*, New York, March, 1878.

The studies in this volume are valuable.

From the *Christian Intelligencer*, N. Y., March 21, 1878.

In this volume, crowded with statistics, facts, and opinions upon sociology, and evidently the product of long and careful preparation, the author presents the subject of "deterioration" of the human race in order to show the necessity of aiming at its "amelioration," etc., etc. The facts which the writer has collected from Government, medical, and sociological authorities are painfully interesting, and of great value for reference.

From the *New Jerusalem Messenger*, N. Y., Sept. 4, 1878.

This book presents a fearful array of facts and statistics as to the deterioration of our race. . . . . Mr. Royce has evidently studied his subject in all its branches. . . . . It is a painful book, but like some other bitter doses it is good for us. It is well that thinking people should know and thoroughly appreciate the dangers which threaten us in this day of our boasted civilization. The book is of deepest interest, and a valuable contribution toward the solution of the Social Problems of our time.

From the *Religio-Philosophical Journal*, Chicago, Sept. 21, 1878.

This is really a good book, one which the reviewer gladly takes up amid the monotony of his task of wading through the unending trash which flows from the press, for a good book does not greet him every day. . . . . It marks the dawn of a new era in Education, and has no equal in the whole range of recent educational literature in the broadness of its views, the profound and exhaustive erudition of its treatment, the freshness of its style and thoughts, and general practical truthfulness. . . . . We cannot quote even the passages of pure gold which almost irresistibly tempt us, for they are so many, it would be impossible. . . . . The book should be read by every youth of the land.

From the *Post*, Boston, August 6. 1878.

In a recent book, entitled "Deterioration and Race Education," by Samuel Royce, the condition of the people and the industrial problem are very intelli-

5

gently presented. . . . . We are disposed to fully agree with the author in his general conclusions. . . . .

From the *Advertiser*, Boston, August 10, 1878.

. . . . As an earnestly written book by a man who has given much consideration to the topics treated, it is worthy the consideration of educators, and, in fact, of every class. . . . .

From the *Commonwealth*, Boston, July 20, 1878.

The life of the author of "Deterioration" has evidently been devoted to a thorough and conscientious investigation of the great social problems of the age, and the facts he has here brought together, painful and humiliating as many of them are, cannot be ignored by those who have charge of the Education and government of the people, if they would save future history from repeating the horrors of the past. A book so faithful, true, and far-seeing is a greater boon to the public than any single invention, however brilliant or labor-saving, inasmuch as wisdom is better than wealth, and men and women are of more importance than their physical environments. . . . .

From the *Record*, Philadelphia, August 30, 1878.

. . . . The author touches the root of the great problem of the day, in attributing the alarming growth of crime and pauperism to the want of an educational system adapted to the needs of the lower classes. . . . . The book is full of potent matter, set before the reader as a "plain, unvarnished tale," and all the more valuable for its plainness. . . . . The tables of statistics have been evidently prepared with great care, and present a startling picture of misery and crime undreamed of, perhaps, even by those who are most interested in the relief and improvement of the dangerous classes. Not the least useful part of the book is a beautifully complete index, a model in its way, and one that we hope to see imitated in future publications of this character.

From the *Mirror*, Manchester, N. H., August 28, 1878.

. . . . "Deterioration" is well-written and packed full of statistics. . . . . The facts and arguments of the book are calculated to establish its proposition of the deterioration of the human race, and the necessity of an ameliorating Education. . . . . To any one interested in social, industrial, and educational questions—and they are the most important of the time—this work will be found valuable.

From the *Farmer's Cabinet*, Amherst, N. H., Aug. 13, 1878.

. . . . The author displays a thorough knowledge of his subject, and his conclusions, backed by a startling array of facts, deserve the most serious consideration of all. We commend it to a most earnest reading.

From the *Kansas Times*, September 1, 1878.

This book is really in the interest of humanity, and answers the great questions of the day. . . . . A book everybody should read.

6

From the *Medical Record*, Atlanta, Ga., September, 1878.

. . . . Whether viewed simply in its bearing upon our civil polity as a people, or from a moral and religious standpoint, this work can not fail to attract the interest of the enlightened reader. We bespeak for it a God-speed and a world-wide circulation.

From the *Educational Monthly*, Parkersburg, W. V., Sept., 1878.

" Deterioration " is well worth the thoughtful perusal of every citizen in the land who has at heart the welfare of his fellow-man. The author has collected a vast amount of interesting material, interspersed with valuable observations and suggestions, which are presented earnestly and with marked ability.

From the *Christian Leader*, Utica, N. Y., Sept. 21, 1878.

Truly a book every one, and especially all engaged in the work of Education, either in the home or in the school, should read ; a most excellent manual for the reformer ; a work crowded with startling facts and wise suggestions. . . . .

From the *Argus and Patriot*, Montpelier, Vt., Sept. 18, 1878.

. . . . The pauperization of the masses and their deterioration, together with the prevention of this double bane through the Kindergarten, the Developing School, the Manual Institute, and Race Education, and a variety of kindred subjects are treated in this volume with much research and matured reflection.

From the *Central School Journal*, Iowa, Sept., 1878.

. . . . " Deterioration " is strong in facts and the main subjects are ably discussed, and best presented to the reader by quoting largely from the author. . . . . We bespeak for Mr. Royce, from our readers, a careful and serious perusal of his work.

From the *Buffalo School Journal*, September, 1878.

This is decidedly the freshest book on the subject of Education which we have perused for many a day. . . . . According to the author our systems of culture lead to deterioration. . . . . It will pay to give this book a careful perusal ; the discussion of the subjects indicates much study and research, and the book is most excellent.

From the *New York Times*, September 22, 1878.

The views of this book are sound and true, and the expression of its ideas is so pithy and striking that they cannot fail to impress the reader. . . . . We agree with the author that there are deteriorating elements at work in modern civilization, and that it must be considered the greatest problem of our age how to counteract them. . . . . On the field of Education our time may fairly be described as a clamor between three different ideals, each presenting itself under various guises ; and the stand which Mr. Samuel Royce takes on this battle-field, in this confusion, is, that he rejects summarily the pretensions of all the combatants. His reason is very simple ; they all educate the mind only, and that which he will have educated is the man, by a process which will be

7

able not only to counteract one of the greatest evils of the age—the deterioration through inheritance—but also to embrace the highest educational ideal which can be conceived—the bringing up of the individual for the sake of the race.

From the *San Francisco Sun and Chronicle*, Sept. 8, 1878.

Mr. Royce has given a book that is valuable, not because it is a plea for the Kindergarten, but for the thoughtful and earnest spirit that pervades it and for the vast amount of facts and inferences contained therein. The title-page bears this motto: "The sacredness of human life increases with civilization," and it forms the key-note of the volume. . . . . The book is filled with material interesting alike to the statistician, the educator, the moralist, and the metaphysical student.

From the *Iowa State Register*, Des Moines, Sept. 21, 1878.

. . . . There is much instruction in this volume to those who are looking ahead to the rising generation, and to their destiny; and all progressionists as well as those who are fearful of a recurring historical lapse in civilization, will find much mental food and many good suggestions in its pages.

From the *Christian Standard*, Cincinnati, O., Sept. 21, 1878.

. . . . The book is thoughtful and timely, and looks in a direction in which there can be but little doubt that our educators will be compelled to walk at no distant day.

From the *Universalist Quarterly*, Boston, October, 1878.

This is a book which we have long desired to see and to possess; a book which gathers up into one body the thousand facts concerning pauperism, insanity, disease, crime, and the physical as well as moral degradation and deterioration of the race, scattered through newspapers, magazines, social science publications, medical works, and Government statistical reports. Mr. Royce would have done a useful and important work, if he had only done this; but his treatment of them, the public use he had put them to, and the manner in which he had made them tell upon his argument for race Education, and the necessity of improving the condition of the dangerous and perishing classes, has added double to their value. . . . . We hope the work will be circulated far and wide, and read of all men and women. Every preacher should have it, and use it in his sermons, that he may be able to instruct his people in the aims and results of social science, and make practical his talk of Human Brotherhood.

From the *New Jerusalem Magazine*, Boston, Mass., October, 1878.

. . . . "Deterioration" is in many things a remarkable book. . . . . The writer has the evils of society much at heart, and does not leave us in doubt as to what will bring about relief. He ought to have the best wishes and support of all Christian people. . . . . The book will be of great use to parents and teachers, and a proper development of its principles will do much to remove the evils which it very graphically depicts.

From the *Baltimore Sun*, Sept. 14, 1878.

. . . . "Deterioration" deserves to be studied, for it strikes at what is beginning to be regarded as a grave defect in our Public School system. . . . .

From the *Brooklyn Times*, Nov. 7, 1878.

This book is "solid," inasmuch as the practical application of its theories to the condition of the people and their industries are plainly pointed out. It touches upon many topics neglected by political economists, ... is full of ripe thought, and appeals to the people to do their duty by the rising generation.

From the *Lewiston Journal*, Me., October 12, 1878.

Are we degenerating? is a momentous question, which has lately been ably discussed by Mr. Samuel Royce in a work entitled "Deterioration," which directs attention to a matter of vital consequence to us as a people and as a race.

From the *Cincinnati Medical Advance*, Sept., 1878.

. . . . We have read the book with pleasure, and cordially assent to many of its arguments, and commend the work as worth the attention of our readers.

From the *Philadelphia Medical Times*, October, 1878.

. . . . Kindergarten and Schools of Industry, advocated by the author of "Deterioration," seem to have the germ of vast good in them, and we watch their growth throughout the country, and do believe that little by little, more and more, they should be made a part of our Common School Education.

From the *Independent*, New York, April 11, 1878.

. . . . Mr. Royce sees the same remedy as Ruskin—and indeed there is no other—to give people a sound industrial training, and induce them to live by the labor of their own hands in the country ; . . . . we wish every hard-pressed working man in our cities could read this book.

From the *Chicago Standard*, October 17, 1878.

. . . . "Deterioration" has for its problem the greatest of the humanitarian questions of our age—the rescue of the race from the evident deterioration. . . . . As a contribution to social science this book takes rank with the best of our times, ... and we earnestly commend it. especially to those to whom is committed the important work of shaping public opinion. . . . .

From the *Christian Register*, Boston, October 17, 1878.

. . . . The facts of "Deterioration" are of great moment, and its suggestions cannot fail to be of value to all who hope to serve their kind. The philanthropic aim of the book deserves all praise, and the industry it has inspired should reap a rich reward in a harvest of good works.

From the *Sunday-School Helper*, Boston, November, 1878.

Here is a book "for the times," if ever such a book was written, ... a presentation of the evils in society, with the remedy for most of them. . . . . To all readers of books we say, get this one, and make yourselves familiar with its contents. We welcome it as one of the educators of the present and the future.

From the *Friends' Intelligencer*, Philadelphia, Ninth Month, 28, 1878.

. . . . We have given some attention to the book entitled " Deterioration and Race Education," and are impressed with the justness of many of the strictures upon modern Education. . . . . Kindergarten and Industrial Education, by which the author hopes to see deterioration arrested, express the wishes of a very large class, if not a majority of his fellow-citizens. . . . .

From the *American Journal of Education*, St. Louis, Mo., October, 1878.

This book should be universally studied. Its arguments are cogent, and merit individual and social consideration. The philanthropic author subjects the present condition of society to a scrutinizing investigation, and proceeds to the development of a system that promises permanent relief . .

From the *University of Michigan Chronicle*, Nov. 9, 1878.

. . . . Every page bears witness to the earnestness of the author, as well as to his deep and careful study of the subject. . . . The work contains questions which involve the future of the great masses of the people, and is deserving of careful attention.

From the *Wisconsin Journal of Education*, October, 1878.

. . . . That the author's sympathies are profoundly and justly stirred is evident, ... and we quite agree with him that our Education should not be confined to imparting a little dry book knowledge . . . . We hope the volume before us will have a wide circulation, and help forward the efforts of the thoughtful to check the downward tendencies of the age.

From the *Iowa Normal Monthly*, October, 1878.

"Deterioration" is a passionate appeal for the elevation of the race, and no one can read it without being stirred up to eager thought upon the subjects of which it treats, nor without asking himself, not in excuse, but in solemn self-accusation, "Am I my brother's keeper?"

From the *Monthly Repertory*, Adrian, Mich., Sept., 1878.

. . . . The author is original and fresh in style, always vigorous, and has evidently read much in the literature that belongs to his subject. . . . . He denounces the present system of Education as insufficient, ... and stimulates thought in a direction that is greatly needed.

10

From the *New England Journal of Education*, Boston, Nov. 14, 1878.

. . . . The author's enthusiasm and love for the race are so sincere, that a reading of the work will awaken multitudes of minds to the vast importance of the truths it enforces, and to an examination of the theories it advances. . . . .

From the *High-School Journal*, Omaha, Neb., Oct., 1878.

. . . . . After a careful study of "Deterioration," we cannot but admit "Deterioration" has many truths which cannot fail to receive serious consideration, especially from men who take an interest in the great problem of Education, and to whom we would advise to read this work. . . . .

From the *Phrenological Journal*, December, 1878.

. . "Deterioration" is worth the careful reading of the teacher, politician, statesman, economist, reformer, and parent. No book of its character which has come under our notice in late years contains so extensive an array of facts and opinions, and so frank and forcible a discussion of their significance.

From the *Popular Science Monthly*, December, 1878.

We noticed this instructive work upon its first edition, and are glad to see that it has gone to a second edition, as it contains a great deal of information bearing upon the subject of Education that cannot be found compiled and digested elsewhere. . . . .

From the *Sanitarian*, December, 1878.

"Deterioration and Race Education" is evidently the result of extensive research by one thoroughly imbued with the spirit of philanthropy, and determined to bring to the surface the appalling prevalence of human depravity, with the view, if possible, of ameliorating it by Education, an Education which shall take cognizance of the vices of mankind, and fortify the individual against them. Drunkenness, idleness, pauperism, vice, crime, and insanity are here aggregated by an array of statistics which ought not, and cannot fail to arrest the attention of all thoughtful persons on the welfare of mankind. . . . . The work is altogether the most valuable and practical contribution to social science which has hitherto appeared, and commendable to the attention of all educators of youth, and all students of social science.

From the *North American Review*, November, 1878.

. . . . "Deterioration and Race Education" is surely well worth reading, and ought to make its mark upon public opinion. . . . . It deserves the notice of well-informed and thoughtful men. . . . . It has great value, and cannot fail to do good, especially in its bold and strong conflict with the narrowness of our dominant schooling and the rabid radicalism of our labor reformers. . . . .

From the *Rev. J. G. Adams, D.D.*

I consider Mr. Royce's book one of the notable works of the century.

From the *Rev. A. A. Miner, D.D.*

Nobody can read Mr. Royce's masterly statement of the evils that afflict humanity, and the remedies set forth in his great work on " Deterioration and Race Education," without the highest profit.

I have carefully perused the contents of that most excellent work, " Deterioration," set forth and elaborated in such a scholarly manner, by a mind thoroughly master of its subject, and cannot but heartily recommend it. A fearless as well as a faithful man, who shall find?

GEORGE WHITE,
Principal of Grammar-School No. 70.

I have read with great pleasure and profit the work entitled " Deterioration and Race Education," and from my position as a public-school teacher, have had ample opportunity to judge of its great importance, and the work it purposes to accomplish. It comes none too soon, and I can only hope that I may live to see its recommendations carried into practice.

J. D. HYATT,
Principal Grammar-School No. 60.

I fully concur in the above recommendation.

JAMES BUCKHOUT,
Grammar-School No. 65.

I most heartily concur in the opinion of the work entitled " Deterioration and Race Education," which is expressed above. The heavy sledge-hammer arguments with which the author enforces his views are essentially necessary at this time to awaken the people to the danger menacing society from the present theories of Education.

W. J. RENNARD,
Principal Grammar-School No. 64.

From *William Lloyd Garrison*

. . . . The scope of Mr. Royce's book is as broad as the world; its spirit, pure and uplifting; its aim, the rescuing of our race from poverty, crime, and debasement by a radical change in educational training; its exhibit of the increase of pauperism, intemperance, insanity, and felony startling; its reasoning lucid, sensible, and impressive · its grasp of the subjects discussed, alike comprehensive and sagacious. It is crowded with vital statistics, noble sentiments, and most instructive suggestions. The preparation and condensation of such a work, the research and reflection required for its completion, must have been a very laborious and exhaustive undertaking, prosecuted in the service of humanity by a devotion acting " like a fire in the bones " for a long period. The high commendations of it bestowed by scores of eminent persons, and by numerous literary, scientific, and reformatory periodicals, indicate a rare concurrence of critical judgment as to its merits, and the desirableness of an extended circulation being given to it.

12

www.ingramcontent.com/pod-product-compliance
Lightning Source LLC
Chambersburg PA
CBHW052339110726
47901CB00005B/1285